the complete book of
TOPIARY

the complete book of
TOPIARY

BY BARBARA GALLUP
AND DEBORAH REICH

Introduction by Rosemary Verey
Illustrations by Kimble Pendleton Mead

WORKMAN PUBLISHING, NEW YORK

Library of Congress Cataloging-in-Publication Data

Gallup, Barbara.
The complete book of topiary.
1. Topiary work.   I. Reich, Deborah.
II. Title.
SB462.G35   1988   715′.1   86–40539
ISBN 0–89480–318–2

Book design: Kathleen Herlihy Paoli
Front cover illustration: Cheryl Griesbach
and Stanley Martucci
Back cover illustration: Kimble Pendleton Mead

Workman Publishing Company, Inc.
1 West 39th Street
New York, NY 10018

Manufactured in the United States of America

First printing November 1987

10 9 8 7 6 5 4 3 2 1

ACKNOWLEDGMENTS

We would like to thank all the gardeners, librarians and friends who gave us unlimited information, advice and time, as well as the generous topiarists we encountered who shared their ideas, skill and experience. A special note of appreciation goes to Alec Gallup and Sara Van Allen, who encouraged us to put our ideas on paper and helped with the original outline of the manuscript; to Peter Workman, who believed in the project; to Michael Cader, Kathy Herlihy Paoli and Mary Wilkinson, who trimmed and shaped it into an actual book; and to Kimble Mead, who added his charming illustrations.

We also want to express our deep gratitude to Ladew Topiary Gardens for their invaluable advice and for generously allowing us to use many source books from the Vlasta E. Schmidt Library.

Finally, we express our appreciation to Rosemary Verey for the excellent introduction she contributed. It is a great honor to have a noted garden authority, designer and historian acknowledge our foray into the venerable art of topiary.

First, I wish to give special thanks to my father, Victor E. Schmidt, from whom I gained my interest in horticulture. Warm appreciation also goes to my mother, Vlasta E. Schmidt; my brother Peter Schmidt and his wife Christine; my close friends Ann and Donald Calder and Ann and George Hackl; and my fellow members of the Garden Club of Harford County, Maryland, for their continuing encouragement and support. Special thanks to Edwin A. Daniels, Jr., for repeatedly coming up with projects that have challenged my creativity.

In addition, I would like to thank the following: Mia Hardcastle, Thomas Miller, Adolph Garza, Thomas Thorpe, and Brad and Sara Gove, all of whom contributed their imagination and labor in executing so many of the topiary examples mentioned in the book.
                                                                    BARBARA GALLUP

I wish to express my boundless gratitude to my mother and father, who inspired by example and encouraged with kindness a love of gardening. Appreciation is extended to the Brooklyn Botanic Garden: I have benefited enormously from my practical experience there, as well as the opportunity to consult its knowledgeable gardeners and botanists. I also give thanks for patience and support to Miranda Magagnini, Patricia Murphy, Janet Lustgarten, Emily Jernigan, Tom Nicklas, Janet Reich, Marcia Walsh, and most of all Andrew, who was always there.
                                                                    DEBORAH REICH

Contents

CHAPTER 1

PORTABLE TOPIARY   21

Tabletop Whimsy on a Frame

The Shape of Portable Topiary • The Range of Frames • Selecting Plants • Showing Off • Decorative Accents • Supplies • Hollow Creations • Training • Stuffed Sculptures • Planting Wrapped Forms • Care and Feeding

Projects

CHAPTER 2

STANDARDS, POODLES & SPIRALS   55

Splendor on a Single Stem

Creating with Herbs • Old Faithfuls • Geraniums • Elegant Oddities • Roses • Hardy Specimens • All About Containers • Raising Your Standards • Maintenance

Projects

CHAPTER 3

MOCK TOPIARY   79

Faux Forms for Indoor Style

Accents and Decorations • Standards • Geometric Sculptures • Birds and Beasts • Plant Materials for Lasting Accessories • Festive Seasonal Specialties • All About Containers • Tricks of the Trade

Projects

CHAPTER 4

FRAMEMAKING   113

Elegant Armatures for Handcrafted Accents

Wire • Tools and Supplies • Constructing a Wire Skeleton • Using Chicken Wire • Preparing the Frame for Planting • Simple Frames for Pots • Zoological Frames for Pots • Freestanding Frames • Chicken Wire Forms • Standard Frame

Projects

CHAPTER 5

IVY TRAINING   157

A Vine Art

All About Ivy • Outdoor Ivy Sculpture • Ivy as Architectural Accent • Decorations on the Ground • Decorating Walls • Ivy Standards • Portable Figures • Trimming • Recommended Ivies • The Hardiest Plants • Fancy Shapes •

Splashes of Color • Big, Bold Leaves • An Ivy
Garden • Caring For Ivy

Projects

CHAPTER 6

ESPALIER
183

Murals of Tracery, Flowers & Fruit

Planning an Espalier • Selecting Plants •
Basic Training • Supports • How to Make
Classic Shapes • Mural Maintenance • Prun-
ing for Flowers, Fruit and Berries • Indoor
Espalier

Projects

CHAPTER 7

KNOT GARDENS
217

Twined Between the Old and New

Knot Gardens • Flat Topiary • Victorian
Revival • Creating a Knot • Boxwood • Herbs •
Dwarf Shrubs • Annual Herbs and Bedding
Plants • Laying Out the Pattern • Planting

Projects

CHAPTER 8

VERDANT SCULPTURE
241

Ornamental Shaping of Trees and Shrubs

The Traditional Repertoire • The American
Style • Displaying Green Sculpture • Selecting Plant Material • Trading the Chisel for the

Shears • Creating a Sculpture • Caring for
Sculpted Trees and Shrubs

Projects

CHAPTER 9

HEDGECRAFT 265

Building Halls and Walls of Green

Hedges • Topiary Maze • Arches, Tunnels and
Houses • Plants • Techniques • Dressing Up
Hedges • Green Archways • Architectural
Forms • Preservation and Renovation

Projects

SOURCES AND RESOURCES

INTRODUCTION

Topiary is one of the oldest, most carefully conceived means of creating firm, decorative elements in the garden. The ancient Egyptians and the Romans practiced the art with imagination and ingenuity. In Renaissance Europe the clipping and ordering of alleys and avenues was as important a part in the making of a garden as the cultivation of flowers. Today, once again, there is a strong revival of the art and it is no exaggeration to say that topiary, in its widest sense, is becoming as successful in the United States as it ever has been in Europe.

When Barbara Gallup asked me to contribute an introduction to this book, I was immensely flattered that she should think a friend from the other side of the Atlantic could possibly add anything to her knowledge of the subject. I was very diffident to accept—I know a bit about the making and clipping of knots and easy shapes, but nothing about indoor portable topiary, spirals and complicated shapes. Then when the text of the book arrived and I started reading, it became irresistible. If you can grow plants you can make topiary shapes of all sizes. If you have no garden, then you can create small tabletop-size features, birds, monkeys, garlands, elegant single-stemmed standards—horticulture for the home. With a garden your horizons will widen, making larger, more permanent features that will grow with the years.

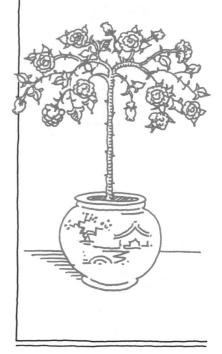

I must congratulate Barbara Gallup and Deborah Reich on their joint achievement in gathering together so many historical facts gleaned from early manuscripts and the first printed books written by 16th- and 17th-century writers. The wealth of practical advice that Barbara and Deborah give is invaluable and is selected from their own personal experience.

Here is the definitive book on this fascinating subject. It covers every aspect—from the strictly practical to the artistic and imaginative, from portable leafy sculptures to the verdant architecture of archways, hedges on stilts, and carefully clipped

*I*n classical Latin, opus topiarium *was the general term for ornamental gardening. Gradually,* topiarius *became the prestigious title of a gardener whose specialty was the carving of trees and shrubs. Today, topiary can refer to any plant, indoors as well as outside, that has been coaxed into a decorative form.*

peacocks and hunting scenes.

My own philosophy about gardens is that they should have diversity, a happy mixture of strong design and careless rapture. Permanent planting is the framework, the boundaries and the dividing hedges; and topiary, either as single specimens or a collection of clipped forms, gives the character, the accents of interest. This book is brim full of ideas and you discover where you can see old specimens of clipped yew and box, holly and privet, trimmed and barbered into cones, obelisks and spheres—the traditional European topiary subjects. In America a new style has developed, and the African giraffe has become a topiary classic. The hunting scene created in Maryland by Harvey Ladew was inspired by a fox and hounds he had seen in an English garden; and in turn the many sculptured shapes in his garden have been seen by thousands of visitors who have copied his ideas in their own gardens. Many public gardens have ever-increasing collections: Longwood Gardens in Pennsylvania, Callaway Gardens in Georgia and Disneyland in California. Specimens are growing in every sense, in numbers and in size.

It is easy enough to visualize an idea, but to carry it out may be harder to achieve. After reading this book you will have far more confidence in how to begin. You will know exactly what equipment you will need, which to buy and where, and which you can expect to find in your own toolshed and cupboards. All the fundamental techniques are carefully explained, step by step, and there are those finishing touches that add the professional look.

Although the art of topiary is so old, this book gives it a new look. I guarantee many more people will be indulging their whims and artistic talents, creating versatile portable topiaries using the fast-growing plants recommended. These will be instantly seen, but over the years there will be an ever-increasing number of slow-growing sculptured forms developing in gardens all over. They will be geometric, realistic and imaginative, inspired by the diversity of ideas in these chapters.

ROSEMARY VEREY

THE LURE OF TOPIARY

Since ancient times, trees and vines have been trained for useful purposes, raising crops off the ground, increasing the yield of fruit and furnishing precious shade. The Romans were the first to develop these skills into topiary, the art of shaping plants to create living sculpture. In succeeding years, generation after generation of gardeners have favored topiary as a means of aesthetic expression, using it as a softer alternative to marble statuary and architecture, or as a pleasing counterpoint to the wilderness of unrestrained nature.

Over two thousand years of garden history and expertise have resulted in a rich variety of plant-shaping possibilities, and now you can participate in the latest step in this long tradition. A wealth of designs, both classical and contemporary, elaborate and simple, are waiting to be brought to life with the snip of your scissors and the snap of your pruning shears. From indoor pleasures such as a tabletop ivy-covered swan and a miniature rosemary tree to outdoor masterpieces of geometrically sculpted shrubs, tree-size teddy bears—even hedges carved into arches and decorative walls—the fantasy world of topiary can become a reality in your own house and garden.

No special skills are required to enter this enchanting realm—even the most inexperienced gardener can quickly create masterful displays that will only improve with time. Imagination is the most important asset, and you'll find the process of creation every bit as enjoyable as the finished product.

For instant results that don't even require a garden, there is portable topiary, the newest form of plant sculpture that's versatile, whimsical and easy to make. By training fast-growing vines over simple wire frames, you can quickly create interior accessories of any size, at any time of year, ranging from a lush green dragon for your desk, to a bird outlined in fragrant flowering jasmine for the windowsill or a huggable leafy dog for your bedroom. Portable toparies are easily moved around as light or

> **❝I love the topiary art, with its trimness and primness, and its open avowal of its artificial character. It repudiates at the first glance the skulking and cowardly 'celare artum' principle, and, in its vegetable sculpture, is the properest transition from the architecture of the house to the natural beauties of the grove and paddock.❞**
>
> —T. JAMES
> *The Carthusian*, 1839

the season dictate—and they make perfect decorative touches for special occasions. Use one as a centerpiece for a festive evening, returning it to its growing spot in the morning. And when you shift your focus outdoors in the summer, you can take your topiary with you onto the terrace or patio.

There are also quick and easy ways to make perfect-looking topiary that resemble growing plants but are actually made of cut flowers, foliage, dried and artificial materials, ribbons and even vegetables! These faux forms are the latest fashion in plant ornaments—popular as distinctive party decorations, such as a colorful globe of flowers and leaves atop a slender stem, and endearing permanent accents, like a friendly rabbit with a soft fur coat of moss.

Even if you don't or can't garden outside, time-honored outdoor training techniques of pruning and shearing can be used to create potted indoor topiaries that resemble stylized trees and other geometric shapes. Miniature models made with herbs and houseplants are especially popular. You can use the same methods to turn geraniums and other flowering plants into spectacular long-legged beauties that display their glittering blooms at eye level. As with portable topiary, your potted classics can be toted outdoors during warm weather.

Outdoor topiary also enjoys a newfound appeal, since most of us have to make our gardens compact and interesting in a limited space. It adds a unique elegance to your landscaping, yet it requires no more skill, time or expense than a well-maintained lawn. Though the results of lawn care and other gardening chores go unnoticed, topiary proudly displays your horticultural handiwork. Topiary reinforces the layout of formal gardens, provides either a tailored backdrop or a focal point for informal plantings, and adds an element of surprise to any garden. It can also become the main feature, turning your outdoor space into a magical green gallery.

An array of styles can turn unruly plants into works of art. Keep the evergreen next to your front door in bounds by turning it into a splendid spiral. Unify the house and garden by clipping

Ordinary hedges can be transformed into an endless variety of interesting architectural features, depending on how ambitious you are. You will find guidelines for creating a maze of your own on page 291.

your hedge into a complementary architectural form. Dress up bare vertical surfaces—and turn them into useful growing space—by training a fruit tree flat against the side of your house or fence. Along with fall's bounty of luscious tree-ripened fruit, you will have the visual delights of winter tracery, spring blossoms and leafy summer shadows. Transform ordinary beds and borders by carpeting them in patterns of miniature hedges and flowers that outline an animal, your initials or a sundial. And if you garden in containers on a terrace or balcony, you'll appreciate the fact that topiary shrubs don't outgrow their pots and planter boxes.

Musing, anon through crooked walks he wanders,
Round-winding rings, and intricate Meanders,
False guiding paths, doubtful beguiling strays,
And right-wrong errors of an endless Maze;
Not simply hedgèd with a simple border
Of Rosemary, *cut-out with curious order*
In Satyrs, Centaurs, Whales, *and* half-men-horses,
And thousand other contarfeited corses.

—GUILLAUME DE SALLUSTE DU BARTAS
La Première Semaine, ou la Création, c. 1590

> **66But after all, it is no more natural for a yew to be clipped into the shape of a hedge than a peacock, and if you do not object to yew hedges, and may regard topiary as a form of sculpture, then it takes its place somewhere among the arts—perhaps not much higher than the art of amusing oneself.99**
>
> —ERIC PARKER
> *The English Scene: The Gardener's England*

Whether you envision your creations as small or large, indoors or out, we hope THE COMPLETE BOOK OF TOPIARY will give you the skill and inspiration to be playful in your own house and garden. Within these pages you will discover a wealth of possible shapes, ranging from the elegant geometric forms of landscape designers, to the fanciful creatures fashioned by gardeners with an irrepressible sense of humor. Each chapter presents specific topiary projects, complete with detailed, easy-to-follow instructions. In the back of the book is a hardiness zone map and a guide to a dozen of the most reliable plants for topiary, so you can choose those best suited to your region of the country or indoor living conditions; a source guide for frames and tools; and a list of American gardens and greenhouses that display topiary—to tempt and inspire you to get out the shears, hedge trimmers, scissors and pots.

We live in a Golden Age of Gardening: never before has such a variety of plants, styles and techniques been available to American gardeners. In every era in which gardening has been cherished as an art, people have been drawn to the lure of plant sculpture, rediscovering old forms, and devising new shapes and styles. Join these noble gardeners of the past, who had the courage and imagination to unite nature and art in the horticultural adventure we know as topiary.

THE LORE OF TOPIARY

One of the first references to topiary was recorded by Pliny the Elder, who lived from 23 to 79 A.D. and told of "hunt-scenes, fleets of ships and all sorts of images" cut from cypress trees. He traced the invention of topiary to a friend of Julius Caesar's named Cnaius Matius during the first century B.C. Soon topiary became a fashionable feature on the country estates of well-to-do Romans.

With the fall of Rome the development of topiary was halted for almost nine centuries. Interest in topiary reawakened in medieval times: plants were clipped into smooth balls and cones raised on single trunks. As battles raged throughout the countryside, entire towns existed within castle walls. In order to grow fruit without taking up living space, a unique form of practical topiary emerged. Apple and pear trees were trained flat, or espaliered, against the inner ramparts. Later, two dimensional wall-trees were treasured for beauty as well as utility, and dozens of patterns were devised.

As part of the rediscovery of the aesthetics of Ancient Rome, topiary was renewed and refined in the Italian Renaissance. Lacking the range of plant material available today, they introduced variety into their gardens with an assortment of clipped shapes. Once again ornate hedges, leafy pyramids, globes, peacocks, bears and ships adorned the garden. Since it was no longer necessary to be protected behind walls and moats, these hillside pleasure gardens were open to the surrounding landscape, and striking views were framed by windows and arches cut into hedges.

Renaissance gardens contained flower beds laid out in intricate geometric patterns. These were edged in clipped boxwood and myrtle, creating flat topiary on the ground. The Tudor English versions were enclosed in small gardens and reflected a fascination with knot patterns, which are often seen in the tapestries and plasterwork of the period. At first the intertwining lines were made of contrasting, low-clipped herbs in the kitchen garden; eventually, the patterns became purely decorative, and the spaces in between the lines were filled with flowers and colored soil, clay and pebbles.

The Dutch have always excelled at raising plants, and since the 15th century have shown great expertise and fondness for topiary. Within the trimmed order of their gardens, topiary added a delightful jumble of playfulness. The Dutch went beyond the carefully arranged classic subjects of the Renaissance, filling their gardens with every conceivable bird and beast, as

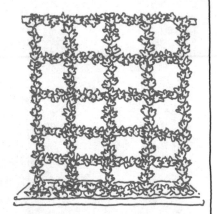

66This [topiary] is the richest and most distinguished in the whole Business of Gardening99

—DEZALLIER D'ARGENVILLE
The Theory and Practice of Gardening,
1712

well as vegetative renditions of tables, chairs and pottery. They surrounded the garden with tunnels or arbors trained from trees, so that they could admire their green sculptures while under shelter from wind, rain or summer sun.

Topiary's popularity peaked in England under William and Mary, natives of Holland who reigned from 1688 to 1702. Evergreen sculptures spread across the countryside, from vast estates to tiny cottage gardens, and ranged from architectural hedges and arbors to flocks of whimsical fowl, sporting hunt scenes, and all the childlike Dutch favorites. To this day, no other place in the world can boast such an abundance and variety of topiary.

While the Dutch and English favored a hodgepodge of amusing shapes, the 17th-century French topiarist preferred bushes clipped into simple, perfect cones, globes or obelisks. They were influenced by the terraced gardens of the Italian Renaissance; yet unlike the hill-perched Italians, who borrowed views of neighboring fields and villages by framing them in topiary windows, the French imposed strict symmetry on a vast landscape that extended as far as the eye could see. French gardens consisted of a manicured panorama, where seemingly endless rows of geometric figures marched through a carpet of flower beds arranged in sinuous scrolls and arabesques. These beds, known as parterres, succeeded knot designs for horizontal ground decoration.

In the early 18th century, topiary became unfashionable. A new movement in garden design, as well as in philosophy, painting and literature, favored the "natural" and picturesque. Topiary was attacked as a symbol of all that was artificial, though in fact it is no more unnatural than a clipped lawn. Many sculpted plants, the culmination of years of attentive pruning, were destroyed as the fervor for the naturalistic style increased. Fortunately, the art of topiary was continued as a folk craft in modest English cottage gardens, whose owners had no interest in the tides of fashion.

The Victorians made topiary fashionable once again. They

revived styles from earlier eras, adapting them to new plants and adding ornate details. Carpet bedding, a new method of ground decoration, covered the gardens in stars, circles, letters, baskets and tadpoles. Like the Tudor knot and French parterre, Victorian carpet bedding reflected the contemporary designs of fabric and architectural details. Amidst these beds of colorful exotic plants, sculpted peacocks, roosters, dogs and cats appeared. Garden architects added order to these eclectic arrangements, bringing the impact of architectural forms into the garden with evergreen walls, arches, summerhouses and arbors. A troop of gardeners, armed with ladders and shears, kept these elaborate scenes immaculate.

Topiary first arrived in the New World in Williamsburg, Virginia, around 1690, as geometric forms dotting diamond-shaped knot gardens. Soon many colonial gardens also included these features. In the following centuries, new estates appeared where topiary was created on a grand scale following styles popular in Europe. Thanks to a growing interest in our past, and time-saving trimming tools, many of these showplaces have been maintained or restored. And since the houseplant boom of the 1950s and 1960s, topiary has been brought indoors and developed into a truly American art form.

Today more and more gardeners have come to know the joys of plant sculpture, enthusiastically choosing from a rich variety of historic and modern styles. In THE COMPLETE BOOK OF TOPIARY we have endeavored to simplify and tailor these techniques to today's modern lifestyles, helping you to create the wonders of this most venerable branch of gardening in your own home and garden.

> **❝Just as people forced to do their own cooking turned ultimately to sophisticated foreign sources and became experts at techniques undreamed of by their mothers, so may American gardeners come to hanker after the horticultural arts unknown to earlier generations.❞**
>
> —ELEANOR PERÉNYI
> *Green Thoughts: A Writer in the Garden,* 1981

In the 19th century, a Mr. Cutbush was importing Dutch topiary jugs, chairs and doves into England to keep up with the renewed demand, enticing customers with his slogan "Cutbushes for cutbushes."

PLANT NAMES

While common plant names are familiar and full of charming associations, they can lead to confusion. The name daisy, for example, can refer to any of at least a dozen different flowers. Latin botanical names are more precise, letting other gardeners and nursery salespeople know exactly which plant you have in mind. A plant's generic name is listed first and is always capitalized—this can be likened to our family name. It identifies the genus or group to which the plant belongs. The second or species name is not capitalized, and is given to only one plant in each genus—although, just as more than one family has a John or Mary, the species name can be used in more than one genus. When a plant is a variation from the species (which could indicate anything from different-colored flowers to a compact growing habit or a special leaf shape) it is called a variety. The variety is identified by the third word in the botanical name; it is capitalized and enclosed within single quotation marks.

GENUS	SPECIES	VARIETY
Taxus	*cuspidata*	'Aurescens'
yew	Japanese yew	golden-tinted leaves

Portable Topiary

TABLETOP WHIMSY ON A FRAME

The ancient and noble art of topiary has been revolutionized by modern techniques that make it simple to populate your home with green beasts, birds and geometric shapes—and you don't even need a garden. Portable topiary is easy, versatile, rewarding and fun, as fast-growing plants are trained over a wire frame to produce plant sculptures that immediately look enchanting. Because the metal frame, rather than a plant's branches, provides structure and definition, your creation can be any size and any shape. From tabletop teddy bears to mantelpiece swans, they may be elegant or endearing—and as unusual as you can imagine.

In the 1960s, amateur contestants in American flower shows sought unusual ways to shape their houseplant entries. They recreated traditional topiary shapes with familiar indoor plants trained on moss-filled metal armatures. The earliest examples were various tabletop-size birds, including a proud rooster, a noble ibis and a regal eagle.

Since then, the popularity of stuffed topiary figures has grown by leaps and bounds. In 1975, Philadelphian Morris Brownell longed to create a spectacular entry for the Bicentennial Flower Show the following spring. He modeled his life-size giraffe after a Kansas-born infant named Sunflower. The 6-foot-tall steel frame was covered with seven kinds of ivy. Obviously, large creations such as this are not easily portable, but they can be moved around with some planning and friendly assistance, and they do add an undeniable surprise element to any interior.

Seemingly overnight, tabletop topiary figures inhabited plant shop windows and scampered across the pages of home-and-garden magazines, while large-scale versions cropped up in unexpected public places. In the fall of 1984, Rockefeller Center startled New York City with wild animals strolling through the Channel Gardens off Fifth Avenue. An elephant, giraffe, lion, camel, rhinoceros and flamingo wandered calmly between the skyscrapers, at home in their preserve of African daisies and ornamental grasses. At Christmastime in 1984, sightseers were greeted in the lobby of the World Trade Center by full-size rein-

The skeletons of portable figures probably have their origins in the florists' frames of the late 19th century, when displays were constructed in the shape of baskets, swans, lyres and even the Gates of Heaven open to receive the departed.

It takes three to five years for a topiary made in the traditional, pruned-shrub style to meet the exacting requirements of horticulturists at Disneyland in California and Walt Disney World in Florida. Whenever they want to produce a figure quickly for special events or to launch a new character, they make a large, stuffed portable topiary, which is ready to greet the public in less than a year.

Portable topiary figures can be created in sizes suited either to tabletops or plazas. These enchanting swans, stuffed and planted in creeping fig, stand six feet tall.

deer pulling a teddy bear-laden sleigh. The shopping center in Owings Mills, Maryland, has featured swans and herons among the fountains of the food court. And the Statue of Liberty celebrated her 1986 birthday with a horticultural likeness at the New York Botanical Garden.

Many public gardens have growing collections and ever-changing shows of portable topiary. Longwood Gardens in Kennett Square, Pennsylvania, the Chicago Botanic Garden in Glencoe, Illinois, and Callaway Gardens in Pine Mountain, Georgia, are all good places to visit for inspiration.

Large or small, portable topiary radiates an essential

charm from every inch, serving as a fanciful or serious decorative element anywhere in your house. You might want just one favorite pet to come home to—or a whole menagerie. Collections can inhabit bay windows; a pair of globes rising on slender stems is an elegant touch on either side of a fireplace. You can display a collection of topiary exclusively, or place a few figures among other objets d'art or houseplant groupings. For an amusing scene, suspend monkeys on a chain or let them swing in your ficus tree. Try an herb-covered shape in your kitchen for beauty and convenience, or a scented green companion by your bath. By making use of artificial lighting, you can even create topiary scenes in windowless hallways and dim corners.

Take a cue from prestigious florists who love portable topiary for distinctive party decorations. Once you create one, you need never worry about a centerpiece for your table. Dress up your favorite green pet for a party display, or create a fantastic new sculpture expressly for one glorious evening.

While a great advantage of framed forms is that they may be started at any time as houseplants or greenhouse denizens, they need not be confined to interiors. Portable plant sculptures can be placed outside, as the climate permits, to adorn a terrace or serve as seasonal garden accents.

Best of all, you can have fun with your topiary. Every time you play with it, giving a snip here and a tie there, the shape improves. Should your life become hectic, and your topiary neglected, it can usually be revived with a good haircut and the replacement of a plant or two.

One of the first practitioners of topiary in America was Thomas Hancock of Boston. Records show that in 1736 he requested for his Beacon Hill garden: "100 small yew trees . . . which I'd frame up here to my own fancy.

THE SHAPE OF PORTABLE TOPIARY

All portable topiary is created by training plants to cover the outside of a frame. This is usually a metal skeleton of an animal, a globe on a stem, which is known as a standard (see Chapter Two), a geometric form, or any other shape you wish to grow. While the frame supplies the basic shape, you add character and detail in the planting and training stages.

The frame may be used in two ways. In the first, the skeleton is stuffed with moss and potting mix, serving as both form and growing container. In the other, the frame serves as a hollow trellis over which vines in the pot beneath it are trained.

Most frames are adaptable to either technique. The decision as to whether or not to stuff them depends largely on the effect you wish to achieve. Empty-frame topiary is usually created for a two-dimensional silhouette or an open-outline effect, although it can be used for a solid cover of green. Stuffed topiary takes a bit longer, but gives a fuller, more realistic sculpture.

Hollow topiary is valued because it can be assembled quickly; and it is particularly suitable for training plants like rosemary, which don't like to have damp foliage. Noted Pennsylvania horticulturist J. Liddon Pennock, Jr. laughingly relates: "People used to ask me how long it took to get a finished chicken, and I told them one and a half to two hours."

Moss-filled forms offer unparalleled versatility. If enough small plants or cuttings are planted directly into the stuffed form, the figure is immediately attractive. Even if you start with only a few plants, it will be fully covered within a short time. Or, as with the hollow method, the stuffed form may be placed on a pot of plants that can be trained up the surface. The advantage of topiary planted in this way is that it needs less frequent watering. It is also possible to combine the two methods in one sculpture.

THE RANGE OF FRAMES

The early creators of portable topiary had to design and, in many cases, fabricate their own frames. Today, you have a choice—either take advantage of ready-made frames, or discover the pleasures of making frames yourself. If you can't locate the frame you want, design and construct your own from scratch. Chapter Four describes how you can easily construct different shapes at home, without special tools or metalworking skills.

There are two basic types of frames. One is flat bottomed, designed to either stand by itself or fit into containers. It can be stabilized in a pot or planter with long pins or wire bent into U-shapes.

The other frame has horizontal and vertical spikes at the base for anchoring below the surface of the soil; it is primarily designed for use with containers. Top-heavy shapes, such as a globe on a stem, often benefit from the stability offered by this type of frame. Several pieces of styrofoam jammed between the frame stem and the pot can be added for even more support. Should your topiary be really top-heavy, however, the stem will need to be set in plaster of Paris or quick-setting cement.

Wire frames, fabricated of rust-resistant metal, may be purchased in a wealth of shapes and sizes. The simplest, most effective frames for hollow topiary consist of a flat outline or open silhouette made from a single wire. The classic shape is a

> **❝Wire frames have entirely superseded the old methods . . . the frame gives the florist at once the desired form, and makes it easy for any person of taste to arrange flowers in the shape of an anchor, star, etc. The frame is filled with damp moss, wound slightly to keep it in place, and the flowers . . . are inserted in the moss.❞** *This Victorian handiwork is the ancestor of modern portable topiary.*
>
> —PETER HENDERSON
> *Practical Floriculture,*
> 1897

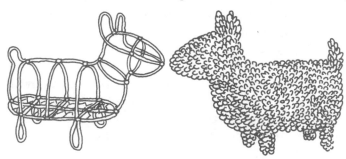

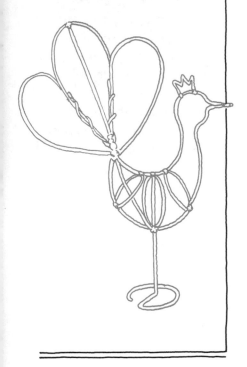

hoop; several may be combined in one pot for a more interesting silhouette. Hearts and weather vane shapes, such as an angel with a trumpet or a running horse, are also used as outline designs.

As for three-dimensional designs, the favored Victorian baskets and swans are being made in modern versions. You are also likely to find globes, teddy bears, rabbits, poodles and terriers. Ready-made frames can be altered to give them your original touch. Carefully bend the frame to give a tilt to the head and a wag to the tail. If you stuff a frame, you can modify the shape by adding extra moss padding in various places. A good selection is available at many garden centers or gift shops at public gardens. If you can't find the shape you want locally, order it from the Source Guide.

Simple but elegant frames can be made with ordinary items found in the hardware store or garden center—even by scrounging through your own closets or garage. For example, semicircular wire hanging baskets can be used to produce several shapes. Join two to make a hanging or kissing ball. Create a lollipop by nailing them on top of a wooden handle or dowel. Grow a slender cone on an upside-down tomato cage whose spikes are tied together at the top. Wreath frames are available in a range of diameters year-round, so don't save them just for the holidays. Stuffed and planted with un-Christmasy plants, they can be hung on the wall or used as the basis of centerpieces. Fill the center with fresh flowers, fruit, candles or a punch bowl.

Whether buying, designing or constructing frames, remember that you are working with live plants. They will always add to the overall dimensions of the figure, softening detail and definition. Therefore, an animal frame should be slimmer than your ultimate creation but exaggerate the size of ears and tail; and limbs should be positioned away from the body. While plants differ in their flexibility, all stems have a breaking point. For this reason, frames with sharp angles and small details are difficult to work with. Instead, give the shape life and character with strong features.

SELECTING PLANTS

While frames are the backbone of portable topiary, it is the plants you pick to cover the surface that will bring your sculpture to life. Experiment with different kinds of plants to give your creations a special look. Any houseplant of vining or trailing habit is a potential star for indoor topiary. Although you can make an entire figure with just one small plant, it is better to start with either a large plant or several small ones. In the first place, you won't have to wait as long for a fully covered topiary. In addition, if one plant dies, stems from the others can be quickly trained to cover the bare patch.

Not all the formal gardens of earlier days were executed on a grand scale. This French etching shows the wide use of portable figures in complementary pots and boxed planters.

> **66In a sense, these groves were tree sanctuaries, for in this land [Egypt], where trees were scarce, trees were everywhere held in veneration. Each temple had its particular kind of tree sacred to its divinity. . . .99**
>
> —RICHARDSON WRIGHT
> *The Story of Gardening,* 1934

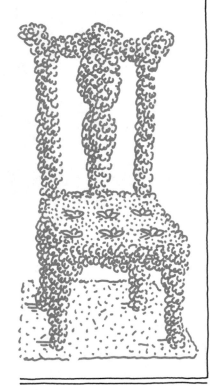

Several kinds of plants can be combined on the same sculpture. Just as different-size stitches in needlework create raised patterns, so the use of different varieties on the same form will give contrast to the surface of your project. Antique dealer Herbert Schiffer created a Chippendale chair, whose seat consisted of an assortment of variegated plants arranged in a tapestry, for the Philadelphia Flower Show. The frame for the project is now in the collection of the Winterthur Museum in Delaware. As unusual a choice as it may seem, chairs were frequent outdoor topiary subjects in England and Holland in the 17th century.

Creeping fig (*Ficus pumila*) and English ivy (*Hedera helix*) have proven to be the most reliable and versatile plants for portable topiary. Commonly available and easily grown, both plants thrive in a range of temperatures and light levels.

Creeping fig roots easily, rarely succumbs to insects or disease and has fine texture, good color and rapid growth. On stuffed topiary it develops tiny rootlets wherever the stems touch the moss, resulting in a close-hugging growth habit. The varieties 'Quercifolia' (oak leaf creeping fig) and 'Minima' (miniature creeping fig) create an even finer texture, but are extremely slow growing. 'Variegata' has white-splashed leaves. These three cultivars are useful in providing contrast on the same form, as all have identical care requirements. Outdoors, creeping fig is hardy to Zone 9 (see the Hardiness Zone Map). Indoors, it should never be allowed to dry out.

Ivy is very popular for topiary because there are hundreds of varieties with ruffled, pointed or heart-shaped leaves, some highlighted in gold or white. Choose ones that enhance the characteristics of your subject. Try a white-marked ivy for the body of a panda, planting a darker type on the arms and legs. Look for varieties with leaves set closely along their stems for best coverage. Among those that have been a great success are 'Glacier,' 'Little Diamond,' 'Gold Dust,' 'Needlepoint,' 'Ivalace,' 'Itsy Bitsy,' 'Kobold' (great for small topiary because of its tiny leaves), 'Stuttgart' and 'Fleur de Lis.'

Ivy is a favorite plant for hollow topiary, but there are

many other delightful possibilities. Jasmine (*Jasminum* and *Gelsemium* in variety) has fragrant winter blooms. Rosary vine or string-of-hearts (*Ceropegia woodii*) also flowers, but its most attractive feature is small, velvety red leaves. Try herbs for a change of sight and scent. Prostrate or spreading rosemary (*Rosmarinus officinalis* 'Prostratus') is easily trained around a hoop. Pennyroyal (*Mentha pulegium*), winter savory (*Satureja montana*), and myrtle (*Myrtus communis*) are also dependably attractive year-round. Orange mint (*Mentha aquatica* 'Citrata') is pretty, but don't count on it in winter when it goes through an unattractive dormant period.

A popular choice for stuffed creations is baby's tears (*Soleirolia soleirolii*). It has a bright green moss-like appearance and close-growing habit. The thin stems root easily wherever they touch moss or soil. No pinning is necessary—simply snip off unruly growth. The 'Aurea' variety has golden-yellow leaves that are perfect for a tiger's stripes.

Corsican mint (*Mentha requienii*) has all the characteristics of baby's tears, with the bonus of a strong peppermint fragrance and finer foliage that is especially good for tiny topiary. Both mint and baby's tears prefer warm temperatures and constant moisture. Creeping Charlie (*Lysimachia nummularia*) is another close-hugging plant with round, slightly hairy leaves. Lawn leaf (*Dichondra carolinensis*) is used as a grass substitute in hot climates, but is also useful for covering stuffed topiary as the seeds can be sown directly in the moss.

Many other plants can be used to provide detail and accents. Sometimes the perfect combination of shape and plant suggests itself. On small figures, select plants with small leaves and a delicate texture that won't obscure the shape. If your topiary is larger, you can add drama by using plants with bolder foliage. In any case, plants with flexible rather than brittle stems will be easier to work with. Stroll through greenhouses and plant shops to see what strikes your fancy—growers are usually happy to give care hints for unfamiliar plants. Succulents, for example, offer a variety of colors, sizes and habits. Since they grow slowly

The ancient Greeks crowned themselves with rosemary wreaths during exams, believing the herb would improve their memory.

In 1713, Alexander Pope's invective against topiary in The Guardian *turned popular opinion against formal gardens and clipped plants. His essay included a mythical catalogue of topiary shapes. Although he intended them to be distasteful, they offer hilarious but tempting inspiration to the budding topiarist!*

and prefer to dry out between waterings, they require less attention than other plants. Stud a turtle's shell with various rosette-shaped succulent species such as hens and chicks, echeverias, sedums and haworthias. Miniature bromeliads are also colorful accent plants that don't need frequent watering.

Dracaena (*Dracaena marginata*) is a plant with cream, green or red stripes on long, narrow leaves. Small specimens lend a spiky, dramatic look to indoor topiary. Some varieties have a stunning overall pink effect that makes for convincing flamingo feathers.

For a lion's mane try that graceful favorite, the spider plant (*Chlorophytum comosum*), in either light green or the white variegated type. Kenilworth ivy (*Cymbalaria muralis*) is also lovely for a mane. It has small, kidney-shaped leaves and occasional blue flowers that resemble tiny snapdragons. Artillery fern (*Pilea microphylla*) grows in a dense layer of minute, fleshy leaves. It can be used quite convincingly as a horse's mane or peacock's crest.

SHOWING OFF

The container for your indoor topiary is nearly as important to the display as the figure itself. There are no hard rules regarding your selection. Some suggestions are offered here, but the final choice depends on your taste and inventiveness.

The size of the container should befit the size of the topiary. The plant sculpture itself should be the focal point, so avoid any container that dwarfs the figure or has an overwhelmingly elaborate design. To prevent water stains on tabletops and floors, the pot must be large enough to catch excess water dripping from the foliage. In general, low pots give sleek, pleasing proportions to animals and birds.

Choose a shape that will harmonize with the sculpture, or

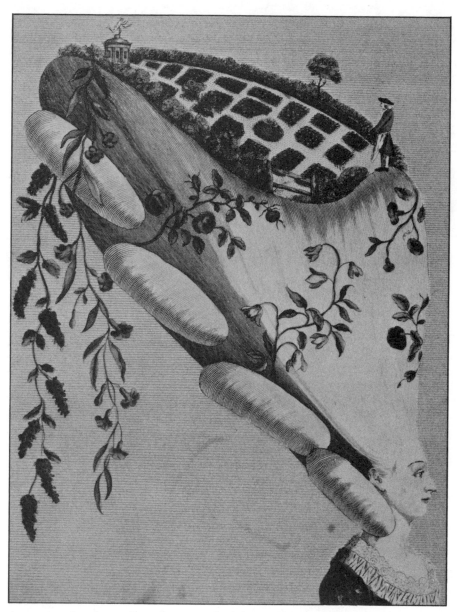

A passion for formal gardens—and elaborate hairstyles—carried to an extreme, is portrayed in 1777 by Matthew Darly in The Flower Garden.

Finely crafted topiary always inspires a desire to show off, though everyone has different ideas about what constitutes portable. In the 18th century the Duchesse de Choiseul sported a 3-foot-high horticultural headdress, which featured a parterre garden complete with flowers and grass, plus a clockwork windmill and a mirrored brook.

*I*f you can't find a pot that suits the dimensions of your topiary, construct a handsome wooden box. It should be slightly larger than the longest part of the topiary. Make the sides from barn siding and the base from plywood. Nail pieces of siding to the base to add height and facilitate drainage. Drill a $\frac{1}{2}$-inch-diameter hole in the bottom so excess water can drain out.

one that will provide contrast. A round pot could be used to echo the head of a roly-poly bear; on the other hand, a square pot can be a striking counterpoint to a rounded form. Decide if you want to focus attention on the topiary itself, or on its environment. A swan takes on a whimsical spirit when placed in a fanciful setting of aquatic plants; standing alone on a simple wooden planter, it becomes an architectural accent.

When selecting a container, choose a terra-cotta pot over a plastic one. Clay has a natural, neutral tone, and is heavy enough to counterbalance the weight of the sculpture. The one advantage to growing topiaries in plastic is that they don't need watering as often; but you will have to put pebbles or some

No matter what age group you are entertaining, portable pets such as this squirrel, rabbit, frog and puppy will add an endearing touch to the occasion.

other weight in the bottom so they don't tip over. Any pot should have a hole in the base for proper drainage. If your favorite clay pot doesn't, drill a hole with a carbide bit.

Freestanding stuffed topiary can sit on almost anything waterproof. Trays and saucers may be as shallow as you like, but should have a rim to catch excess water. One of the best stands is a waterproof spice turntable or lazy Susan. The small lip is unobtrusive but sufficient to catch drips, and since the turntable rotates, all sides of the sculpture can easily be groomed and exposed to the light.

Garden centers, craft shops, gift boutiques, antique stores, flea markets and mail-order catalogs are all potential treasure troves for topiary containers. Sometimes you need look no further than your own kitchen—glass baking dishes, china and plastic trays are all wonderful possibilities. Use them, as well as clear plastic saucers, to line non-waterproof containers such as wooden planters, baskets and unglazed clay saucers. To avoid any leaky surprises, test each container before using to make sure that it will, indeed, hold water. And if you choose to display topiary on a favorite china piece, line it with a sheet of plastic to prevent rust stains caused by the metal frame.

Freestanding topiary does better when placed on a trivet or layer of pebbles. In the first place, the entire figure will be visible if it's raised almost level with the top edge of the container. Also, the plant won't be sitting in a puddle while it enjoys the humidity from water collected in the container. Possible platforms include cake cooling racks and pot trivets. Pebbles can be found in a wealth of colors and sizes, adding another element of interest to your display. You can choose from ordinary stones, polished river stones, black Japanese rocks, glass flower-arranging pebbles or drops, clear and multicolored marbles and aquarium gravel. If you are concerned about weight, use perlite, the white granules sold as a soil lightener.

> **❝. . . for grand effect, nothing, in our estimation, can ever be produced in promiscuous planting to equal that obtained by planting in masses or in ribbon lines.❞**
>
> —PETER HENDERSON
> *Practical Floriculture,*
> 1897

> Gervase Markham, in his 1631 volume The Whole Art of Husbandrie, encouraged Englishwomen of his time to train rosemary "for their pleasure, to grow in sundry proportions, as in the fashion of a Catt, a Pecocke, or such like thing as they fansie."

DECORATIVE ACCENTS

Once you have provided your topiary with a practical and attractive container, it's time to add some finishing touches. To create a fanciful scene or to evoke a natural setting, surround your topiary with miniature plants. Specialists in terrarium varieties can offer a good selection for your topiary's habitat. Try a ground cover of creeping thyme or baby's tears, highlighted with miniature hosta and ferns. A rabbit could be happy surrounded with tiny lettuce plants. Disguise plain containers to blend naturally with plants by gluing burlap or sheet moss, a natural green material that comes in flat layers, to the outside.

Cheer up your home by adding flowering plants to your display. Miniature African violets add a note of color year-round. Celebrate spring by tucking crocus, lily-of-the-valley and narcissus bulbs in among the plants at the base of your sculpture. Lobelia, alyssum and miniature impatiens are annuals that will provide months of color.

Many touches can be added to depict detail. For a whimsical look, use buttons for your animal's eyes; for a more realistic look, add taxidermist's eyes and false eyelashes. Dried natural materials can also be used as eyes—try berries, tiny cones, cloves or anise seed. Gray Spanish moss makes a spritely horse's tail, and the silvery lichen called reindeer moss gives an illusion of water when it surrounds a swan, water bird or frog. For an easy woodland atmosphere, place an acorn-clutching squirrel on a layer of twigs. Tiny dried flowers can be pinned on to create necklaces and ties.

There are countless ways to temporarily jazz up topiary for a festive effect. Spruce up pots or trays with decorative coverings that are easily removed when the party ends. For a natural look, stick shiny galax leaves on the outside with florist's clay. If you want a coordinated effect, cover containers with swatches that match your tablecloth and napkins. Tie fabric on with raffia

Whether potted or freestanding, portable topiary brings a touch of fantasy that enlivens any room.

or ribbons. If you want to add plants to the scene just for the occasion, nestle small pots of them among the permanent under-plantings and conceal the pots with sheet moss or Spanish moss. This way you won't have to spend time transplanting, and the disturbance to existing plants will be minimized.

Special touches will transform your plant sculpture into the guest of honor. A dog could hold a small basket filled with flowers or chocolates in its mouth. Keep your monkey content during the party with a banana. Cut flowers can be pinned into stuffed forms—the moisture inside will keep them fresh for hours. If your topiary isn't covered yet, flowers will conceal the bare spots for your party. Add carefree glamour with streaming

ribbons, available in a multitude of colors, widths and textures. Festoon geometric shapes with swags and bows. Garland animals with a variety of crowns and collars; plait streamers into flowing tails and manes.

For evening affairs, highlight your creations with battery-operated minilights, available at party shops. You can drape the entire animal, or simply highlight the display with a glowing collar or wand.

SUPPLIES

Portable topiary is made up of a frame, growing medium and plants. Between the garden center and the five-and-ten, you should be able to purchase supplies locally. Portable topiary is a young craft, and the majority of the articles you'll use were originally designed for other uses.

Long-fiber sphagnum moss is the best basic filling for frames. When a frame is filled with moss and potting mix a haven is created for plant roots, whether they are planted inside or appear as rootlets along climbing stems. This filling should consist of ingredients that will retain moisture and provide nutritional as well as physical support for the expanding root system. It should also be lightweight to exert a minimum of stress on the frame and so that the moist figure is not too difficult to move. Long-fiber (or coarse) sphagnum moss answers all the above requirements and should be the main ingredient in filling stuffed topiary. It has a fluffy texture and is composed of whole fibers of dried moss that become spongy when wet. A plastic dishpan or pail is handy for soaking sphagnum. If you are making a large topiary, you can soak a quantity in a plastic wading pool. Don't try to substitute milled sphagnum—it has the texture of fine powder and is impossible to use for filling frames. If your skin is particularly sensitive, you might want to wear thin rubber gloves when working with sphagnum moss.

Sterile soilless growing mixes (Pro-Mix, Fafard and Metro-Mix are some brand name examples) are added to the filling for a more nourishing mixture. A good proportion is one part of soilless mix to two parts of sphagnum moss. Ordinary potting soil is fine for use in a container, but too heavy for use in a frame. Forget about garden soil—it is full of insects that run rampant in damp moss.

Pieces of styrofoam can be placed in the center of large forms prior to filling to cut down on the weight. You can also insert plastic bags or cheesecloth filled with styrofoam pellets or perlite.

Sheet moss is another type of natural material used to construct portable topiary. The moss comes in flat layers: one side will be either a fresh green color or dried to a more golden shade; this is the side that should face outward. Stuffed frames are sometimes wrapped with a skin of sheet moss to hold the filling and to create a smooth, attractive surface. Because the sheet moss is itself decorative, you can display the figure while only partially covered by plants—or even completely unplanted. For a fuller, richer appearance on hollow frames, wrap each wire with sheet moss.

Fishing line and florist's wire are the best materials for holding the stuffing or securing sheet moss around the frame. Although wire is easier to work with than line, it rusts quickly, so don't use it on forms you intend to keep for a long time. Fishing line, also called nylon monofilament, is transparent and virtually invisible. It can cut into your hands as you pull it tightly, so wear gloves or adhesive bandages on your fingers. A good strength for most projects is 8- to 10-pound test. For large topiary, use 25-pound test. If you are constructing a giant form, use 50-pound dacron line, which doesn't stretch. Where there are large spaces between the wires of your frame, crisscross fishing line or waterproof adhesive tape to hold the filling. If plants are tied to the hollow frame, you can use either raffia or thin green string. These are attractive and gentler on tender stems than line and wire.

SUGGESTED PLANTS FOR SCULPTED CREATURES

WATERBIRD
Use dracaena or spider plant for spiky feathers

POODLE
Train miniature creeping fig for the "clipped" parts of the body; ordinary creeping fig on pompoms

LION
Baby's tears on the body; Kenilworth ivy on the mane

FAST & EASY COVERAGE

CREEPING FIG

If you space plants every 6 inches or so, the figure should be covered within 4 to 6 weeks.

BABY'S TEARS

Grows rapidly, with a delicate texture, but needs high humidity and care not to overwater. Because of its creeping habit, it must be used on a stuffed form. The gold-colored variety is useful for contrast.

IVY

In general, the all-green varieties are easier to grow than variegated forms, which are fussier about light and water. Once established it covers rapidly, but not as fast as creeping fig or baby's tears. Good for hollow and stuffed types.

Portable topiary both surprises and delights when it stands in unexpected contrast to the environment. Here animals from the African plains parade through an urban plaza.

U-shaped hairpins make the best choice for securing vines on a stuffed topiary and tucking in stray bits of moss. Florist's or fern pins are adequate, but a little clumsy to work with on small pieces. If you can't find hairpins or fern pins, florist's wire can be cut into short lengths and bent into pins. In a pinch, paper clips can be reshaped to suit your needs.

A layer of chicken wire can be wrapped around a hollow, three-dimensional frame to encourage a solid cover of leaves, since it gives stems something to cling to in the open spaces in the skeleton. If you cover an outline frame, you will get a solid, flat shape.

Although ordinary household scissors or knives will suffice for most portable topiary work, a few inexpensive tools will facilitate many construction and maintenance tasks. Wire cutters are useful for trimming wire and shortening pins to be used in narrow areas. Seam snippers or manicure scissors are invaluable for delicate planting, arranging and pruning. Tweezers, particularly the long surgical models, help to groom out dead leaves.

HOLLOW CREATIONS

Growing on an Empty Frame

This is the basic procedure to follow for any shape you want to make without stuffing. The plants are trained up from the pot under the frame. The steps can be applied to any homemade or commercial frame.

Planting

Select a pot that is slightly larger in diameter than the widest part of the frame. Moisten your favorite soilless growing mix. Look for plants with long stems in 3- to 4-inch pots to quickly give a finished look. If you are training a hoop, cut the growing time in half by starting with two plants, one at each end of the hoop. As in ordinary potting, the plants should be set at the same depth at which they were growing in their original pots. Be sure that the the roots are covered with soilless growing mix, but don't bury the stems.

You will need:
—*a pot*
—*a wire topiary frame*

FAST & EASY COVERAGE

CREEPING CHARLIE
Another quick, dependable plant, with a compact growth that resembles baby's tears.

SEDUM
Effect is instant when slow-growing plants are closely spaced in a stuffed form. Easy to grow. Can dry out between waterings.

DRACAENA
Place close together in a stuffed form for instant effect. Discard after a year, when they get leggy.

SPIDER PLANT
Use like dracaena. Plain green or striped types are equally simple to grow.

KENILWORTH IVY
Simple, but like baby's tears it requires good humidity and a stuffed form.

MORE CHALLENGING COVERAGE

OAK LEAF AND MINIATURE CREEPING FIG
Unequalled for their fine, close texture, but grow very slowly. Can take one year to cover a topiary.

CORSICAN MINT
Charming scent and tiny pale green foliage make it desirable, but it rots easily.

VARIEGATED IVY
White or gold markings are striking, but plants tend to be less vigorous and adaptable than green varieties. Calico's red stems and green-and-white speckled leaves give a unique look, but it is fussy about watering.

HERBS
Pennyroyal, prostrate rosemary and thyme are worth growing for scent and flavor. Take care not to overwater.

—*soilless growing mix*

—*(optional) two lengths of wire bent into U's; sheet moss; long-fiber sphagnum moss; fishing line or florist's wire; chicken wire*

1. Partially fill the pot with soilless growing mix. Place the frame in the pot. If it has spikes, push it down to anchor firmly. If it has a flat bottom, cut two lengths of wire and bend into U-shapes. On either side of the frame, push these U-shaped wires down around the base and into the soil to secure it. If the frame has a flat-bottomed base, set it in the container before adding soil.

2. Remove plants from pots and transplant. Add soilless mix as necessary to settle the plants at the proper depth, leaving an inch of space between the mix surface and the rim of the pot. Locate plants next to any vertical supports or next to the base of the frame, so stems can be neatly trained upward and onto the frame.

3. If desired, the wires that make up the frame may be individually wrapped with moss. This adds something moist for plants to cling to. Take long, narrow pieces of sheet moss and cover the inside with a thin layer of sphagnum. While holding the sheet moss in place around the wire, lash it tightly with fishing line or florist's wire. This is recommended only for very simple shapes.

4. If you want to cover the frame easily with a solid surface of leaves rather than an outline, wrap the open space between the wire with string or chicken wire before planting.

TRAINING

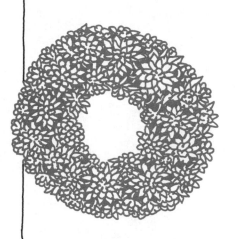

There are three ways to train plants on a hollow frame. The methods are similar, but the finished effect will be different. The first technique is to weave stems around and through the frame until it is completely covered. The second is to twine stems around each wire for an airy silhouette. The third is to tie plants to the frame. This last technique creates a more even, uniform outline and allows you total control, making it possible to train different plants to form patterns on the same frame. For instance, train ordinary wax plant (*Hoya carnosa*) around the inner side of a hoop, and surround it with an outer circle of variegated wax plant.

Weaving

Lift up a stem and wind it around and through the frame, working from the bottom to the top. Repeat until all stems have been woven into the frame. As new growth appears, tuck it into the frame. Once the entire form is covered, new shoots should be trimmed off.

Twining

Take individual stems and twist them around and up each wire. Twine new stems around the frame in the same fashion until the top is reached, where they are snipped off.

Tying

Tie stems to the frame with raffia or string. Check ties frequently to make sure they don't accidentally cut through enlarging stems. Cut tight ties and replace with looser loops. Once stems are woody, they will stay in place and the ties can be removed.

STUFFED SCULPTURES

Plant-As-You-Build
Layered Sphagnum Form

Longwood Gardens' Patricia Hammer uses this method, which she calls "build as you go," to form lions, penguins, deer and all her other vining creations. It is a quick, efficient and easy way to stuff a frame to be covered with vines. The procedure for inserting the plants is the same as for any ordinary potting task, except that the plants are put in on their sides. As in conventional potting, take care to put the plant in at the proper depth so that the roots are covered without burying the stems. Use either cuttings rooted in flats or small, sturdy plants in 2- to 3-inch pots. Before you begin, get a rough idea of how many plants you'll use and where you'll place them. Plant in a more or less even pattern on the form. Don't stuff or plant narrow portions of the frame and extremeties, such as beaks, noses, arms and legs, which dry out rapidly. Put plants with long runners next to appendages, training them out to cover these difficult spots. For texture and color contrast, use a combination of plants. If you want a bear frame to become a panda, for example, create a lighter tummy by planting a variegated variety to contrast with darker plants on the rest of the form. If there are large spaces between the wires of your frame, crisscross fishing line or waterproof adhesive tape to hold the sphagnum.

You will need:
—long-fiber sphagnum moss
—a wire topiary frame
—rooted cuttings or small plants in 2- to 3-inch pots
—(optional) fertilizer; fishing line or waterproof adhesive tape

1 Soak sphagnum moss in a pan of lukewarm water until soft. You may also use a weak solution of fertilizer.

2 A handful at a time, squeeze excess water out of moss and build a 2-inch-thick layer in the bottom of the frame.

3 Remove plants from pots. Arrange around the perimeter of the layer, so that the roots rest inside and the stems protrude sideways through the frame. Be careful not to insert the plants too deeply. Sprinkle any loose soil from the pots over the roots.

4 Working your way up and around the frame, build layers of moss and plants, pressing down gently on each layer of moss until the frame is filled.

5 Pin and shape to cover the frame.

Building a Wrapped Form

> 66Every part of the [sphagnum] moss is permeated with minute tubes and spaces, resulting in a system of delicate capillary tubes, having the effect of a very fine sponge. The cells readily absorb water and retain it. The water can be squeezed out, but the Moss does not collapse and is ready to take in fluid again.99
>
> —MRS M. [MAUD] GRIEVE
> *A Modern Herbal*, 1931

Wrapped forms take more time to complete than layered sphagnum versions, but they are sturdier and better for non-vining plants that don't completely cover the surface, such as succulents, dracaenas or spider plants. Remember, wrapping adds to the dimensions of the form, so figure on an increase of about an inch overall.

Sheet moss can be used dry, but it is easier to mold to the frame if it is soaked in a weak solution of fertilizer diluted in lukewarm water. Squeeze out excess moisture as you use each piece. For filling, mix one part of soilless growing mix with two parts of sphagnum moss and moisten.

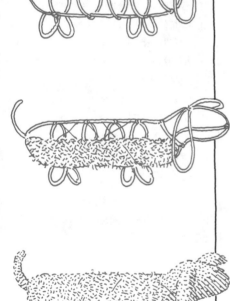

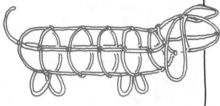

You will need:
—*sheet moss*
—*soilless growing mix*
—*long-fiber sphagnum moss*
—*a wire topiary frame*
—*fishing line or florist's wire*

1 Line the base of the frame (inside bottom) with the thickest pieces of sheet moss.

2 Cover the lower half of the frame on the outside with sheet moss. Tie a piece of line to the frame and wrap it loosely around the sheet moss, basting it in place to cover the frame and hold the filling.

3 Fill the cavity created by the covered portion with the stuffing mixture.

4 Repeat Steps 2 and 3 until the entire frame is covered in sheet moss and filled with growing mix.

5 Lash the entire form with line to hold the sheet moss and filling securely in place and create a smooth surface: tie one end to the frame, leaving a long "tail"; keeping the line taut, wrap it snugly around the form several times; tie off securely, using the tail; repeat this step as necessary, starting with separate lengths of line, until the entire form is sturdy and smooth.

6 Add bits of thinner sheet moss to details, such as ears and paws, to lend character and definition. Small areas like these don't need a filling of growing mix.

PLANTING WRAPPED FORMS

There are three ways to plant wrapped forms. The first is to train vines up from an underlying pot or planter. You can water it like any houseplant, supplemented by an occasional misting. The second technique, called plugging, is to insert small plants all over the form itself. Plugged topiaries are easily soaked to keep the growing plants properly watered. To achieve maximum coverage in the shortest time, put plants both in the form and in the pot. The third method is to set one large plant directly in the form. When you are stuffing, leave a hole for the plant in the largest part of the frame. It will take longer to cover the shape but, because the root system is better developed in a large plant, the sculpture won't need to be watered as frequently.

Planting in the Pot

Select a pot that is slightly larger in circumference than the base of the frame. Moisten your favorite potting soil or soilless growing mix. Look for plants in 3- to 4-inch pots with the longest runners to give good coverage right away. As in ordinary potting, the plants should be set at the same depth at which they were growing in their original pots. Be sure that the roots are covered with potting soil or soilless mix, but don't bury the stems.

Although the directions call for a stuffed and wrapped wire topiary frame, you could use one that has simply been filled with long-fiber sphagnum.

You will need:
—a pot slightly larger than the base of the frame

—*potting soil or soilless growing mix*
—*a stuffed and wrapped wire topiary frame*
—*small plants with long runners in 3- to 4-inch pots*
—*(optional) two lengths of wire bent into U's*

1 Partially fill the pot with soil or growing mix. If your frame has a spiked base, place it in the pot and push down to anchor firmly. If the frame has a flat-bottomed base, set it in the container before adding soil.

2 Remove plants from their small pots and transplant into the larger clay pot. As you work, tilt each plant so that the foliage trails over the rim and downward and the underside of the leaves is facing up. In this way the upper surface of the leaves will be correctly oriented when you lift the vines to cover the frame. Locate plants around and close to the edge of the pot.

3 Continue planting around the entire circumference of the pot, forming a circle of plants close to the rim with leaves upside down. This will leave a space in the center for the stuffed frame. Add soil or growing mix as necessary to settle the plants at the proper depth, leaving an inch of space between the mix surface and the rim of the pot.

4 Center the flat-bottomed frame (if that is what you are using), and secure with two lengths of wire bent into U's. Push these wires around and down either side of the frame for stability.

5 Lift up the vines that are hanging over the rim of the pot and place them up and around your frame. As you do so the leaves of the vines will once more be facing upright. Pin the vines to cover the frame.

Plugging in the Form

Select small plants in 2- to 3-inch pots or rooted cuttings. Use as many plants as possible, planting closely for an instantly finished look. Avoid planting in extremities or narrow portions of the form, which dry out quickly. Instead, if you are using a vining plant, train runners planted in adjacent areas to cover these spots.

You will need:
—rooted cuttings or small plants in 2- to 3-inch pots
—a stuffed and wrapped wire topiary frame
—a pencil
—sheet moss
—U-shaped hairpins

1 With your finger or a pencil, poke a hole through the sheet moss and enlarge it as necessary to accommodate the roots. Take a rooted cutting or remove a plant from its growing container and insert it into the opening. As in ordinary potting, the plants should be set at the same depth at which they were growing in their original pots. Press the moss gently but firmly to secure the plant and to eliminate air pockets.

2 Seal the opening around the plant with a plug of sheet moss. Secure the moss plug with a U-shaped hairpin. This step encloses the plant securely and keeps stuffing from falling out.

3 Repeat these steps until the main areas of the form are plugged.

4 Pin and shape to cover the frame.

One Large Plant in the Form

In this method the plant is placed in the central or fattest portion of the form. This is the best location since it is the last area to dry out and allows you to use a large plant. Because the plant has a well-established root system, it will quickly grow out over the entire figure. Select a plant growing in a pot several inches smaller than the intended planting area.

You will need:
—a large plant and its pot
—a wire topiary frame
—long-fiber sphagnum moss
—U-shaped hairpins
—(optional) sheet moss and fishing line or florist's wire

1 Remove the plant from the pot, being careful not to break the pot, and set both aside.

2 Begin stuffing the form with sphagnum. As you approach the center and top, insert the empty pot as a guide, packing the filling firmly around it.

3 (optional) Wrap the form with sheet moss and lash with line, being careful not to cover the top of the pot with moss.

4 Remove the guide pot and insert plant. Add filling around the roots as necessary to settle the plant, as you would in ordinary planting.

5 Cover the top of the root ball with sheet moss and pin securely.

Training Vines on Stuffed Forms

Stems are trained on moss by pinning them to the surface. They usually send out small roots wherever the shoots touch the moss. Don't pin down tender tips—they bruise and break too easily. Pin between leaves, not through them. Try for one even layer of growth—leaves trapped beneath others will rot. As the plants grow, train and pin new shoots to fill in bare patches. Once the surface is covered, stray stems should be trimmed back with scissors.

CARE AND FEEDING

Provide a growing location with good light, moderate temperature and good air circulation. The latter is especially important for the successful culture of stuffed topiary. The leaves are against damp moss, and if water stagnates on them rather than evaporating, a host of fungal problems can result. Most plants used for portable topiary do not require full sun—they generally prefer strong indirect light. Bear this in mind when summering them outdoors—just like a person who has been under wraps all winter, they will sunburn.

The skills required to maintain indoor topiary are no more extensive than those needed to develop and care for any houseplant collection. For a lush, even coat, figures should be rotated to expose all sides of the sculpture to the light source. It is difficult to maintain growth on the underside of some shapes. Freestanding topiaries can be hung upside down to grow vines over tummies. An ordinary shower curtain hook clipped to the base of the frame makes it easy to suspend.

Once the topiary is settled and growing, it requires five kinds of attention: watering, feeding, grooming, insect control and disease control.

> **A hedge doesn't grow down—it follows the sun.**
>
> —GUS YEARICKS
> on the difficulty of training a topiary elephant's trunk downward

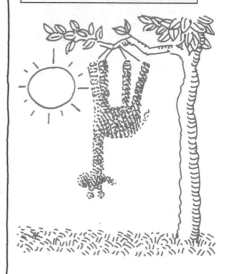

I f your topiary pet has long ears or a slender neck, these parts will dry out before the rest of the figure needs watering. To keep them moist, turn the creature upside down and dip the thinner portions in a bowl or a pail filled with water.

Watering

How often you water depends on the size of the figure, the kind of plants you are training and the location. The bigger the form, the longer it can hold water. Skip watering on overcast days. All types of portable topiary appreciate frequent misting to raise humidity, wash off dust and discourage bugs. Keep a misting bottle near your topiary—it will be more convenient to spritz the plant when you pass by.

Misting is an added bit of attention that your sculptures will appreciate, but misting isn't enough to keep plants adequately watered. Remember, it is the roots that take up most of the moisture a plant needs, and these are inside the moss or soil. If you have planted in the pot, add water when the soil surface feels dry to the touch. If you have planted in the form, carry the figure to the kitchen sink and wet thoroughly with the sprayer. Leave the figure in the sink for a few minutes to drain off excess water.

Feeding

Once a month apply a balanced water-soluble fertilizer, such as Peters or Miracle-Gro. Most plants rest for a period in late fall and early winter, so withhold fertilizer at that time. For free-standing stuffed topiary, fill a pail, sink or bathtub with tepid water. Add fertilizer to make a weak dilution. Gently immerse the figure, leaving it until no air bubbles rise to the surface, but no longer than a couple of hours. Set upright and drain excess water. Potted specimens can be fed by adding fertilizer to the watering can. You may find time-released granules, which are scratched into the soil and last for several months, more convenient. A touch of fertilizer added to the misting bottle gives leaves an immediate treat.

Grooming

It is part of the natural growth process for new leaves to replace older ones. Dead or yellowing leaves are easily removed with tweezers or small scissors. Tie or pin down any stems that help cover the frame, and remove any excess growth that doesn't contribute to the shape. Cut out sections where stems have become woody, with leaves set far apart. Train new tendrils to cover the resultant bare patches. If these techniques are practiced regularly, your topiary will always look fresh and attractive.

Properly cared for, portable topiary will last several years. When forms lose their shape as the stuffing deteriorates, don't despair. Fill in the cavities with fresh sphagnum. But eventually, plants do become woody and lose vigor. At this point, you are better off taking them apart and starting all over again. If a frame is in good condition, refurbish it with a coat of paint or wrap with tape, and use it to grow a new figure.

Insect and Disease Control

Misting and soaking are necessary for pest and disease control, as well as for irrigation, but occasionally pests survive these measures. Most insects reproduce at the rate of several million per month, and fungal diseases spread rapidly, so early diagnosis and treatment is crucial. The following afflictions are sometimes found on indoor topiary.

Fungus gnats are small brown flying insects that flutter out of moss and soil whenever the topiary is watered or moved. The adults are ugly but harmless. The larvae, however, which live deep in the growing medium, feed on roots and can be damaging.

Aphids are greenish brown insects that crawl along the stems and under leaves and young shoots. They suck juice from the plant and are quite destructive. Ivy is a common victim. Aphids are easily identified by the presence of a sticky substance

Horticulturist Bob Beck cares for large topiary birds at the shopping center in Owings Mills, Maryland. To keep stuffed topiary thriving for a long time he recommends using fish emulsion, which is a natural fertilizer, rather than chemical formulations, which leave an undesirable residue in the stuffing. He also sprays water-soluble chemical fertilizers directly on the leaves for a quick boost.

TRANSPORT-ING TOPIARY

If you are bringing your creations to a party, remember that they are fragile and take a few precautions:
* *In cold weather or extreme heat, bring the car close to your house or greenhouse and run the heat or air conditioning until the car is a moderate temperature.*
* *Wrap topiary with grocery bags or many layers of newspaper as insulation against the wind and cold.*
* *If possible, lay the topiary on its side. Support and cushion the figure with garbage bags filled with styrofoam pellets, shredded paper or crumpled newspaper.*

known as honeydew that gives the underside of leaves a speckled, shiny appearance.

Mealybugs are closely related to aphids, also sucking fluid from plant parts and leaving a residue of honeydew. They are easily identified by their white, cottony exterior. They share the aphid's favorite spots, and also congregate in the axils where leaves join stems. On hollow topiary, check between tie and stem for hidden mealybugs. They can be killed by dabbing individually with a cotton swab moistened in rubbing alcohol.

Spider mites are so tiny that they may not be visible to the naked eye. They can be detected by the presence of fine webs and light speckled patches on leaves. Fortunately, they are highly susceptible to water, so well-tended topiary rarely succumbs to this pest.

The safest course of action when combating insects is to begin by spraying with soapy water, insecticidal soap or an organic preparation such as rotenone, pyrethrum or resmethrin. If the problem persists, resort to a stronger chemical pesticide. Never apply these toxic preparations as a preventive measure. Identify the insect and treat the plant with a product specific to the pest. If you have a large collection, consider using a fogger—flea bombs are readily available and quite effective. Whatever you use, carefully follow the directions on the label.

Fungal diseases appear when topiary is routinely overwatered, misted on overcast days, or located where light and air circulation are insufficient.

There are three common fungal problems. Leaf spot appears as rounded brown patches. Powdery mildew is evidenced by a grayish-white substance that coats leaves; eventually, the affected foliage dries up and dies. Botrytis is not as common as leaf spot and mildew and is usually due to overwatering. Untreated, the leaves and stems rot. The presence of symptoms on a few leaves is not cause for alarm—simply remove the affected parts and correct the water or location problem. If the condition spreads and persists, treat by drenching leaves and roots with a fungicide solution such as benomyl.

Standards, Poodles & Spirals

SPLENDOR ON A SINGLE STEM

Astandard is the tailored classic of the topiary world, bringing a sophisticated grace to any setting. Resembling a stylized tree, it is characterized by a crown of growth atop a single erect stem. Standards are experiencing renewed popularity, perhaps because of their reassuring association with trees, which have been admired since antiquity as symbols of elegance, grace, strength and permanence. Most of these long-legged beauties prefer to be pampered indoors, but a few are content to live outside.

Because of the pleasing simplicity of its shape, clearly defined by the contrast of a smooth, straight stem and leafy head, a standard can be made from an array of plants that are unsuited to fancier shapes. Choose any plant with a strong upright stem—including houseplants, herbs, flowering exotics and hardy garden plants—for a variety of effects in any location. Most often the head is fashioned into a sphere, but it can also resemble a mushroom, pyramid or cone. There are other shapely variations of single-stem topiary. Poodles have multiple disks or balls along the stem instead of a single crown of growth. A spiral's foliage coils up and around its trunk like the serpent around Eden's tree. And while tradition dictates that the stem be as straight as possible, it is sometimes twisted into corkscrews and knots. A fancy effect may be achieved by twining or braiding plants into a single stem and head.

The first shaped plants to appear with the rebirth of pleasure gardening in the Middle Ages were standards with heads clipped into a single smooth globe or a series of flat circular tiers. Illustrations from medieval and Early Renaissance manuscripts show devoted gardeners arranging them, often in tubs and urns, among the herbs and flowers. These potted specimens were often prized citrus fruits; as gardens became more colorful, tree-form topiaries were made from showy flowering plants such as roses, camellias and geraniums. Most of these slender aristocrats were placed in the garden as summer decorations and moved into greenhouses during harsh Northern European winters. Today standards are usually sheltered inside, since many

Although training herbs into trees is depicted in antique European gardening books, it was a forgotten art until its current revival by Americans in miniature versions. In the 1950s horticulturist Bunny Mellon was one of the first to rediscover the art of training rosemary, thyme, santolina and myrtle into shapes that ranged from 10 inches to 3 feet tall. The whole collection began, in a most American fashion, with a sprig of myrtle given to her by the gardener at Mount Vernon.

With a resurgence of interest in formal gardens around the turn of the century, many architects extolled the charms of topiary statuary. In 1904 a Mr. W. Gibson, head gardener at Levens Hall, gave some general advice on the formation and care of topiary in The Book of Topiary. But Nathanal Lloyd, in his 1925 book Craftsmanship in Yew and Box, was the first garden author in centuries to give detailed instructions for forming arches, birds, hearts and spirals.

A wide variety of classic standard shapes can be easily executed in miniature versions. Together they comprise a wonderful showcase of plant training techniques.

of the tempting showy plants for training can't survive winter outdoors. This is scarcely a hardship, as such elegant creations serve double duty as garden accents and interior ornaments.

Recently, miniature herbal versions for indoor decorations have joined the standard repertoire. These tiny topiaries bring into the house all the spirit and splendor of a full-fledged tree. This modern adaptation has a precedent in antiquity: the Greeks raised herbs in small pots as offerings to Adonis and other spring gods. And trees have traditionally been planted to celebrate the birth of a child. You can adapt these customs by raising miniature standards in pots and giving them as birthday and house-warming presents.

A lone specimen is a source of pride, but standards and their single-stem kin are most often seen in pairs. They seem to mate for life—if one dies, the survivor is unlikely to be matched up again. A couple looks quite at home on either side of a gate, door or fireplace. A group of standards adds a dimension of height to an otherwise flat garden picture. Use them to punctuate different areas or beds. They look especially appropriate dotted among the patterns of a knot garden. A simple terrace or deck becomes more elegant with a standard at each corner.

Interior designers find that slender potted topiaries can either strengthen the historical character of traditional decors or soften and accentuate the geometric angularity of contemporary schemes. A forest made of various-size standards allows you to make attractive use of a patch of indoor sunlight. They prefer to grow in a sunny location, but there's no harm in borrowing them for the evening to dress up your table. You can arrange a group in staggered heights, like candlesticks. If you have successfully raised a pair, place them on your mantel. A widowed tree can stand alone as a centerpiece, or march a regimented row down the center of a runner.

The unfussy lines of single-stem shapes gives no hint of the care and time taken to develop them. From six months to two years of attenion are required to create a lush, ample top. The challenge is one of perseverance more than skill, for the basic training technique is as straightforward as the shape. From infancy, a plant is encouraged to grow a straight central stalk. Once it has reached the desired height, you pinch off the tip and begin forming the head. The reward is a horticultural treasure.

The size and proportion of the standard, poodle or spiral depends on your own patience and surroundings—and on the plant you choose. The design is a balancing act of texture, color and shape; rely on your eye and judgement. Consider the plant's characteristics, including the scale of foliage and flowers, and the rate and habit of growth. A general rule: the larger the leaf,

> **Little low hedges, round like welts, with some pretty pyramids, I like well. . . .**
>
> —SIR FRANCIS BACON
> "Of Gardens," 1625

Rosemary takes its name from the Latin ros, *meaning "dew" or "spray," and* marinus, *meaning "sea." It is native to the cliffs along the Mediterranean.*

the taller the stem. The width of the head should also be in proportion to the length of stem. Cascading plants can be trained into a weeping standard. When designing these, remember that the drooping branches obscure a portion of the stem, so make it correspondingly taller. In its youth, the standard will look a bit awkward, like a newborn colt, because it takes a while for the crown to fill out. The traditional dimensions are tall and slender for an elegant effect; but shorter, more rotund versions have the charm of miniature inhabitants of a magic forest. It is very nice to have a preconceived height for a standard, although sometimes one just can't resist pinching back young plants to begin forming the head.

CREATING WITH HERBS

The most endearing potted topiary are trained herbs. Dating back to medieval kitchen gardens, when the neatly clipped forms stood among the knotted beds, they served a useful as well as a decorative function—sprigs were snipped off for use in cooking, medicinal and cosmetic concoctions. Many kinds adapt readily to a range of indoor conditions, where they can be trained into standards, spirals and poodles. The young branches are flexible, but eventually the trunk becomes quite woody. Whether or not you make use of the cuttings, you will enjoy the scents that emerge whenever you trim.

Rosemary (*Rosmarinus officinalis*) has always been a popular herb for potted topiary. The star billing is well deserved, for it is suitable for simple or complex designs, both large and small. The fine, needle-like leaves resemble those of yew, a favorite for outdoor topiary; the foliage color is a distinctive gray-green. There are lots of varieties, most of which are nearly impossible to tell apart, but it is easy to distinguish between the upright types, appropriate for standards, and the prostrate ones, which lend themselves to training on a frame. The plants generally have small, lavender blooms, but 'Albus' and 'Roseum' have white or pink flowers, respectively. Rosemary is often used to flavor roasts, stews and vinegars; and its robust aroma adds a strong note to potpourri. Many medicinal and cosmetic properties have been ascribed to this herb, including the power to beautify hair, dispel nightmares and improve memory.

Dwarf myrtle (*Myrtus communis* 'Microphylla'), though not as well known as rosemary, is equally willing and reliable. It can be trained to any height, from 6 inches to 6 feet. With bright, true green, shiny leaves, white flowers and blue-black berries, it is visually interesting at any time of year. Though more difficult to grow, 'Variegata,' with white markings on the leaves, is worth fussing over if you want a more unusual effect. Twigs exude a spicy smell when cut, making pruning a joy.

Thyme (*Thymus vulgaris*) and sage (*Salvia officinalis*) are well-known culinary herbs that make delightful small trees. As with rosemary, there are spreading and upright forms of thyme—choose the latter for miniature standards. Sage is trained into larger tabletop models. The plant takes its botanical name from the Latin *salveo*, meaning "I am well," because it is reputed to cure all illnesses. Surely it cures houseplant boredom, for there are over 500 varieties, with leaves in different shades of green, gray, pink and white. There is even a sage with a pineapple scent (*Salvia elegans*). Mexican oregano (*Poliomintha longiflora*) is extremely unusual but worth tracking down because it is a gorgeous standard. This highly aromatic culinary herb is ornamented with a profusion of trumpet-shaped bluish flowers.

Some herbs are not edible, but are prized for their appearance, scent and mystical associations. French lavender (*Lavandula dentata*) is a good indoor plant, grown for the fragrance of both foliage and flowers. There is also a larger variety (*Lavandula dentata* 'Candicans') with silver leaves. Lavender is used in perfume and soap making. Add some to homemade potpourri to banish melancholy thoughts from the house. Santolina (*San-*

> **[Rosemary] is also good to helpe dimnesse of sight, and to take away spots, markes and scarres from the skin. . . . for the heart, rheumaticke braines, and to strengthen the memory. . . .**
>
> —JOHN PARKINSON
> *Paradisi in Sole,*
> *Paradisus Terrestris,*
> 1629

> *Orange trees were potted treasures in Europe, moved into shelter during harsh weather and set out as garden accents during the mild months. This practice lead to the modern cultivation of topiary in pots.*

tolina chamaecyparissus), also known as lavender cotton, has lacy gray foliage and a pleasant, piny scent. Despite the open delicacy of the leaves, it will form a dense-headed tree 1 to 2 feet tall. Other herbal candidates to delight the eye and nose alike include curry plant (*Helichrysum angustifolium*) and licorice plant (*Helichrysum petiolatum*). Lemon verbena (*Aloysia triphylla*) has the truest lemon scent of all herbs and is a delicious addition to cocktails. When grown indoors, it goes through a resting period from fall to February.

Dutch gardens of the 16th century featured standards and poodles of myrtle, bay or citrus set out each spring to add height to flat formal beds.

The bay laurel (*Laurus nobilis*), sometimes known as sweet bay, is an herb for large, handsome tree sculptures. Because of the bay's large leaves, a respectable minimum height for standards is 5 feet. The leaves have a pungent flavor that is released only after long cooking, so it is added to simmering soups. Bay trees are classic doorway sentinels. Gervase Markham, in *The Whole Art of Husbandrie*, wrote in 1631: "The Bay, in Latine Laurus, is a most gratefull Tree to the house, a porter to Emperours and Bishops, which chiefly garnisheth the house, and standsalwaies at the entrie." Perhaps this tradition arose from the belief that bay laurel's protective powers could guard the inhabitants. In 1670 John Smith's *England's Improvements Revived* charged that "Neither witch nor devil, thunder nor lightening hurt a man in the place where that tree grows." The plant grows slowly, so it will take many years to develop a stately specimen. Think of it as an heirloom: slow in the making but long-lived, to be cherished for many years.

OLD FAITHFULS

Your favorite flowering plants can become handsome garden ornaments with balls of flowers on 4- to 6-foot stems. Warm summer days bring visions of them sparkling in wooden boxes or barrels and in clay pots, basking on porches, verandas, and around swimming pools. When cold days arrive they must be taken inside for protection until the following spring. Some plants take a winter rest, while others keep on flowering and growing, providing an exciting addition to any sunny room.

Heliotrope (*Heliotropium arborescens*) is an old-fashioned bedding plant that can be raised to enticing heights—where delicious vanilla-scented purple flowers reach your nose. You can also add height and pizzazz to your garden with fuchsia (*Fuchsia* in variety), bougainvillea (*Bougainvillea* × *buttiana*) and lantana

66Sage is much used of many in the moneth of May fasting, with butter and Parsley, and is held of most much to conduce to the health of mans body.

It is also much used among other good herbes to bee tund up with Ale, which thereupon is termed Sage Ale, whereof many barrels full are made, and drunke in the said moneth chiefly for the purpose afore recited. . . .99

—JOHN PARKINSON
Paradisi in Sole, Paradisus Terrestris,
1629

Heliotrope got its name from the Greek words helios, *meaning "the sun," and* trope, *"to turn," because its sweet-smelling flowers follow the sun, turning during the course of the day from east to west and back again to greet the sunrise.*

(*Lantana camara*). Lantana offers an assortment of two-tone and solid-color flowers ranging from white and pale yellow to deep orange, purple and red. Fuchsia, bougainvillea and lantana all have a weeping effect initially; as you trim back the branches over the years, however, they develop a more rounded crown. For striking touches in a sunny location, choose from the lusciously hued single and double hibiscus varieties. Euryops (*Euryops pectinatus*) has yellow, daisy-like flowers that are set off by gray-green foliage. If you want to enjoy colorful standards in a shady spot where flowers won't thrive, select from the hundreds of fast-growing coleus varieties.

Citrus trees have been the classic indoor/outdoor standard of grand European gardens. They were valued for their exotic fruit and their scented flowers, which were as prized as orchids for decorating the heads of brides. Lemon, orange or kumquat are easily grown and will grace the house and garden with an antique air.

Azaleas are frequently seen as standards; the ones you receive as gifts are usually forced carefully in a greenhouse for a one-time profusion of flowers, so enjoy them while they last. They can, however, be brought into bloom again in the house as long as they receive plenty of sun to set new buds. These tend to open in a scattered fashion, rather than all at once. Stunning poinsettia trees appear around Christmas, and should be treated as temporary decorations. Their raising is best left to the commercial grower, who knows the very precise schedule of light and dark the plants require to flower successfully again.

GERANIUMS

Around the world, geraniums are favorites for house and garden standards. Properly speaking, these plants belong to the genus *Pelargonium*, first brought to England from South Africa in the 17th century. By 1753, the great botanist

Linnaeus recognized 25 species. These are the forerunners of the hundreds of hybrids we have today. Trained geraniums were the rage in Victorian times—and it is no wonder, for they are fast growing, with many reaching a respectable 4 to 5 feet in six months and developing a luxuriant head of cheerful blooms in a year.

The varieties sold for bedding (*Pelargonium* × *hortorum*) make standards that will flower unfailingly through the hottest summer weather, in many shades of scarlet, salmon, pink and white. The best plants for training have compact growth, such as the 'Sprinter' or 'Orbit' series. 'Martha Washington' or 'Regal' geraniums (*Pelargonium* × *domesticum*) have an altogether different appearance, with wrinkled leaves and pansy-shaped flowers in luscious colors that appear in time for Mother's Day.

Scented geraniums were popular in the early 19th century until they were eclipsed by the larger-flowered, bedding types. Their nostalgic charm is well worth discovering as they are the best group for turning into little trees providing year-round indoor enjoyment. The flowers are mostly unremarkable, but the variety of the foliage in appearance and aroma is astonishing. The leaves can be coarse, filigreed, curled and splashed with white and gold. This enormous range allows you to create standards of many heights, depending on the scale of the leaf. The fragrance can evoke rose, apple, mint, strawberry, apricot, coconut, nutmeg, orange, lime or lemon. Some of the rose and lemon varieties also have a convincing flavor when used in cakes, candies and jellies, so save your trimmings for the kitchen. Any of the crinkly leaved varieties, such as *Pelargonium crispum* 'Prince Rupert,' make delicate-looking trees, while the robust 'Grape Leaf' is good for a larger standard.

One famous orange collection, at the Belgian seat of the Duke of Enghien, had 108 poodle- and lollipop-shaped trees, some of which thrived for two hundred years.

66. . . opere topi-arii *writhen about in degrees like the turnings of cockil shells to come to the top without payne.*99

—JOHN LELAND
Itinerary, c. 1560

ELEGANT ODDITIES

Many unusual plants for standards are now appearing on the houseplant scene, although some have been raised in pots for centuries. Victorian rosemary (*Westringia rosmariniformis*), is not a rosemary at all, although it looks very similar. It is easier to grow than the real thing, being stronger and more disease resistant. New Zealand tea tree (*Leptospermum scoparium*), a relative of myrtle, has scented foliage similar in appearance to rosemary, but it is decked with charming red or white rose-like blooms from late fall through early spring.

Braided standards and poodles, though simple in shape, serve as remarkable room accents and are fast becoming a staple of interior design.

Florists' genista (*Cytisus racemosus*) is a woody plant whose branches used to be forced into bloom around Easter for use as a fragrant yellow cut flower. Mickey Mouse plant (*Ochna multiflora*) really looks like a miniature version of a shade tree, with locust-shaped leaves and sweet-scented yellow flowers. The name was inspired by the red-and-black berries that follow, which resemble a Mouseketeer's cap and last up to six months.

Many landscape plants that have good dense foliage, interesting flowers and fruit can also be grown successfully indoors in good light. Try Surinam cherry (*Eugenia uniflora*), and natal plum (*Carissa grandiflora*). The latter has fragrant white flowers and edible fruits. Serissa (*Serissa foetida*) is another good choice, with tiny solid green or variegated leaves and rose-like white flowers. Ceanothus hybrids are also unusual, with sweetly scented, fuzzy blue flowers.

ROSES

Nothing is more enchanting than a tree-form rose, which brings this most beloved of all flowers to eye and nose level. Rose standards are produced by grafting two plants together, rather than by training a single individual. This is done so that a hardy trunk and root system can be quickly attained from a vigorous variety that had undistinguished blossoms. A magnificent bloomer, of regal lineage but slow growth, is grafted on top of a sturdy trunk to form the head. Almost any hybrid tea or floribunda may be used, but for the best show and a lollipop shape, select a variety that blooms in compact clusters rather than in single flowers on long stems. The trees are usually about 5 feet tall although there are also shorter versions, made from small-flowering types, that are about 3 feet in height. These are variously referred to as dwarfs, half-standards or patio trees, and they are charming for small gardens and terraces. Many garden centers and nurseries offer an abundance of rose trees in

If you want to use a standard as a centerpiece or other festive decoration, but don't have any moss or pebbles on hand to conceal the soil surface, reach into the refrigerator for inspiration. Artfully arrange grape clusters, cherry tomatoes or other fresh fruits and vegetables around the base of the stem to hide the soil.

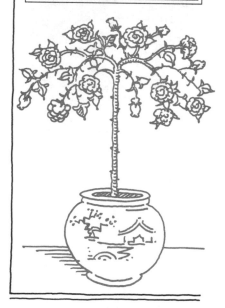

> **❝A large rose-tree stood near the entrance of the garden: the roses growing on it were white, but there were three gardeners at it, busily painting them red. . . .**
>
> **'Would you tell me, please,' said Alice, a little timidly, 'why you are painting those roses?' . . .**
>
> **'Why, the fact is, you see, Miss, this here ought to have been a red rose-tree, and we put a white one in by mistake; and, if the Queen was to find it out, we should all have our heads cut off, you know.'❞**
>
> —LEWIS CARROLL
> *Alice's Adventures in Wonderland*, 1865

the spring, so it may be convenient to simply purchase them. If you want to delve into this horticultural craft, however, directions for a grafted standard can be found on page 76.

The magnificence of the grafted rose standard has a price—because the most vulnerable part of the plant, the grafting union, is well above ground level, the tree is susceptible to frost damage. Except in the mild winters of Zones 8 to 10, rose standards must be protected. One method is to loosen the roots, lie the trees on their sides and cover them with a thick layer of soil or mulch. Another approach, if the rose trees are grown in containers, is to store them in an unheated garage or basement. Check these a few times during the winter, adding water when the soil is dry. In the spring, cut off any dead branches and introduce the trees into bright sun gradually by placing them in the shade or on a porch for a week or so. Ask your local garden center which is the best procedure for your locale.

HARDY SPECIMENS

Some hardy plants are trained into standards that can be left outdoors all year, in planters or in the ground. Columnar junipers (*Juniperus chinensis* and *Juniperus virginiana*) are relatively inexpensive, grow rapidly in an upright fashion and willingly yield to shaping. You would do well to practice on one of these before attempting a spiral on a slow-growing or more expensive plant. Alberta spruce (*Picea glauca* 'Albertiana') grows slowly, but has a fine, dense yet soft texture that's perfect for elegantly groomed standards, poodles and spirals. Forsythia (*Forsythia* in variety), the well-known garden shrub, is quickly trained into simple, large standards. Stake the lax stem in the early years of growth and your impatience will be rewarded with a mature standard in just two growing seasons.

Grafting is practiced to raise dwarf or low-growing hardy plants on tall stems. Cotoneaster (*Cotoneaster horizontalis*) looks like an elegant weeping willow when grown in this fashion. Fancy dwarf varieties of evergreens such as pine, hemlock, spruce and juniper are joined to the trunks of an ordinary species to create sensational effects. One or more top-grafts are performed to create either a single globe or several tiers of growth.

The Chinese court visited by Marco Polo venerated peach trees, placing them by the door as a sign of immortality.

ALL ABOUT CONTAINERS

Although standards are sometimes grown in the ground or have their containers plunged into the earth for the summer, they look best when the mass of the head is balanced at the base by a pot. Historically, standards and their variations were raised in *caisses versailles*, square wood boxes ornamented with feet and knobs, or in clay urns with handles through which a pole was slipped so two men could handle a heavy specimen. Italian terra-cotta pots are also traditional containers—their ornate garlands and plaques offset the simplicity of single-stem forms. Planting in any of these three ensures a classic look. If you paint the container a color that harmonizes with the foliage, like pale gray, delicate blue or light green, the standard will assume an air of tranquil elegance. For a more casual appearance, plant large standards in wooden tubs such as whiskey half-barrels. Cast stone or concrete planters can be found in many designs, some of which have a complimentary antique air. They are quite heavy, but this is an asset if you don't want someone to walk off with your entranceway accessories. Although plastic pots are often used commercially for azalea and poinsettia standards, don't use them for your creations—they don't have the necessary weight to counterbalance the head and can tip over easily.

Buddha saw the light while sitting under a tree; therefore trees were associated with him and many of his followers believed trees had souls.

RAISING YOUR STANDARDS

Most plants will, if left alone, produce a central stem or leader that grows more-or-less straight up. If you pinch off the growing tip, the plant rechannels its energy into branches and shoots that grow out sideways. All along the central stem are growth nodes, called lateral buds. The growing tip, called the apical bud, produces a hormone called auxin, which suppresses the growth of lateral buds. Removing the growing tip diminishes the auxin supply, allowing these lateral buds to sprout. Auxin is produced at the tip of every branch, so new ones must also be cut to wake up dormant lateral buds.

There are two important points to glean from this technical information. First, you must start a standard with a plant that has not been pinched, one that retains a straight central stem. If you can't find one, root your own cutting. Second, to develop a full, voluptuous head, keep pinching.

It is important that the young plant develop a thick, healthy stem. Until the crown has formed, remove the lower branches but retain the side leaves along the central stem, also called basal or primary leaves, that help feed the plant. Place it in as much light as possible. Start your projects, if you can, in the early spring. That way the plant has a long season of warmth and sun to shoot upward. Placing it outdoors in a sheltered location will also help it along. Give the standard a one-quarter turn weekly to develop a straight trunk and a balanced head.

Tying the main stem to a stake helps to keep it straight and support the weight of the head. All plants need this assistance initially. Some, such as myrtle, rosemary and lantana, become woody and firm after a few years and will stand on their own. Other plants never lose a soft stem and will always rely on the aid of a stake.

When you tie, make the knot against the stake, never against the stem, since the pressure can injure the stem. Use a soft but strong material to make the ties. Raffia, string or twine

Formal standards and poodles acquire a casual flavor when they are planted in rustic tubs or barrels, allowing them to settle comfortably into informal country settings.

are all good choices—brown or green is less conspicuous than white string or twine. You must check the ties every few months, to make sure that they haven't become too tight as the stem has grown in circumference. The plant will be seriously injured if the tie cuts into, or girdles, the stem.

Bamboo poles or wooden dowels are easy to find in a range of lengths and diameters. Some are dyed green to blend with the plant's foliage. For tall or heavy-headed standards, enlist the more capable and permanent support of metal stakes soldered to a base. If you are contemplating a weeping standard with a wide head, it's a good idea to use an umbrella or wheel-shaped support for the pendant branches.

THE IMPOSTOR'S GRAFT

❝Even at the present day, the gardeners of Italy . . . sell plants of jasmines, roses, honeysuckles, &c., all growing together from a stock of orange, or myrtle, or pomegranate, on which they say they are grafted. But this is a deception, the fact being that the stock has its centre bored out, so as to be made into a hollow cylinder, through which the stems of jasmines and other flexible plants are easily made to pass, their roots intermingling with those of the stock. After growing for a time . . . they assume all the appearance of being united.❞

—BERNARD MCMAHON
McMahon's American Gardener, 1857

A Basic Standard

You will need:
—a plant with a straight, unpinched leader
—two bamboo or wooden stakes, one shorter than the other
—raffia, twine or string
—scissors
—a clay pot
—potting soil

1 Select a plant with a straight, unpinched leader. If the plant is in a small plastic pot, repot it into a slightly larger clay one for stability. Insert a stake alongside the leader, firming the soil to keep it upright.

2 Starting at the bottom, tie the stem at intervals wherever it requires straightening and support.

3 Remove side shoots, but not the primary leaves that grow along the central stem. As the plant approaches the desired height, allow some side shoots to grow out where the head will be. Repot as necessary, until it is in a container appropriate to the ultimate size of the standard. When the leader has grown above the original stake, add a taller one alongside. Tie the plant to the new stake, and then cut ties to the original stake. If the stem is weak leave both stakes in, retying to the original one for maximum stability.

4 When the the leader reaches the ultimate height, pinch off the tip. When the resultant shoots are several inches long, pinch these just above a leaf node. Repeat periodically until the head is well branched.

Poodle Variation

This is a variation on the standard where multiple growths are developed along the stem. The traditional design has three growths shaped into balls or flat tiers, but you can have more or less as you desire. The two shapes may even be combined for a more interesting individual. Follow the steps for making a standard, but retain side shoots along the leader where you want to form the additional balls or tiers. Pinch these tufts of growth often to encourage fullness.

Give a twist to the classic shape. You can create tricky effects with a little patience and advance planning. The secret is to start while a plant is quite young, and keep a close eye on its growth.

Knotted Trunk

Carefully and gradually, make a loose knot in the central stem while it is very young. Avoid bruising the stem. Once the open, loose knot has been formed, develop the head as described for a basic standard.

Braided Standard

This single shape is composed of two or three plants. Plant them close together near the center of the pot. Remove all side branches and loosely twist or braid the stems to form a single trunk. Stake as you would for a standard. Once the desired height has been reached, pinch off all central stems and shape new growth into a single head.

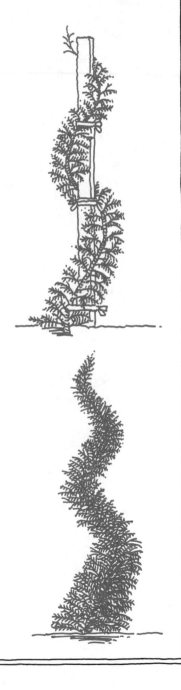

Spiral

In contrast to standards, the best plant for a spiral is one that is well branched along the entire stem. There are two ways to achieve a spiral topiary. In the first, the stem itself is trained to grow around a pole. In the second, the stem remains straight and the foliage is clipped to create a spiral around the stem.

Corkscrew Spiral

You will need:
—colored plastic adhesive tape
—a wooden dowel at least 1 inch in diameter
—a plant with a straight, unpinched leader that is well branched
  along the entire stem
—raffia, string or twine

1 Twist colored tape, candy-cane fashion, around the dowel as a guideline.

2 Wrap the main stem around the dowel, following the tape. Tie the stem to the dowel with the raffia, string or twine, as needed to hold it in place. Continue to wrap new growth.

3 Remove the pole after the stem thickens into a woody trunk. Rosemary or myrtle usually hardens after two years.

4 Once the desired height has been reached, pinch off the tip of the leader.

5 Trim and shape for a neat, well-defined spiral.

Straight-Stemmed Spiral

This is a bolder way of achieving a spiral, since the trimming is essentially done freehand.

You will need:
—a plant with a straight, unpinched leader that is well branched along the entire stem
—a bamboo or wooden stake
—raffia, string or twine
—ribbon
—a nail

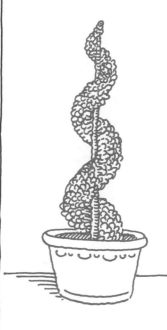

1 Tie the plant to a stake with raffia, string or twine, keeping the central stem as straight as possible.

2 Nail a ribbon to the top of the stake, and wind it down in a spiral around the outside of the plant. Working from the bottom up, using the ribbon as a guide, clip all around the ribbon back to the stem to create a spiral. Remove the ribbon.

3 As the plant grows, repeat Step 2, continuing to tie the central stem to the stake, and trimming any new side growth to maintain the spiral pattern.

4 Once the desired height has been reached, pinch off the leader.

5 Trim and shape for a neat, well-defined appearance.

Vaccum cleaners are handy for removing dead leaves and dust from the heads of standards. Gently insert the hose past the outer layer of healthy foliage to reach trapped debris.

Grafted Standard

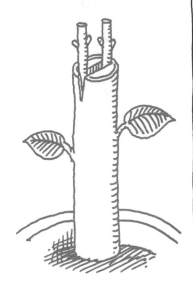

Whenever a slow-growing or low plant such as a spreading juniper or miniature rose has flowers or foliage that make it desirable as a standard, it can be grafted on top of the stem of a more vigorous relative. Use plants that are known to be compatible partners. The plant used to form the roots and main trunk is known as the understock, while the plant chosen for the top is called the scion. The simplest union is the cleft graft, whereby a stem of the desired top plant is slipped into a notch in the trunk of the bottom plant. The actual joining takes place in the cambium, the actively growing layer underneath the bark of both plants. In order for the graft to succeed, the cambium layers of the scion and the understock must be lined up. Do not remove shoots and leaves from the understock until enough new leaves emerge on the scion to nourish the plant.

You will need:
—a sturdy-trunked, single-stemmed plant for the understock
—one-year-old stems of a compatible plant for the scion
—a sharp knife
—a screwdriver
—paraffin canning wax, grafting wax or a clear plastic bag and
  rubber band

1 Select a sturdy-trunked plant for the understock and make a straight cut across the top, leaving the length of stem you want for the standard. Cut two pieces from the middle of one-year-old wood for the scions, 6 to 8 inches long, with four to six buds on each. In the case of outdoor plants, the buds should be in a dormant state. Two scions are used as insurance—the stem that grows more quickly is retained, and the weaker is cut off.

2 With the buds of the top pieces pointing up, make two cuts to taper the bottom and expose the cambium. Do not touch

the freshly cut surfaces, as the residue on your hands can prevent the graft from taking.

3 Using a sharp knife, make a slit 2 to 3 inches deep in the top of the trunk. Insert a screwdriver to hold the cleft open.

4 Insert the top stems, one at each side of the slit, aligning the cambium, visible as a bright green layer just under the bark. Remove the screwdriver.

On outdoor plants: Melt paraffin canning wax or grafting wax, allow to cool slightly, and pour it over the entire union and the tops of the cut scions to seal.

On indoor plants: Waxing isn't necessary. To keep the tissues moist, cover the graft with plastic wrap and tie it with a rubber band.

5 Within a few weeks it will be evident if your graft is successful. Retain the more vigorous scion and remove the weaker. On outdoor plants, the dormant buds on the scions will begin to swell. Indoors, new leaves will develop. After about a month, remove the plastic bag.

MAINTENANCE

There are lantana and bay laurel trees over eighty years old, and records of tubbed oranges maintained in European collections for two hundred years. Plants with non-woody stems such as geranium, coleus and heliotrope don't last as long, losing their vigor after four or five years. They may survive past this point, but with a less attractive show of foliage and flowers. To ensure that your horticultural tour de force lives up to its potential, follow the care guidelines below.

> **A**ncient Hebrew law forbade the destruction of trees even when sacking a city.

66*The worship of trees was apparently among the first forms of religion. The Tree of Life is found in all of them. . . . [Trees] became both an object of worth and a feature in gardens, eventually to be elaborated into many magnificent and costly forms.*99

—RICHARDSON WRIGHT
The Story of Gardening,
1934

Once your single-stem creation has attained its ultimate height and breadth, you will want to maintain its pleasing proportions in the same pot. In order to keep it from outgrowing the container, repot yearly, preferably in spring or fall. Tap the plant out of the container, loosen the root ball with your fingers and remove any strangling roots. Replant in the same pot, using fresh soil.

It is extremely important to regularly examine the stem where it is tied to the stake. Once a tie has cut into living tissue, the damage is permanent and growth retardation and death result. Make a habit of checking ties frequently, replacing tight ones with a looser loop. At the same time, inspect the base of any wooden stakes, which eventually rot off at the soil line.

As part of your vigilance look for mealybugs, the small white cottony insects that love to hide between stem and tie while they suck away at a plant's juices. They can be eradicated by touching the bodies with an alcohol-moistened swab. Mealybugs are common pests on myrtle. Whiteflies, small insects that flutter around a plant when it is moved, prefer geranium, lantana and fuchsia. There are two different types of scale—immobile bugs that cling to the underside of leaves, especially bay laurel. One is a small, hard oval disk; the other resembles a speck of cotton. Rosemary is usually unbothered by bugs, but is prone to powdery mildew disease, which appears as a grayish-white substance that coats the leaves. Spider mites are a plague on many plants in dry atmospheres. They are so tiny that they are hard to see, but their presence is confirmed by fine webs and light speckled patches on the leaves. Fortunately they are killed by contact with water, so misting will eradicate them in the early stages of infestation.

Regular clipping keeps a standard shapely and lush. Don't try to do the whole trimming job in one session after the shape has been ignored for a while—it's too discouraging. Periodically clean out the inside of the head. Cut out dead twigs and thin out live growth so light and air can penetrate and encourage dormant shoots to sprout from the middle.

Mock Topiary

Faux Forms for Indoor Style

Mock topiary is the newest trend in interior decorating with plants. The sophisticated-looking creations are used by fashionable florists and party planners to quickly dress up dinner tables and transform ordinary rooms into spectacular settings. They may resemble growing plants, but they are actually assembled from cut branches, flowers and fruit—so you can enjoy a finished look instantly.

These fabulous fakes recreate any topiary size and shape, from elegant standards and geometric shapes to humorous animals and enchanted creatures. And although live topiary is predominantly green, mock topiary introduces an exciting rainbow of colors because it incorporates so many different kinds of leaves and flowers.

ACCENTS AND DECORATIONS

There are two kinds of mock topiary: lasting creations that will give any room in your house a finishing touch, and short-term decorations for festive occasions. And since you don't have to worry about giving it enough light, you can display it anywhere—on coffee tables, end tables, mantelpieces, kitchen and bathroom countertops and shelves, or even as unexpected doorstops.

Long-term topiaries are made with dried branches, leaves, blossoms, berries and herbs. The lovely tones of these materials can be used to enhance any decor or color scheme.

Temporary transformations can be as bright or subtle as you like, since you can choose from an infinite variety of fresh foliage, flowers, fruits and vegetables. Choose a style or shape that's purely of the moment—something that captures the spirit of the season or holiday, picks up the theme and colors of your

66*On the other hand, Emma did know how to run the house. She sent patients statements of their visits in well-written letters that didn't look like bills. When some neighbor came to dine on Sundays, she managed to offer some tasty dish, would arrange handsome pyramids of green-gages on vine leaves, serve fruit preserves on a dish, and even spoke of buying finger bowls for dessert.***99*

—GUSTAVE FLAUBERT
Madame Bovary, 1857

party or incorporates the guest of honor's favorite flowers. You don't even have to wait for a special occasion; a make-believe topiary can brighten the most ordinary day.

It is easy to be spontaneous about faux plant sculptures, since they are made with materials you already have around the house and garden, or can easily find at the florist or the hardware store. Some designs don't even require a frame, thanks to ingeniously simple florist's techniques.

Dinner table decorations have long been an important part of festive occasions, and now that mock topiary is featured, they have never been more exciting. The Victorians created elaborate

Mock topiary is a fast and inventive way of transforming your party setting into something special. Here the use of a variety of textures and colors turns a tented party into a fantasy jungle.

garden scenes on the table: formal patterns, called parterres, were laid out with garlands of evergreen roping or ivy. You can bring them up to date by dotting the simulated gardens with elegant geometric topiary. For sit-down dinners, the pattern should be confined to the middle of the table (even small sculptures can create great impact). If you are having a buffet, make use of the entire table surface, arranging your dishes and platters within the design.

Large-scale mock topiary turns any room into an inspired fantasy setting for the evening. Even giant tree shapes are inexpensive and easy to make. In a matter of hours, you can use cut evergreens or mosses to transform your living room into a stately formal garden. Place two tall standards, florist's favorites that simulate a tree with a single trunk and globe-shaped crown, on either side of the door. Continue the theme throughout the room with a series of classically shaped topiary figures, such as multi-tiered poodles and obelisks. For a more informal, spirited atmosphere, recreate a tropical scene. Make the trees out of palm leaves and ferns. Inhabit them with mock topiary creatures, such as swinging moss monkeys and parrots covered in brightly colored leaves and flowers.

STANDARDS

This simple tree-like shape, which usually resembles a clipped globe on a straight trunk, is a favorite form in traditional gardens and conservatories. With faux techniques, standards can be as classic or as innovative as you wish. The top may be made of flowers or leaves; the trunk may be a natural branch, broom handle or wooden dowel, depending on the effect you want to achieve; and they can range in size from miniature lollipops made from dried herbs for permanent decoration to huge flower arrangement-crowned trees for a gala event.

> **F**aux plants have been popular ever since the Crusaders returned from the East with tales of gold trees studded with precious jewels.

Especially for weddings, New York City designer Renny Reynolds loves delicate, flowery "orbs on stems." They stand about 2½ feet tall at the center of each table, balanced by miniature lead garden urns from Renny's antique collection. The trunk is actually a plain wooden dowel, transformed by a wrapping of moire ribbon and narrow streamers of shimmering satin. The orb is covered with roses, stephanotis, baby's breath and lily of the valley. The container you choose for the base of a standard is as important to the overall effect as the flowers and foliage you select for the top. You can capture the look of antiques, in any shade you desire, by painting a faux finish on plastic urns. On page 95 you'll find many other ways to turn an ordinary plastic or glass jar or a tub into something spectacular.

Designer Robert A. Zimmerman does parties for private clients and museums in Baltimore and Philadelphia. He also likes the festive yet traditional look achieved with floral standards. He feels that the arrangement of flowers is most crucial to the success of a standard and he always places his flowers first, adding the greens of leaves or mosses later, but only as needed to hide the foam core of his design. Zimmerman prefers flowers that are long lasting, blending familiar ones like freesia, carnations and roses with more unusual nerines, alstroemeria, liatris and sweet-smelling stock. When he wants to give the standard a contemporary feeling, he uses a plexiglass pole as the trunk. His favorite pots are brass ones, which many people already have in their homes. For maximum impact he creates 9-foot-high standard masterpieces. At this height, the flower decorations don't disappear in the crowd.

If the formal look appeals to you, make traditional standards a part of your home. For an English air, use sprigs of holly to form the ball on top, and set the little tree in a clay pot. A boxwood tree, festooned with tiny mandarin oranges and housed in a white box, has a French flair that evokes the trees in the famous orangery at Versailles. For an Italian decoration in the style of Della Robbia, use the same boxwood tree in a terra-cotta garland pot. Adorn the standard with an assortment of small fresh fruits: lady or crab apples, key limes, kumquats, cranberries or cherries. Substitute candied or glacéed fruits for a decoration that will last for weeks.

Poodles are variations on the standard, with multiple balls or tiers on a single "trunk." This was one of the first topiary designs—many examples can be seen in medieval illustrations. Any of the formal combinations described above could also be used for poodles.

Sometimes an informal standard is more appropriate. With a looser, more open shape, you can play with scale, color and texture, and make use of a variety of flowers. Create a weeping canopy of blooms atop a gnarled or twisted branch. Make a little tree from a tuft of dried sage leaves atop a small branch and plant it in a pot made of galax or magnolia leaves.

For a standard with an Oriental flavor, use a ginger jar or lacquered basket as the container. Try a natural color bamboo stake for the trunk, and top it with a bunch of clipped juniper or santolina twigs. If an Arabian Nights effect appeals to you, arrange a pyramid of palm fronds, peacock feathers and eggplants on a thick trunk. Crown this with a pineapple, and set the whole affair in a brass planter.

GEOMETRIC SCULPTURES

Geometric topiary is a regular feature of French and Italianate gardens. Obelisks were once carried from Egypt back to Imperial Rome, and were eventually used in topiary versions to accentuate Italian and French gardens. Today, mock versions allow you to enjoy these noble shapes indoors. The key to an obelisk's elegance is to keep it tall and thin, with clean, well-defined edges. Cover it with only the flattest flowers, making sure they are level. Gardenias and roses are favorites, but you might try camellias or chrysanthemums as well.

New York City designer Ronaldo Maia also favors obel-

A mock topiary bust or figure of a friend would be a clever personalized gift—and add a classical yet humorous air to any party in their honor. It will also give you a chance to practice your pruning technique. Fasten together several blocks of floral foam with hot glue, stick in cut evergreen branches to cover, and clip the branches until you have achieved a sculpture.

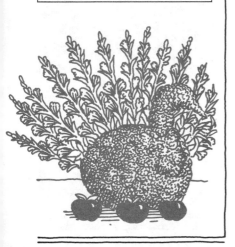

isks, which he designs for long-term display as well as party decorations. He covers 1½- to 2-foot forms in flat green moss, then dresses up the obelisks with bows and garlands of dried rosebuds.

For simple yet striking topiaries, tie a dense bunch of leaf-covered twigs such as boxwood together at the base. As soon as it is tied, the cluster will suggest the form of a globe or fat flame, just as a full bunch of violets naturally falls into a rounded mass when you place them in a small-mouthed vase. All you have to do for a sculptured look is to take scissors and bravely shear the bundle of twigs into the desired shape.

The geometric patterns of espaliers, flat topiary usually done with fruit trees against a wall (see Chapter Six), are well suited to mock interpretation. Lena Caron, director of Maryland's Ladew Topiary Gardens, one of the finest and most diversified topiary showcases in the world, made a beautiful espalier to decorate the manor house one Christmas. She covered a low, predominantly horizontal, two-armed silhouette in boxwood sprigs and accented it appropriately with miniature fruits. It lasted well through the holidays. A rustic variation, which remains attractive all year, is achieved by covering the same shape in moss and decorating it with nests of twigs, wispy Spanish moss and dried flowers. You can easily make either version for your home—or as a gift.

BIRDS AND BEASTS

Animals are the most amusing and endearing kind of mock topiary. There is always one creature or another in vogue, and with mock topiary you can quickly join the fashion. Eagles are Renny's recent favorites. Originally feathered in ivy, they look handsome in sleek, dried moss plumage. The eagles are now maintenance free—they can be stored between parties without any need for light, water or grooming. If you have a

At Ladew Topiary Gardens, Christmastime visitors are greeted by mock topiary foxhounds, a playful evocation of the garden's famous outdoor yew hunt scene.

Y*ou can duplicate the medieval estrade with a wood or metal plant stand made to resemble a standard or a tiered topiary. Fill it with bushy potted plants, changing the foliage tones and flower colors as the season or occasion dictates.*

living topiary that isn't looking its best, you can quickly get it in shape for a party by cutting away dead plants and covering it with moss.

Teddy bears seem to grow more popular every year. They appeal to almost everybody, from sophisticated grownups to the youngest child. Ronaldo loves them in assorted sizes for centerpieces or on coffee tables. His are covered in velvety moss and hold little baskets of flowers or potpourri. For a child's birthday, delight small partygoers with a bear completely covered in bright flowers. If you prefer a casual and long lasting version, make a shaggy bear of gray Spanish moss or honey-toned raffia.

If horses are your hobby, create handsome mock topiary replicas. The slender figure of a horse is a handsome accent for many rooms and occasions. Combine different kinds of moss to depict a smooth coat and a flowing mane and tail.

Swans always look elegant and graceful, especially when they float on a mirrored or glass surface. Several of the frame sources listed on pages 310 to 312 carry swans in a choice of sizes. You can display a spectacular swan even without a frame, by carving the shape out of foam and covering it in flowers. Use contrasting flowers to outline the wings and body.

When the house at Ladew Topiary Gardens is decorated for the holidays, foxhunting is the main theme. This was the late Harvey Ladew's great passion, as evidenced throughout the house in paintings, figurines and furniture. At Christmastime, mock topiary hounds run down the front staircase as if rushing to greet each guest at the door. These are made from yew branches, so they look exactly like the famous outdoor versions on the front lawn.

Geometric and whimsical designs can even be combined into one topiary. On the West Coast, designer David Jones, creates standards with birds and beasts atop the balls.

Any figure covered in sheet moss can be dressed up by sewing on details. Use a large needle and heavy-duty thread in a contrasting color to embroider eyes, a smiling mouth, feathers, or a fish's scales. For purely textural contrast, use fishing line or dental floss.

PLANT MATERIALS FOR LASTING ACCESSORIES

I f you want simulated topiary that will remain attractive in your home for a long time, use plant materials that hold their color and shape when dried. Mosses are useful topiary coverings that can be bought in a variety of textures and in colors ranging from golden brown to gray to green. Mosses can camouflage styrofoam and wire forms before you add foliage and flowers, or they can be displayed alone for their intrinsic decorative value—combine different kinds for accent and contrast. Smooth-textured sheet moss comes in large flat pieces and is easy to use. It is either a fresh light green, dried to a golden brown, or tinted a deep green. Mound moss is a fresh green color, and grows in mounded forms. Spanish moss is a loose, distinctive gray, curly type. Reindeer moss has a popcorn texture, and will absorb moisture readily. Damp it down before working with it, as it is too brittle to use in a dry state. Reindeer moss is naturally a grayish green, but you can buy it dyed in a multitude of colors.

Thick branches make sturdy, natural looking trunks for standards and other upright shapes. Lighter, thinner shoots and small twigs are used to decorate mock forms. For a woodsy look, try to find branches with bits of moss and lichen clinging to them. Birch and fruit tree branches are especially decorative because of the interesting texture of their bark, but you can use any wood available.

Berries make colorful accents ranging from yellow, orange and red hues to purple, blue and black. Between your yard, the woods and well-stocked florists, you should find a good selection—including those from holly, multiflora rose and bittersweet. Small pine cones and tiny hemlock cones are also easily gathered, realistic additions to simulated topiary.

Dried flowers provide a long lasting way to add variety and color. The colors are generally not as bright as fresh flowers, but there is still a rainbow of hues and forms. Lavender, chive flowers, rosebuds, blue salvia and yarrow are attractive choices that may already be growing in your garden. Harvest just before the flowers are completely open, tie them into bunches and hang upside down in a dark location to dry. More choices can be purchased where herbs or craft supplies are sold. Strawflowers are very sturdy and the flowerheads come

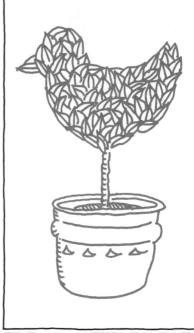

On February 25, 1745, a masked ball was held at Versailles. Louis XV strode into the Hall of Mirrors with seven companions, all disguised as topiary yew trees. It was there that the king wooed Madame Pompadour, who became his lover and official court mistress. Perhaps she was taken by his costume, since she was an accomplished gardener.

mounted on wires, making them even easier to use. Statice, German statice, globe amaranth, cedar rose, Japanese lanterns and baby's breath are also pretty and commonly available. Eucalyptus has no flowers, but the rounded gray-green leaves are handsome and subtly fragrant.

There is nothing more charming than a faux topiary made of herbs, which have a wealth of texture, scent and symbolic

Charles-Nicolas Cochin depicted Louis XV's unusual entourage in this piece, known as The Yew Tree Ball.

value. Rosemary, the traditional herb of remembrance, makes a lovely standard for a birthday or anniversary gift. Thyme has more delicate foliage, so it is useful for small standards or detailed shapes. Sage and sweet marjoram are also attractive and fragrant. Fresh herbs are pliable and easy to work with, whereas dried ones are brittle and must be handled with care. Fresh herbs can be allowed to dry in place and will keep for years. But since they shrink, bunch them very tightly in the form to prevent gaps later on. To achieve a thick cover, wire herb stems together into little bunches before adding to the form.

Loose leaf dried herbs, the kind that come in jars for cooking, may also be used to cover faux forms. Instead of wrapping styrofoam balls in sheet moss before you insert flowers and branches, coat them with white glue and roll in dried herbs. Thyme, oregano or blended herbs are pretty; the same ball can also be rolled in potpourri for an equally fragrant but multicolored display. Whole bay leaves can be glued individually onto topiary forms for a convincingly leafy look. Stick cinnamon makes a natural trunk and continues the culinary theme. You can find short ones, about 3 inches long, at the grocery store. Longer sticks, up to 12 inches or so, are usually sold at stores that specialize in spices. To add to their length and strength stick a longer wire through the center, concealing the wire in the pot and standard head.

FESTIVE SEASONAL SPECIALTIES

Instant topiary allows you to create dazzling party effects, from one stylish centerpiece to imaginative displays that transform an entire room. And these rich-looking decorations don't have to be expensive—with a little resourcefulness, you can find an assortment of materials in your garden and

66If you get simple beauty and naught else, you get about the best thing God invents.99

—LIPPO LIPPI
Italian Renaissance painter

nearby woods and fields. If you can't find some of the plants mentioned below, don't despair. Many of them, particularly around holidays, can be purchased at a florist or garden center.

Evergreen boughs are invaluable for winter holiday decorations, and fortunately, Christmastime is a good season for pruning outdoor evergreens. Cut branches will last several weeks if they are stuck into a material that can be kept wet. Boxwood, holly, juniper, white pine, hemlock, fir and yew are all sturdy and long lasting. Firethorn and burgundy-colored barberry offer a bonus of decorative berries. Northerners pay dearly for a few sprigs of white-berried mistletoe around Christmas, but if you are lucky enough to live where it grows naturally you can use it freely in mock creations. Remember that the berries are poisonous, so keep mistletoe out of the reach of children and pets.

Boxwood has a fine, shiny appearance that gives any topiary a classic look. So that you don't have to disfigure your valuable bushes, use only the very tips of cut boxwood. Or cut a few long branches into many pieces so you can get maximum coverage from just a small number of them.

For a clean, sculptured appearance precut all evergreen twigs the same length before sticking them into the form. It's hard to avoid unsightly stubs and cut leaves if you trim after assembly. Break thin branches and cut heavier branches on an angle so that you have a point that will easily pierce the form.

Blooming branches such as forsythia, quince, cherry, apple, pussy willow and corkscrew willow bring a note of early spring color indoors. If the buds are very tight, you can use a technique called forcing to open them in time for your party. Cut the branches; mash the ends with a hammer so they can absord plenty of water and swell the buds; soak the entire branch in a bathtub filled with warm water, which will simulate spring conditions and convince the blossoms to open.

When warmer weather arrives, gather flowers from your garden for summery topiary. Every flower will give faux sculptures a different character—each has a unique shape, color, texture and way of carrying itself on a stem. Roses have a flat, satiny appearance; sweet peas and nasturtiums flutter on their stems like butterflies; and bright marigolds and zinnias create a stiff, ruffled surface.

An airy quality is achieved in mock standards by adding the graceful wildflowers of field and meadow. Many wildflowers wilt soon after you pick them and won't hold up in topiary forms, but Queen Anne's lace, black-eyed Susans and wild roses are quite dependable. They look delicate but are sturdy enough to stay fresh in your creations for the length of a party and through to the following day. Grasses and milkweed pods are other free-for-the-taking materials that can be incorporated into large-scale designs.

If you are fortunate enough to live near the woods, you can gather a variety of mosses and lichens. These treasures are as precious to a mock topiarist as a flawless diamond because of their subtle colors and understated elegance. They look delicate, but will last several weeks if you refresh them by misting with water. Mushrooms are more fragile, but will certainly last through the evening.

Florists use foliage in arrangements to offset floral colors and stretch a few flowers over a large area. You will improve your topiary, as well as your party budget, by filling in with greens. Take advantage of homegrown greens to create floral topiary without stripping your flower beds. Pachysandra and ivy stems can be picked without harm to a ground cover planting. Sometimes the sprigs even root in the topiary form and can be replanted in the garden.

Fresh foliage will add a variety of effects to your mock topiary. Autumn leaves that fall from your maple, oak or beech trees can be used as seasonal accents on standards. Take some leaves from houseplants—croton, dracaena or palm leaves make for wild, unexpected effects. If you have an asparagus fern, insert a few stems so their delicate, airy texture will set off surrounding flowers. Buy a bunch of inexpensive greens from the florist to finish off your topiary with a professional

Herbs from your summer garden can be dried for midwinter mock topiary projects. Cut them in the early morning, as their volatile oils are dissipated by the heat of the sun. Tie the stems together into loose bunches, and hang upside down in a dark, dry, airy place. Avoid exposure to direct light, which will cause the foliage to fade.

touch. Leatherleaf fern and galax leaves have a polished appearance and give any design a note of class. They are also sturdy, inexpensive and will last several weeks—put the stems in a glass of water and store them in the refrigerator. Even ordinary parsley adds a fresh, cheerful green to topiary, and the curly texture is distinctive.

To create striking temporary topiary at any time of year, ask your florist for fresh flowers that don't bruise easily and will last for several days. Many can be removed from their stems and pinned directly into the form through the center of the flower head. Daisies and chrysanthemums are familiar favorites; also try star of Bethlehem, a more unusual but sturdy flower, white with a black center, that is smaller and good for depicting detail. Carnations have a spicy scent and are easy to handle. They come in a luscious assortment, from solid white to speckled pink-and-red, and in sizes from miniature to jumbo. Carnations don't sit flat against your form, so allow for an increase in size. Anthuriums are exotic flowers that stay fresh for days. They are available in a variety of sizes, in colors ranging from a delicate pink to deep scarlet and even shades of green. Baby's breath looks fragile, but the stems are sturdy and the sprays can be cut to any length for a variety of effects. Get a lot of mileage out of a single gladiolus stalk by plucking off the individual flowers. Alstroemeria, gerbera and freesia are other dependable florists' mainstays.

Miniature pineapples, the traditional symbol of welcome, are also available on long stems from the florist. Other fresh fruits and vegetables add realistic accents for faux standards and espaliers. Lady apples, mandarin oranges, kumquats, small eggplants and miniature artichokes all contribute to the illusion that your creation is alive and growing. Broccoli and cauliflower florets can also be used to cover the entire topiary.

At the Paco de Sao Cipriano Garden in northern Portugal, a 15-foot-high topiary cock immortalizes a folktale bird that jumped from a stewing pot to testify to the innocence of an accused murderer.

ALL ABOUT CONTAINERS

Whimsical animals and birds often look best standing directly on tables or flat trays, but standards, poodles, obelisks and espaliers are best offset by containers. Clay pots, baskets and brass or wooden planters are all pretty possibilities. The one you choose will play an important role in determining the overall look of your mock display.

If you don't have a container of the right style, size or shape, improvise with ordinary plastic and glass food storage jars and boxes. You can quickly dress up these plain containers in a variety of ways, turning them into fantastic displays. Freezer containers and margarine tubs are inexpensive, versatile and waterproof options. If you buy foods in bulk, save the containers—or just ask for empty tubs at the deli counter or fish store. Metal coffee and juice cans are equally good candidates.

Disguise your grocery store finds, and other plain containers, by covering them in moss, leaves, fabric or paint. Any of these materials can be easily attached to the outside of glass, plastic or wood with ordinary white glue or florist's clay, which has the advantage of being removable.

Another way to transform containers is to dress them in a coat of paint. If you are starting with unfinished wood, the first step is to apply a coat of primer. The next step, for any surface, is a coat of spray enamel, which results in even coverage. Use any color you desire—gold or silver instantly turns trash to treasure.

For effects that look elaborate but are actually simple to do, try a fancy painted finish. Spray enamel is used as a base coat, with one or more different colors of oil-base or acrylic paint applied on top. These are painted by hand to create a variety of textures. For a mottled finish, use a small sponge as an applicator, pressing firmly in some spots, lightly in others, and overlapping different colors. Other interesting textures are achieved by using a small paint brush, feather, scrap of fabric

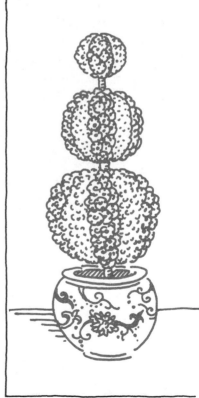

At the height of the Victorian craze for plant decorations, table ornaments were carried to extravagant extremes. Holes were cut in mahogany tables and costly damask cloths so that the pots of large plants could be concealed beneath the table. Thanks to modern mock topiary artistry, it isn't necessary to make such expensive sacrifices in order to dress up your table.

or even your fingers to apply the color. Stippling is a technique used to apply a random pattern of tiny dots. Use a small brush, and lightly touch the surface of the container with the tip. Stippling in several shades will result in a multicolor confetti effect.

Aluminum pie plates and plastic plant saucers are good shallow, watertight bases for any faux form. Attach one to the top of a stem to support the head of a mock standard if you want a graceful, airy, weeping crown of leaves, twigs and flowers. For small, light versions use a pie plate; substitute a rigid plastic saucer for tall, heavy ones. Foil containers from frozen foods come in all shapes and sizes and they make useful platforms for many geometric or fanciful designs. The individual serving-size could be nailed to a thin dowel as a form for charming miniature floral standards.

TRICKS OF THE TRADE

Floral designers are masters of illusion, creating such magical effects as clouds of flowers balanced on slender twigs. You can share their success once you master a few invisible tricks of the trade—happily, these behind-the-scenes techniques are ingeniously simple.

In order to create mock topiary, you must equip yourself for the craft. Don't be discouraged by the number of supplies mentioned—for any given project, you will need only a few of the items. There are several equally good methods for constructing mock topiary, all of which call for different supplies. So familiarize yourself with the following tools and materials and choose the technique you prefer.

An electric glue gun is indispensable for mock projects. The guns are inexpensive and simple to operate, delivering a thin line of hot plastic glue that dries almost instantly to a permanent, clear, waterproof bond on metal, wood, fabric, glass or plastic. Care must be exercised when using one of these guns, however. Never leave it unattended and be especially careful if children are about. You can also use a cold glue that dries instantly for a strong, clear bond. Bathtub caulking doesn't have to be heated and also creates a strong seal, but it must be allowed to cure overnight. It is available in white, clear and a variety of colors. Where an entire surface is to be covered use ordinary white craft glue, which is easy to spread.

Pointed scissors or a knife, as well as wire cutters, come in handy for making the underlying framework and for cutting branches and flower stems. Long tweezers are helpful for inserting soft-stemmed leaves and flowers.

Any animal or geometric wire frame for portable topiary may be used as the basis of a mock shape. You can buy large wire forms in the shape of a cone or stylized Christmas tree. These don't have to be stuffed since they're fitted with rings to hold potted plants—which could also hold cut branches or flowers. Wreaths are so popular now that the frames are available year-round at garden centers, florist supply houses and craft shops. Certainly they are handsome hung on doors and windows, but they are equally at home laid flat on tables to surround standards or candles.

With mock topiary, it is a simple matter to devise your own forms without a metal skeleton. Chicken wire is easily bent into any shape you desire; this covering contains and supports the filling of your choice. The green-coated variety is less visible. Renny uses a core of crumpled chicken wire for his elegant standards. He reinforces them with a few hoops of stronger wire around the outside.

There are several stuffings you can use for wire frames and chicken wire shapes. Crumpled newspaper is a light, cheap, dry filling that can be used to fill wire forms before covering them with sheet moss or sticking in evergreen branches. Autumn leaves are another option. You can use them wet or dry, and if tightly packed, they will firmly hold branches and stems. Damp long-fiber sphagnum moss is used for a filling where you wish to hold a maximum amount of moisture, in order to con-

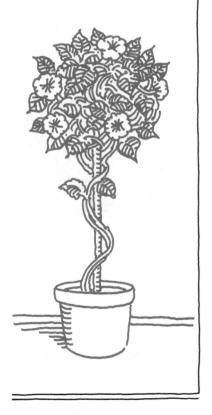

serve fresh-cut greens and flowers.

Plastic floral foam, usually sold under the brand name Oasis, is a material used by florists to create arrangements. It is soft, green, brick-shaped and easy to cut into any size or shape. Floral foam will absorb quite a bit of water, so you can have fresh-looking flowers and foliage all through a long evening without fear of sloshing. But once it has completely dried out, it is difficult to use, since it does not readily re-absorb water. Soak Oasis in a basin or pail of water until it sinks, which means that it is thoroughly saturated. Allow excess water to drain off and set it into your container. Oasis can also be used for dry arrangements, although there is a brown foam sold as Sahara that is made specifically for use with dried materials. Plastic adhesive florist's tape, sold as Oasis tape, is used to keep foam from shifting in pie plates, saucers and other containers.

Foam may be used as a filling for wire forms. It is strong enough to be used without a wire casing for small figures. Small domes of foam, sold as Igloos, are enclosed in a plastic cage that eliminates the need for wire wrapping. Two can be joined together to form the heads of tabletop-size standards.

Firm fruits and vegetables can be used like foam as the core of a mock topiary, because they naturally contain enough moisture to keep cut evergreens looking fresh for several weeks. Potatoes, Osage oranges and rutabagas are firm enough to hold branches. You will have to pierce the skin with a nail before inserting the branches, unless the stems are extremely tough and woody.

Styrofoam is useful whenever you are constructing topiary with dry materials. Blocks can be carved into any simple shape, and balls are available for creating standards and poodles in a range of diameters. They come in green or white; try to get green ones, which won't show through foliage. Rough hunks of styrofoam are used to anchor topheavy topiary in its container. They don't have to be uniform in size or color, since they will be disguised—you can even break up old packing material. When you don't have enough styrofoam to fill the container, use several pieces wedged between the side of the pot and the central spike or legs of the frame. Fill the remaining space with sand for greater stability.

Plaster of Paris is a better base for tall topiary standards and poodles. Crumple newspaper in the container first, so you don't have to add as much plaster. Mix only as much as you need for one figure, because plaster hardens very quickly. You can save valuable pots and planters for another use by molding the plaster in an inexpensive plastic or metal can and setting this base inside the decorative container. To prevent the mixture from leaking out of a basket, line it first with a plastic bag.

Florist's clay, sold in blocks, can be broken off into pieces and comes in handy in a variety of ways. Use it as the basis for small standards, forming the head or anchoring the stem in a container. Conveniently, it also comes in strips on paper-wrapped rolls—useful for wrapping containers in leaves or fabric. Unlike the hot glue, which will form a permanent bond, anything stuck together with florist's clay can be pulled apart easily and reused.

Thin enameled florist's wire is an unobstrusive green and comes in precut straight lengths or coiled on spools. The straight pieces are good for adding length and strength to flower stems. The spooled wire is used for securing filling inside frames.

Flower picks are small spikes of green wood, with a piece of wire attached, that add length and rigidity to dried or fresh flower stems before you stick them into foam or long-fiber sphagnum bases.

Water picks are plastic tubes of various sizes, with a pointed end that may be stuck into foam or vegetable forms. They are filled with water and have a rubber cap that seals around the flower stem. For light weight and to eliminate the risk of water dripping onto the table, many florists prefer to construct a dry base, using water picks to add fresh flowers. Water picks also provide additional support and water for delicate flowers in a wet form.

PRESERVATIVES

Fresh foliage materials can be dipped in preservatives to prolong their longevity. Anti-desiccant products, such as Wilt-Pruf, Envy, Cloud Cover and Vapor Gard, leave an invisible barrier on cut evergreens that reduces moisture loss so they stay fresh longer. Follow manufacturer's instructions to dilute concentrates. Many gardeners prefer to dilute to an even weaker solution than recommended.

Clear floor wax, such as Johnson's Klear Wax or Future, dries to a smooth, glossy coating that keeps certain cut evergreens and leaves shiny and colorful for a long time without water. Boxwood, ivy and croton foliage, and anthurium and spathiphyllum flowers, are especially long lasting after dipping, and have stayed green and fresh for as long as six weeks.

USING MONO-FILAMENT FISHING LINE

When in doubt about the strength of the line needed for a particular project, always use a heavier-test weight. Avoid using blue line, which shows garishly against sheet moss. Clear line is inconspicuous, but may show when it catches the light. For truly invisible wrapping, try dark green monofilament, which is usually sold in the heavier weights.

Mock creations add special warmth to holiday decorations, ranging from a foxhead-emblazoned wreath and a mantel swag to a pair of pineapple-topped cornucopia standards.

Dowels and broom handles are used, as are natural branches, to simulate the trunks of standards and poodles. They can be cut to any length and are sold in different diameters—the thickest are capable of supporting tall, heavy-headed standards. Dowels will give your creation a more stylized look than branches, and they can be finished nicely by painting, staining or wrapping in ribbon or moss. Bamboo stakes can be employed like dowels; cover them in ribbon, or leave them bare for a natural look. Generally, pushing a foam or wire ball firmly down on the top of the dowel holds it in place. If more security is needed, drill horizontally through the pole, and run a wire through the hole and the ball form.

Ribbons give faux topiary a final festive touch. Don't skimp on quality or quantity. It's only a few extra dollars in exchange for a vastly superior display. Cheap ribbon never ties or drapes gracefully, and invariably lacks the luster of good satin, grosgrain, moire or velvet ribbon. Get your topiary animals ready for a party simply by tying bows around their necks. For festive standards, tie masses of narrow satin ribbon into small bows under the head and let long ends stream down. Raffia bows have a charming, rustic look that is more appropriate when you are aiming for a naturalistic, earth-tone atmosphere.

Pebbles and marbles, in an assortment of colors and sizes, can reflect light and add interest to mock displays. They are helpful for disguising supportive bases, and in addition to their decorative function, they act to counterbalance the weight of the head. Small-scale Christmas tree ornaments, some with a decidedly un-Christmasy look, present a tempting assortment of baubles. These are fabulous for putting the finishing touches on elegant designs. For a deluxe touch, bejewel your mock topiary in garlands of imitation pearls or rhinestones.

Many party designers find that successful room transformations are ultimately due to good lighting schemes. For a truly magical evening, spotlight your mock topiary. You can even highlight it by draping the figure in battery-operated miniature lights.

Standard or Poodle

This is a simple way to create a standard or multi-balled poodle, using either styrofoam balls or a piece of foam wrapped in chicken wire to form a rough ball shape. Keep in mind that the height of the trunk should be in proportion with the diameter of the sphere.

DISGUISING A TRUNK

To cover up an unattractive broom handle or dowel trunk:
- *Spray with decorative paint*
- *Festoon with gaily colored ribbons*
- *Wrap with sheet moss, using florist's wire or fishing line*
- *Apply a wood stain*

When wrapping a slender stem or thin tail in sheet moss, run three or four lines of hot glue along the stake or wire. Then press the sheet moss in place to prevent slipping.

You will need:
—*a sturdy dowel, broom handle or branch for the trunk*
—*a decorative container*
—*three or more pieces of styrofoam plus sand or pebbles; or plaster of Paris plus an inexpensive plastic or metal container slightly smaller than the decorative container*
—*a styrofoam ball or a piece of floral foam wrapped in chicken wire (for the poodle, two or more styrofoam balls or pieces of wire-wrapped foam)*
—*U-shaped hairpins or florist's pins or glue*
—*sheet moss*
—*(optional) decorative pebbles; Spanish moss or sheet moss; dried or fresh herbs and flowers; water picks*

1 Stand the dowel, broom handle or branch upright in the center of the pot. Wedge at least three pieces of styrofoam between the pot and the trunk until it will remain firmly vertical. Fill the pot to within half an inch of the rim with sand or pebbles.

2 If the standard is over 1½ feet tall or if the head is large, you may have to weigh down the pot even more. Plaster of Paris can be used, in which case you can eliminate the styrofoam and sand or pebbles. Follow manufacturer's directions for mixing the plaster. Hold the trunk upright in the center of the inexpensive container, and pour in the plaster to an inch below the rim. Set the inexpensive container inside the decorative container.

3 Take the styrofoam ball or wire-wrapped floral foam in one hand and, steadying the trunk with your other hand, jam it onto the top of the branch until it sticks about halfway through the ball.

4 Cover the ball by pinning or gluing on pieces of sheet moss.

5 (optional) You can cover the sand, pebbles or inner container with a layer of pretty pebbles, Spanish moss or sheet moss. For a long-term decoration, use glue to add dried herbs and flower heads. For a temporary effect, fresh flowers can be used if you first put them in water picks.

Triple Poodle Variation

A triple poodle can be created by using three balls of the same size, or of graduated diameters. Stabilize the trunk in the pot as in Steps 1 and 2. Take the largest ball and push the trunk all the way through it, sliding it down until it is 4 to 6 inches above the rim of the pot. Apply glue around the bottom of the ball to keep it from slipping farther down the trunk. Repeat with the middle ball, sliding it down until it is at the midpoint of the trunk, and glue that in place. The top sphere should be pushed on last—stop when the trunk is about halfway through the ball.

Large Standard

Large styrofoam balls are expensive, so if you want to make a big standard, make your own form from Oasis floral foam and chicken wire. It can be soaked to accommodate fresh flowers inserted directly, or used dry, with dried material or water picks. Bob Zimmerman uses the following method to create magnificent floor-standing standards 9 feet tall.

You will need:
—a thick branch or dowel, 1½ to 2 inches in diameter, for the trunk

—*a decorative container*
—*three or more pieces of styrofoam plus sand or pebbles; or plaster of Paris plus an inexpensive plastic or metal container slightly smaller than the decorative container*
—*four bricks of Oasis floral foam*
—*chicken wire*
—*thin florist's wire*
—*fresh cut flowers and greens or dried material*
—*Spanish moss*
—*(optional) decorative pebbles, Spanish moss or sheet moss; water picks*

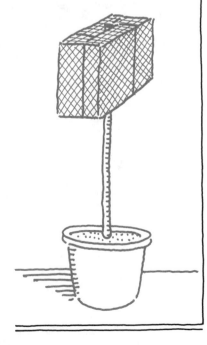

1 Stand the branch or dowel upright in the center of the pot. Wedge at least three pieces of styrofoam between the pot and the branch until the trunk will remain firmly vertical. Fill the pot to within half an inch of the rim with sand or pebbles.

2 Plaster of Paris can also be used, in which case you can eliminate the styrofoam and sand or pebbles. Follow manufacturer's directions for mixing the plaster. Hold the trunk upright in the center of the inexpensive container and pour in the plaster to an inch below the rim. Set the inexpensive container inside the decorative container.

3 Take four bricks of Oasis floral foam and arrange as pictured on the left. Wrap the foam with several layers of chicken wire, scrunching each piece around the foam into a rough ball shape. It doesn't have to be perfect—the leaves and flowers will round it out. If you want to put flowers directly into the foam, soak it in a tub of water, and then let excess water drain off.

4 Grasp the ball with two hands and jam it down on the trunk. Take thin florist's wire and lash it through the chicken wire and around the trunk to stabilize.

5 The form is now ready to be covered with flowers or dried materials. Bob Zimmerman uses a moist form, and he achieves his look by always inserting the flowers first. He adds flowers on their own stems, and then gently fills in any spaces between them with bits of Spanish moss. Other floral designers will put in their greens first, and then add individual flowers in water picks. Use whichever method seems easier to you—the important thing is to completely conceal the foam and wire form.

6 (optional) You can conceal the sand, pebbles or inner container with a layer of pretty pebbles, Spanish moss or sheet moss.

Saucer Standard

The following directions are for a more informal standard. This one is big and solid, 4 feet tall with a trunk about 3 inches in diameter. The top consists of a fanciful arrangement of palm leaves, fruits and vegetables crowned with a gracious pineapple. It is designed to stand on the floor rather than a tabletop. A pair would look good on either side of a fireplace or your front door. A rigid plastic plant saucer holds a block of floral foam as a form for the head. Because the head is heavy, a plaster base is used to stabilize it. You will want to display this creation in an elegant brass planter or fancy clay pot. To save it for other uses, mold the plaster base in a disposable container, which can be set inside the planter.

This method can also be used for lighter or smaller versions topped with an airy arrangement of flowers—in which case you can use an aluminum pie plate and anchor a thinner and shorter trunk in styrofoam.

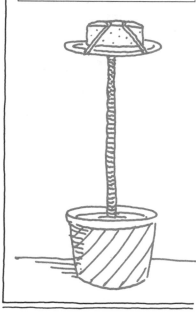

In her classic 1931 reference work on plant lore and uses, A Modern Herbal, *Maud Grieve* relates this charming story about an unusual use for sphagnum moss: "The Lapland matrons are well acquainted with this moss. They dry it and lay it in their children's cradles to supply the place of mattress, bolster and every covering, and being changed night and morning, it keeps the infant remarkable clean, dry and warm."

You will need:
—*plaster of Paris*
—*a branch or dowel, 4 feet tall and at least 3 inches in diameter, for the trunk*
—*a decorative container*
—*an inexpensive plastic or metal container slightly smaller than the decorative container*
—*a rigid plastic plant saucer, 10 to 12 inches in diameter*
—*a washer*
—*a screw*
—*a hot glue gun and glue cartridges*
—*a brick of floral foam*
—*plastic adhesive florist's tape*
—*palm leaves or other cut greens*
—*a small wood or bamboo stake, 12 to 18 inches long*
—*a pineapple*
—*thin wooden skewers or toothpicks*
—*small fruits and vegetables*
—*(optional) decorative pebbles, Spanish moss or sheet moss*

1 Follow manufacturer's directions for mixing plaster of Paris. Hold the branch or dowel upright in the center of the inexpensive container, and pour in the plaster to an inch below the rim. Set the inexpensive container inside the decorative container.

2 Once the plaster has set you can attach the saucer. Slip the washer over the screw, and screw through the center of the saucer, fastening it to the top of the trunk. Apply hot glue around the edges of the washer for a watertight seal.

3 Soak the foam brick in a tub of water. Drain. Center it in the saucer, and secure it in place with florist's tape.

4 Start to build your arrangement by concealing the edge of the saucer with palm leaves. Take a small stake and pierce it

through the middle of the pineapple. Insert the other end in the center of the foam. Using thin wooden skewers or toothpicks if necessary, insert other small fruits and vegetables around the pineapple to create an attractive mound that covers the form.

5 (optional) You can conceal the inner container with a layer of pretty pebbles, Spanish moss or sheet moss.

Hanging Basket Standard

Plastic hanging baskets of Tahitian bridal veil, Boston fern or Swedish ivy are useful for imitation standards. These plants maintain a rounded shape naturally, concealing the pot and soil and instantly achieving the look of a lush head.

You will need:
—*a branch or dowel about 1½ inches in diameter for the trunk*
—*a decorative container*
—*three or more pieces of styrofoam plus sand or pebbles; or plaster of Paris plus an inexpensive plastic or metal container slightly smaller than the decorative container*
—*one full plant, growing in a plastic hanging basket, with a snap-off saucer plus its triple-wire hanger*
—*a nail*
—*(optional) decorative pebbles, Spanish moss or sheet moss*

1 Stand the branch or dowel upright in the center of the pot. Wedge at least three pieces of styrofoam between the pot and

the branch until the trunk will remain firmly vertical. Fill the pot to within half an inch of the rim with sand or pebbles.

2 Plaster of Paris can also be used, in which case you can eliminate the styrofoam and sand or pebbles. Follow manufacturer's directions for mixing the plaster. Hold the trunk upright in the center of the inexpensive container, and pour in the plaster to an inch below the rim. Set the inexpensive container inside the decorative container.

3 Snap the saucer off the bottom of the basket; nail it to the top of the pole.

4 Set the planted basket on top of the saucer and snap them back together. Bend the wire hangers down, and use them to secure the basket to the trunk.

5 (optional) You can conceal the sand, pebbles or inner container with a layer of pretty pebbles, Spanish moss or sheet moss.

Frameless Foam Birds and Beasts

This method eliminates the need for a wire frame, and works well for small shapes you want to cover with fresh flowers and foliage. The simplest shapes to carve are a duck, whale or rabbit, but feel free to try other animals. You will need a waterproof tray, pan or saucer to display your finished topiary.

You will need:
—two bricks of floral foam
—a hot glue gun and glue cartridges

—a pencil or permanent marking pen
—a knife
—fresh cut flowers or evergreen branches
—a waterproof tray, pan or saucer

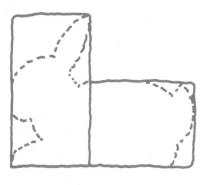

1 The foam blocks must be absolutely dry. Set one down on the long side. Apply hot glue to one of the ends. Working rapidly before the glue dries, press the second block standing on end. Let the blocks stand ten minutes until the seal is complete. Scratch the outline of the creature on the side of the foam with a pencil or permanent marking pen. If you are making a rabbit, mark the two ears on the front side of the tall block.

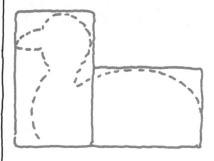

2 Use the knife to cut the foam, following your outline carefully. For the rabbit, cut between the ears; on the whale, carve out the tail fins.

3 Put the glued and shaped blocks in a sink filled with water until they are thoroughly moistened. Drain sink and allow excess water to drip off form.

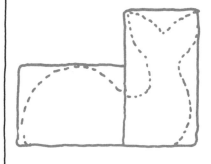

4 Cut branches or flower stems down to a uniform length of 3 to 4 inches. Cover the form densely, until no foam shows. Boxwood or yew will give you a realistic-looking topiary, while fresh flowers will create a fanciful figure that especially delights children. Set the topiary on a waterproof tray, pan or saucer and use any leftover flowers and evergreens to decorate the tray.

Flower-Covered Bear

A flower-covered bear is enchanting and can be made very quickly. Chrysanthemums are good for this, since they are sturdy and inexpensive. Buy a teddy bear frame, or make one as described in Chapter Four. You will need a waterproof tray, pan or saucer to show off your creation.

You will need:
—a wire teddy bear frame
—long-fiber sphagnum moss
—fresh cut flowers
—florist's wire
—a waterprooof tray, pan or saucer
—sheet moss

1 Soak sphagnum in a tub of water until it is thoroughly saturated.

2 Pick up a handful of sphagnum and squeeze out excess water. Stuff into the bottom of the frame. Working from the bottom up, stuff firmly until the entire bear is packed tightly with moss.

3 Remove a flower head from its stem. Stick a piece of wire through the center of the flower and press it into the moss until it is flush against the form. Repeat until the entire bear is closely covered and no moss shows through. Set the topiary on a waterproof tray, pan or saucer and use a piece of sheet moss and leftover flowers to decorate the edge of the tray.

Mock Espalier

This tasteful decoration was designed by Lena Caron for Ladew Topiary Gardens. It is covered with boxwood twigs and festooned with small apples and oranges. For a more informal look, cover your espalier in Spanish moss, and decorate with small twigs and ivy tendrils. Do not use aluminum wire, which bends too easily.

You will need:
—a 27-inch branch or dowel, an inch in diameter, for the trunk
—plaster of Paris
—a 4 to 5-inch, inexpensive plastic container
—a decorative container, slightly larger than the plastic container
—No. 8 galvanized wire, 8 feet long, cut into two pieces, 57 inches and 39 inches in length
—pliers
—florist's wire
—boxwood twigs cut into uniform 4-inch lengths, or Spanish moss
—a ribbon bow
—(optional) decorative fruits such as kumquats or lady apples; Spanish moss or sheet moss

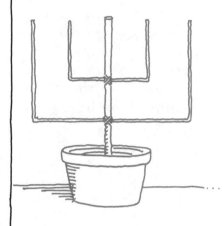

1 Stand the trunk upright in the center of the plastic container.

2 Follow manufacturer's directions for mixing plaster of Paris. Hold the trunk upright in the center of the inexpensive container, and pour in the plaster to an inch below the rim. Set the inexpensive container inside the decorative container.

3 Take the longer (57-inch) piece of wire and mark the center point. Measure out an inch on either side from the center. Using pliers, make a loop between these points.

4 Mark out 13½ inches on either side of the loop. At these marks, bend the wire up with pliers to form right angles.

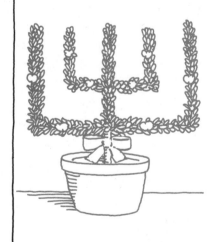

> **66Each tree should have the same cared-for appearance that a well-groomed horse presents in the satin shine of his coat. . . .99**
>
> —FRANCES GARNET, the Viscountess Wolseley, *Gardens: Their Form and Design*, 1919

5 Take the remaining (39-inch) piece of wire, and repeat Steps 3 and 4, bending at right angles 8½ inches from the center.

6 Slide the loop of the longer arm over the trunk. Measure up 11 inches from the base of the stem and lash the arm tightly to the trunk at this point with florist's wire. Slip the loop of the second arm over the trunk. Measure up 5 inches from the first arm and lash the second arm in place.

7 The next step is to cover the framework. Starting at the top of an arm and working toward the center stem, lash bunches of cut boxwood (with greenery facing upward) onto and around the arm with florist's wire, overlapping the rows of branches to hide the wires. When you reach the center, tie off wire, and start at the top of the other side.

8 Repeat with the other arm, and cover the center stem in the same fashion. To mask where the row of boxwood meets the center stem, tie on a ribbon bow.

9 (optional) Decorate randomly with miniature fruits. For a permanent effect, instead of using boxwood you can wrap the arms in Spanish moss and secure with wire. You can conceal the inner container with a layer of Spanish moss or sheet moss.

Framemaking

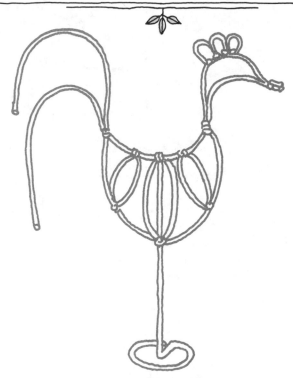

ELEGANT ARMATURES FOR HANDCRAFTED ACCENTS

In portable topiary the frame determines the ultimate shape, molding the character of your green sculpture. You could certainly purchase ready-made topiary frames at garden supply centers or through mail-order houses (see the Source Guide). But for a topiary that is uniquely yours, why not make your own wire frame? You'll have the fun and satisfaction of creating your plant sculpture from conception to completion, seeing it evolve from a coil of wire to a lush, beautiful living creature. Even if you follow a pattern, each handmade frame will have a slightly different appearance—and therefore its own character. And any frame can be customized without altering the design on paper by simply bending the wires: change the angle of a butterfly's wings, turn a dog's head, or bend one ear of a rabbit to give individual personality to your creation.

The simplest frames, recommended for your first endeavor, consist of a flat outline or open silhouette. Designs given here include a classic, versatile hoop—combine several of these to make a sphere. If you'd like to start with a more amusing shape, try the endearing heart, charming sparrow or graceful goose.

While the more complicated three-dimensional frames may look tricky, they basically consist of a wire outline with circular ribs added at right angles to round out the shape. Add to your aviary a rooster, or start a menagerie with a playful seal, a contented rabbit, a lamb or a cat. Move on to frames with a few more pieces, and invite a patient turtle, gleeful dog, well-fed pig, and whimsical dinosaur to join the zoo. A sailboat is easy to construct—present it as a gift to a nautical friend, or incorporate it into a tabletop tableau. Or try a topiary rendition of the Owl and the Pussycat setting out to sea in a beautiful pea-green boat.

Framemaking requires some dexterity and imagination, but mostly just the courage to give it a try. As you work on your first frame, you'll quickly become accustomed to handling wire. Before long, you will find yourself playing with it and devising your own designs. Small imperfections don't matter, because any kinks or lumpy joints will be covered by stuffing and plants. And

> **66***Wire frames have entirely superseded the old methods . . . the frame gives the florist at once the desired form, and makes it easy for any person of taste to arrange flowers in the shape of an anchor, star, etc. The frame is filled with damp moss, wound slightly to keep it in place, and the flowers . . . are inserted in the moss.***99**
>
> —PETER HENDERSON
> *Practical Floriculture,*
> *1897*

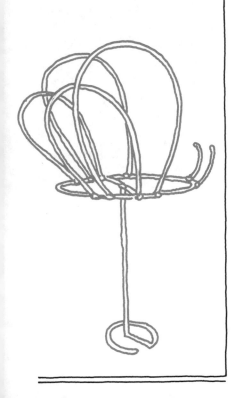

details can be altered by padding with moss.

Sketch your ideas on graph paper so you can figure out how much wire you'll need, or even enlarge the drawing to an actual-size pattern. Needlework magazines and pattern books are excellent sources for designs on grids, and often the patterns are already a good size for topiary frames. Remember that both stuffing and plants add to the overall dimensions of the sculpture and tend to obscure small details. So you must always make frames slimmer than the ultimate design, and exaggerate features such as noses and tails.

Frames are of two basic types: one has spikes or a stand that anchors the frame below the soil surface, and is designed for use with pots; the other is flat bottomed, designed for both freestanding and container use. This second type can be fixed on top of a pot or planter with long pins of bent wire.

One technique used to round out the form and strengthen the frame is to make a skin of chicken wire. Sometimes the chicken wire is wrapped around a skeleton, as in the case of the turtle's body. In other instances, with simple shapes such as a cone or a teddy bear, the form is composed entirely of chicken wire, which can be covered with live plants, cut flowers or foliage for a mock effect.

WIRE

Wire is the main ingredient of your frame. It must be flexible enough to bend easily, but stiff enough to hold the shape you want. There are a few things you should know about wire before you buy it and start making frames. It is sized in reverse order to its thickness—the higher the gauge number, the thinner the wire. The thicker the wire you use, the harder it is to bend, but this makes for a stronger frame. The recommended gauges have proven to be sufficiently flexible yet rigid to create portable frames in the dimensions given for the projects in this chapter. If you can handle bending thicker wire, by all means use it to ensure an even stronger structure.

Aluminum wire is soft, flexible and rustproof. It is more expensive than galvanized wire, but infinitely easier to bend. Depending on the shapes you choose, one 50-foot roll will give you two or three figures with enough left over for a few small outline frames. A No. 8 or No. 9 gauge is recommended for the portable frames described in this chapter. Aluminum wire will leave a dark residue on your fingers, but this washes off easily. To avoid soiling your hands or clothes, look for aluminum wire that is encased in a thin plastic coating. For an attractive finish, spray paint the frame with fast-drying lacquer sold in auto supply stores. Exposed portions will be unobtrusive if you select a dark color.

Galvanized wire is harder to bend than aluminum, but this means a thinner gauge will still hold its shape. It is especially suited for making large, simple outline frames. The recommended thickness for the portable frames is 14- or 16-gauge. The galvanizing process makes the metal rust resistant, but it will corrode eventually. If you want your assembled frame to last for years, paint it with spray lacquer. Coat hangers are made from galvanized metal, and they can be used if you don't have any other wire around—but you will be restricted by the limited length of the wire.

Frames for outdoor use are made of stiffer galvanized wire. Instead of gluing or taping, each joint must be soldered together. If you are handy with a welding torch, you can enlarge the designs given here to a size appropriate for shrubs. Make your outdoor frames with No. 8 or No. 9 galvanized wire, sometimes sold as fence wire.

Chicken wire has two basic uses for topiary. It can be used on its own to construct simple frames, or it can be added to wire skeletons. There are two types of chicken wire: the ordinary kind sold in various widths (from 2 to 5 feet) for fencing; and the green florist's type, which is better if you can find it, and comes in convenient 12-inch-wide rolls.

If you want to make large frames, twist strands of wire together for added strength.

Framemaking is a good project to share with children, especially if you choose one of their favorite shapes. Many children are captivated by dinosaurs or boats—why not delight them with a brontosaurus or a sailboat? And the learning experience and the fun don't end with the completed frame. Children can discover the joy of caring for a living plant, or the excitement of decorating a sculpture with flowers for their own birthday parties.

TOOLS AND SUPPLIES

You will need only a few tools and materials to make frames. Most likely, you already have many of them on hand; if not, they are inexpensive and easy to find. Pliers are invaluable for bending wire; the needle-nose type is best for small-scale framemaking or areas that require precise bending. Wire cutters are indispensable; any style will work as long as they are sharp. A tape measure is necessary for measuring coiled or curved sections of wire, while a yardstick is helpful for

With just a few easy-to-find tools and supplies, you can turn almost any room into a complete topiary workshop.

straight pieces. Some or all of the following supplies are essential: thin, spooled wire (either green-enameled florist's wire or copper wire); waterproof adhesive tape (such as Oasis brand florist's tape, decorative vinyl tape or electrical tape); and bamboo stakes. You may prefer to use gloves when working with wire in order to prevent cuts and scrapes. A permanent marking pen is useful for marking spots to bend or cut along the wire.

Until the invention of the hot glue gun, framemaking was a complicated process that required elaborate metal-working skills and involved hazardous and messy procedures using blow torches and acid. The glue gun is a simple electrical device that dispenses hot glue that dries almost instantly to create a strong, waterproof seal. The more pressure you apply to the cartridge, the faster the glue comes out. Be careful not to burn yourself with the hot glue or metal tip, and never leave the gun plugged in and unattended.

CONSTRUCTING A WIRE SKELETON

Cutting

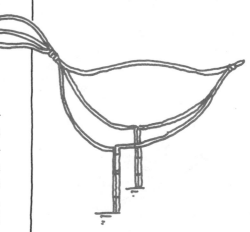

Before starting, cut all the pieces required for the frame. Allowance has been made for two inches of overlap in the patterns unless otherwise specified; if you are working on your own design, be sure to add at least two inches to each piece. You can always cut off the excess, but it is awkward to lengthen a wire that is too short, and this may create a weak spot in the frame. When making the actual cut, close your eyes or turn your head as a protection against flying pieces.

Bending

Bend each precut section of wire to follow the designs illustrated. Several methods are used to form the frames. Every bend uses a slightly different amount of wire. Don't worry if your dimensions vary slightly from the directions.

For curves and corners, hold the wire in one hand, and use pliers to bend it into the desired shape. If you are forming two identical pieces, shape one first. Then take the second piece and bend it to follow the contours of the first. For smooth curves, use pliers to bend the wire a little bit at a time. For a sharp curve that doubles back on itself, use needle-nose pliers at the turning point.

Form circles just under the rim of a clay pot, or around any rigid cylindrical container such as a wastebasket. Overlap the circle for a perfect shape; cut off excess wire, leaving a 1-inch overlap for joining.

When forming straight sections, smooth out any bad kinks with pliers. Run your fingers along the wire, pulling it into a straight line. The heat from your hands helps to soften the wire. Don't be too vigorous or you may get a friction burn. Be careful not to overwork the wire. If you bend it too many times in the same place, it will snap. If it does break, you can rescue the frame by overlapping the pieces, since allowance has been made in each design. Secure the overlap with florist's wire and tape or hot glue.

Joining

Don't try to assemble the entire frame in one step. Join two wires at a time, and wrap where they meet with thin spooled wire to hold them together. A twist tie will also work, but it makes the joint lumpy.

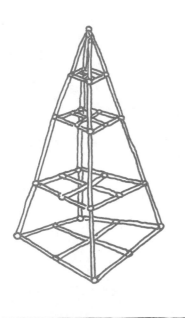

Reinforcing

There are two ways to strengthen the frame. The first is to wrap all the individual wires after assembly, including the joints, in waterproof adhesive tape. This is a tedious but recommended step that adds rigidity to the figure, and makes the wires unobtrusive while the plants are small.

The other strengthening method is to cover the joints themselves with hot glue. If possible, let the joint dry while it is laid flat on a table, or hold the frame for a minute or so, until the glue begins to set. Be careful that you don't glue the wire to the table. Let the glue harden completely (for about five minutes) before picking up the frame and gluing the next piece. Smaller or outline frames can be either wrapped or glued, whichever you find easier; but larger, more complex ones should be glued and then covered in tape.

If you are going to stuff a frame that is tall or top-heavy, add a bamboo stake for stability. The stake should run from the base of the pot all the way through to the top of the figure. Stakes can be added to the central stems of pot frames, or alongside the legs of freestanding animals. Use hot glue, tape or thin wire to attach the stake to the wire; then wrap them both together with tape.

USING CHICKEN WIRE

Cutting

Cut chicken wire so that loose ends are left along the edge. These will be bent around the adjoining section of wire. If you are adding chicken wire to a wire skeleton, it doesn't have to exactly follow the shape of your frame, but be sure it's slightly larger, so there is enough to secure it to the skeleton.

> **❝The frame is simply an outline of the topiary shape you wish to create. Adding various-sized circles makes the shape three dimensional. For easy circles, wrap wire around any round kitchen container, such as a spice bottle or a peanut butter jar.❞**
>
> —MIA HARDCASTLE
> professional
> framemaker

> **It must be remembered that topiaries, particularly indoors, are not ornamental figures or knickknacks; they are living plants, and must be cared for as such. They may be used as decorations for the evening, but must be returned to a proper growing place the following day.**
>
> —ALLEN HASKELL
> award-winning topiary grower, horticulturist and garden designer

Bending

Once scrunched, chicken wire will hold the desired shape. Make tucks where you want to taper the figure.

Joining

Secure chicken wire to itself or to wire frames by wrapping and twisting the cut ends, or by sewing pieces together with thin wire.

The noble peacock is just one of the many birds and beasts that you can bring to life with your framemaking handiwork. A picture or etching can often help to inspire your efforts at wire sculpture.

Preparing the Frame for Planting

Sometimes the frame has enough ribs for structural strength, but not enough to hold the filling. Remedy this by crisscrossing the frame with waterproof tape before stuffing. Pull it taut and twist it around joints. Or add a skin of chicken wire. To plant in chicken wire-wrapped frames, simply cut a hole large enough to accommodate the root ball and insert the plant in the stuffing.

Each frame design lends itself to completion in a variety of ways, which are described in detail in Chapters One and Three. If you aren't completely happy with certain parts of the frame, you can fatten portions or alter details when you stuff the frame by padding with bits of moss.

> Form the bare bones of your topiary on the thin side—the plants or flowers you add will fatten it up.

Simple Frames for Pots

The following shapes are designed for placement in a pot. All have a circular-shaped base so they will stand upright. The circular portion is bent from 9 inches of wire added to the desired height of the stem. For greater stability, glue the base to the bottom of the pot, jam in wedges of styrofoam or partially fill the pot with pebbles. If you use glue, be sure not to cover the pot's drainage hole. Most of the designs that follow are for 5- or 6-inch-diameter clay pots. Azalea pots, which are lower than standard pots, have better proportions for most shapes.

Hoop

One of these jointless designs makes a simple but effective frame for a 6-inch pot. You can also combine them for a sphere, or arrange several in a pot for a geometric configuration of your own design. Hoops can be made any size you like. Simply cut a length of wire equal to the total of the circumference of the circle plus two times the height of the pot plus 9 inches. (The easiest way to form a perfect circle is to bend it around a pot or container.)

You will need:
—wire cutters
—pliers
—one 60-inch piece of wire
—(optional) thin spooled wire or twist ties; waterproof adhesive tape

1 Bend the wire into a circle about 12 inches in diameter, reserving 10½ inches at each end for the stem and base. When a full circle has been formed, bend the ends at right angles, twist together for a straight stem equal to the depth of the pot, then bend both pieces out and around to form a circular base to sit on the bottom of the pot. Adjust the base until the stem stands straight.

2 (optional) For added rigidity, wrap the straight portion tightly with thin wire, twist ties or tape.

Heart

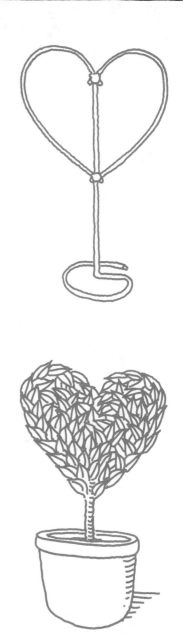

If you plan to either stuff the heart or make it taller than the dimensions given here, reinforce the wire stem with a bamboo stake.

You will need:
—wire cutters
—pliers
—two 17-inch pieces of wire
—one 25-inch piece of wire
—thin spooled wire or twist ties
—waterproof adhesive tape or a hot glue gun and cartridges
—(optional) a bamboo stake

1 Form two equal halves of the heart with the two 17-inch wires.

2 Make the stem from the 25-inch wire: using 8 inches for the circular base, bend 1 inch of the wire in to the center, then up at a right angle, and straight up into a stem. Adjust the base until the stem stands straight.

3 Lay the stem flat on the work surface; attach half of the heart with thin wire or twist ties, overlapping slightly.

4 Attach the second half as above, overlapping the first half.

5 (optional) Attach the bamboo stake to the wire stem with thin wire or twist ties.

6 Wrap all the individual wires with tape, or reinforce joints with hot glue.

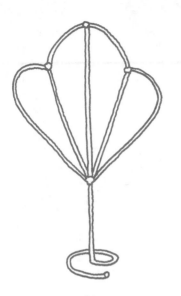

Fan/Peacock's Tail

This figure can be displayed on its own as a two-dimensional form in a 6-inch pot, or used as a peacock's tail.

You will need:
—*wire cutters*
—*pliers*
—*one 35-inch piece of wire for the stem*
  (substitute one 26-inch piece of wire for the peacock's tail)
—*one 39-inch piece of wire for the center loop*
—*two 35-inch pieces of wire for the side loops*
—*one 26-inch bamboo stake*
  (substitute one 18-inch bamboo stake for the peacock's tail)
—*thin spooled wire or twist ties*
—*waterproof adhesive tape or a hot glue gun and cartridges*

1 Make the stem from the 35-inch wire: using 8 inches for the circular base, bend 1 inch of the wire in to the center, then up at a right angle, and straight up into a stem.

2 Attach the stem to the stake with thin wire or twist ties.

3 Bend a 39-inch wire to form a center loop about 17 inches long, crossing the ends slightly. Secure it to the stem with thin wire or twist ties.

4 Bend a 35-inch wire into a side loop about 14 inches long, crossing the ends slightly. Attach it to the stem and alongside the center loop for about 6 inches. Repeat on the other side.

5 Wrap all the individual wires with tape, or reinforce joints with hot glue.

Zoological Frames for Pots

The following designs can be two-dimensional outline frames, or—by adding circles as ribs—converted into three-dimensional figures. When you add the circles, be sure to place them inside the outline wire to hold the shape.

Sparrow

Designed for a 4-inch azalea pot, this simple but charming little bird is formed with just two pieces of wire.

You will need:
—wire cutters
—pliers
—one 34-inch piece of wire for the stem, rear, back, head and upper beak
—one 8-inch piece of wire for the chest and lower beak
—thin spooled wire or twist ties
—waterproof adhesive tape or a hot glue gun and cartridges
—(optional) one 10-inch piece of wire for the circle

1 Form the stem and part of the bird outline from the 34-inch wire: using 8 inches for the circular base, bend 1 inch of the wire in to the center, then up at a right angle, and straight up into a 7-inch-long stem. Bend again into the outline of the bird's tail, back, head, and finishing at the tip of the upper beak, which should measure about 1½ inches.

2 Bend the 8-inch wire to form the chest and lower beak. Join it to the top of the stem and to the tip of the beak with thin wire or twist ties.

3 (optional) Use the 10-inch wire to make a circle, securing the 1-inch overlap with thin wire or twist ties. Attach the circle inside the outline as shown, from the stem to the back.

4 Wrap all the individual wires with tape, or reinforce joints with hot glue.

Goose

A different bird, and a simple design for a 5-inch pot.

You will need:
—*wire cutters*
—*pliers*
—*one 22-inch piece of wire for the stem and base*
—*one 37-inch piece of wire for the body outline*
—*thin spooled wire or twist ties*
—*waterproof adhesive tape or a hot glue gun and cartridges*
—*(optional) one 13-inch piece of wire for the circle*

1 Make the stem from the 22-inch wire: using 8 inches for the circular base, bend 1 inch of the wire in to the center, then up at a right angle, and straight up into a stem.

2 Form the 37-inch wire into the outline of the bird, starting at the belly and working forward to the beak, which should measure about 1½ inches, continuing around the head, back and rear and ending at the belly, leaving 2 inches at the end for the overlap. Secure the overlap with thin wire or twist ties.

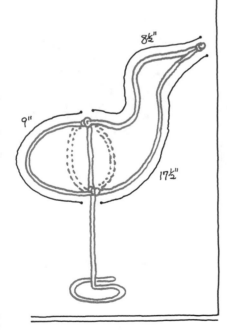

8½"

9"

17½"

3 Attach the outline to the stem, joining the two pieces where they meet at the underside and back with thin wire or twist ties.

4 (optional) Use the 13-inch wire to make a circle, securing the 1-inch overlap with thin wire or twist ties. Attach the circle inside the outline alongside the stem.

5 Wrap all the individual wires with tape, or reinforce joints with hot glue.

Rooster

This three-dimensional fowl, designed by framemaker Mia Hardcastle, looks good in a 6-inch pot. With slight adaptations, the same basic method is used to shape the peacock and seal in the two subsequent projects.

You will need:
—*wire cutters*
—*pliers*
—*one 22-inch piece of wire for the stem and base*
—*one 34-inch piece of wire for the top outline*
—*one 38-inch piece of wire for the bottom outline*
—*two 10-inch pieces of wire for the outer circles*
—*one 14½-inch piece of wire for the inner circle*
—*one 9-inch piece of wire for the comb*
—*thin spooled wire or twist ties*
—*waterproof adhesive tape or a hot glue gun and cartridges*

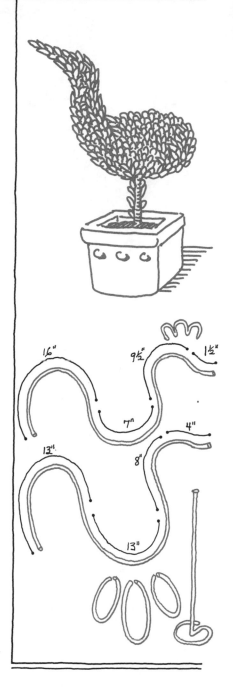

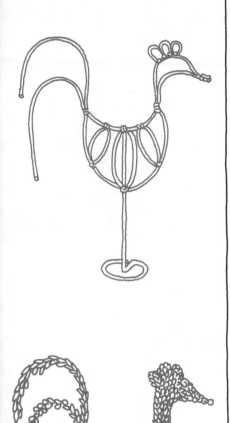

1. Make the stem from the 22-inch wire: using 8 inches for the circular base, bend 1 inch of the wire in to the center, then up at a right angle, and straight up into a stem.

2. Bend the 34-inch wire to form the top outline, starting with a 1½-inch beak and continuing through the head, back, and top tail feather.

3. Bend the 38-inch wire into the lower outline, starting with the lower beak and continuing through the neck, chest, and lower tail feather.

4. Join the top and bottom sections of the outline with thin wire or twist ties at the beak, neck and tail.

5. Bend the two 10-inch and one 14½-inch wires into circles, securing the 1-inch overlaps with thin wire or twist ties. Attach one of the smaller circles inside the outline at the tail end of the bird. Attach the larger circle inside the outline in the center of the bird. Attach the remaining small circle toward the front of the bird.

6. Attach the stem to the belly and the back alongside the middle of the circle with thin wire or twist ties.

7. Form the 9-inch wire into the comb, and secure it to the top of the head.

8. Wrap all the individual wires with tape, or reinforce joints with hot glue.

Peacock

This elegant adaptation of the rooster is a bit complicated, but worth the effort for a spectacular topiary. It looks best perched on a 6-inch pot. By adding a fantail, your barnyard bird becomes a noble creature that recalls the grand gardens of Europe.

You will need:
—*wire cutters*
—*pliers*
—*one 22-inch piece of wire for the stem*
—*one 33-inch piece of wire for the top outline*
—*one 38-inch piece of wire for the bottom outline*
—*two 10-inch pieces of wire for the outer circles*
—*one 14½-inch piece of wire for the center circle*
—*one 6-inch piece of wire for the crest*
—*a Fan/Peacock's Tail frame, without the circular base (see page 126)*
—*one 13-inch bamboo stake*
—*thin spooled wire or twist ties*
—*waterproof adhesive tape or a hot glue gun and cartridges*

*D*on't feel limited to the designs shown here. One woman who wanted an amusing accessory for garden parties devised a hat frame. She has planted it in ivy—the trick is to water it a few days before an occasion, so she doesn't get a wet head.

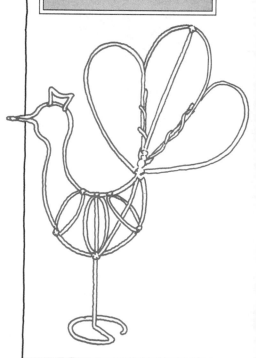

1 Make the stem from the 22-inch wire: using 8 inches for the circular base, bend 1 inch of the wire in to the center, then up at a right angle, and straight up into a stem. Attach the stake alongside the stem, wrapping together with wire, twist ties or tape.

2 Bend the 33-inch wire to form the top outline, starting with 2 inches for the upper beak and allowing 12 inches for the head and back of the neck, 7 inches for the back, and 12 inches curving up beyond the body and into the tail.

3 Bend the 38-inch wire into the lower outline, starting with 2 inches for the lower beak and shaping the neck and belly,

leaving 12 inches curving up beyond the body and into the tail.

4 Join the top and bottom sections of the outline with thin wire or twist ties, securing the two wires at the beak and crossing and securing the two wires at the tail.

5 Bend the two 10-inch and one 14½-inch wires into circles, securing the 1-inch overlaps with thin wire or twist ties. Attach one of the smaller circles inside the outline at the tail end of the bird as shown. Attach the larger circle inside the outline in the center of the bird. Attach the remaining smaller circle toward the front of the bird.

6 Attach the outline to the stem with thin wire or twist ties.

7 Form the 6-inch wire into the peacock's crest, and secure it to the top of the head.

8 Make the Fan/Peacock's Tail using a 26-inch wire for the stem, an 18-inch bamboo stake, and omitting the circular base.

9 Bend the Fan/Tail stem at an angle and slip it through the bird's body, adjusting the two sides of the V until they line up with the middle loop of the tail. Attach the Fan/Tail to the V, and also to the points where it intersects the ribs of the body and stem.

10 Wrap all the individual wires with tape, or reinforce joints with hot glue.

Seal

This clever beast, poised atop a 6-inch pot, playfully balances a ball on the tip of its nose. For best balance, don't stuff the ball. Instead train plants up from the head to cover.

You will need:
—wire cutters
—pliers
—one 22-inch piece of wire for the stem
—one 55-inch piece of wire for the body outline
—two 9-inch pieces of wire for the neck and tail circles
—two 14½-inch pieces of wire for the middle circles
—two 10-inch pieces of wire for the ball
—thin spooled wire or twist ties
—waterproof adhesive tape or a hot glue gun and cartridges

1 Make the stem from the 22-inch wire: using 8 inches for the circular base, bend 1 inch of the wire in to the center, then up at a right angle, and straight up into a stem.

2 Bend the 55-inch wire to form the body outline, starting 2 inches below the uppermost tip of the tail. Allow 19 inches from the tip of the tail through the back to the nose, and 27 inches from the nose through the belly to the lower tip of the tail. The back of the tail should measure 7 inches, with a 2-inch overlap beneath the uppermost tip. Overlap the ends and join with thin wire or twist ties.

3 Bend the two 9-inch and two 14½-inch wires into circles, securing the 1-inch overlaps with thin wire or twist ties. Attach the smaller circles inside the outline at the tail and neck ends of the seal. Attach the larger circles inside the outline at the chest and belly of the seal.

4 Attach the outline to the stem with thin wire or twist ties.

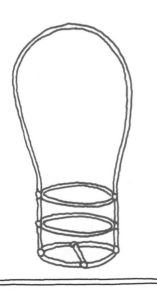

5 Make two circles from the 10-inch pieces of wire, securing the 1-inch overlaps with thin wire or twist ties. Join the circles at right angles, one inside the other, to make the seal's ball.

6 Attach the ball to the tip of the seal's nose with thin wire or twist ties and reinforce with tape or glue. If you use glue, hold the ball in place until it sets.

7 Wrap all the individual wires with tape, or reinforce joints with hot glue.

FREESTANDING FRAMES

The nice thing about these flat-bottomed frames is that you can create a realistic scene, since there is no container to spoil the illusion. If you wish to set them on a pot, just bend a piece of wire into a U and stick it through the base of the frame to anchor it in the soil.

Basket

This diminutive model is 3½ inches in diameter, but baskets can be any size that captures your fancy. You can wrap this little accessory with sheet moss and line it with long-fiber sphagnum. Then set a small plant in the center. Pin the vines down to cover the sides and train up the handle. One clever way to use larger basket frames is to plant small vines near the edge for training over the outside and up the handle, leaving the center hollow. When you are stuffing the basket, leave space for a plastic pot in the center. This way you can have a changing display of potted African violets, primroses or a cut-flower arrangement in the center. An easy way to form uniform circles is to bend the wire just under the rim of a 4-inch-diameter clay pot.

You will need:
—*wire cutters*
—*pliers*
—*three 12½-inch pieces of wire for the circles*
—*one 24-inch piece of wire for the handle*
—*one 3½-inch piece of wire for the base*
—*one 5- by 5-inch piece of chicken wire*
—*one 4- by 13-inch piece of chicken wire*
—*thin spooled wire or twist ties*
—*waterproof adhesive tape or a hot glue gun and cartridges*

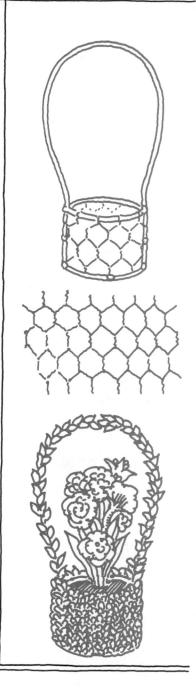

1 Bend each 12½-inch wire into a circle, securing the 1-inch overlaps with thin wire or twist ties.

2 Bend the 24-inch wire into a U shape to form the handle.

3 Attach the 3½-inch wire across one circle with thin wire or twist ties. Attach this circle inside the handle to form the base as shown. Attach the other two circles to the handle at 2-inch intervals.

4 Line the bottom with the 5- by 5-inch piece of chicken wire. Take the 4- by 13-inch piece of chicken wire, and wrap it around the outside of the basket, bending the cut ends over the top and bottom circles.

5 Wrap all the individual wires with tape, or reinforce joints with hot glue.

Pyramid

The size of this figure makes an impressive table decoration. It can be enlarged for a floorstanding sculpture—just be sure to add one square as a support for each 5 inches of side length. For precise squares, measure carefully and use needle-nose pliers.

You will need:
—wire cutters
—pliers
—a permanent marking pen
—one 33-inch wire for the 8-inch-square base
—one 25-inch piece of wire for the 6-inch square
—one 17-inch piece of wire for the 4-inch square
—one 9-inch piece of wire for the 2-inch square
—two 8½-inch pieces of wire to brace the 8-inch square
—two 6½-inch pieces of wire to brace the 6-inch square
—two 4½-inch pieces of wire to brace the 4-inch square
—two 2½-inch pieces of wire to brace the 2-inch square
—four 20-inch pieces of wire for side pieces
—thin spooled wire or twist ties
—waterproof adhesive tape or a hot glue gun and cartridges

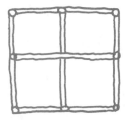

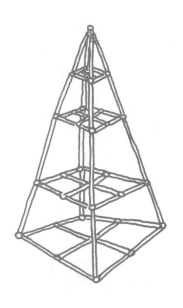

1 Bend the 33-inch wire into an 8-inch square, securing the 1-inch overlap with thin wire or twist ties. Repeat with the 25-inch wire for a 6-inch square, the 17-inch wire for a 4-inch square, and the 9-inch wire for a 2-inch square.

2 Attach the two 8½-inch wires as cross braces to the 8-inch square, securing with thin wire or twist ties at the midpoint of each side. Repeat, using appropriate wires, to cross-brace each square.

3 Attach the 20-inch side pieces to the outside corners of the largest square, securing them with thin wire or twist ties. Loosely tie side pieces together at the top.

4. Mark each side piece at 5-inch intervals. Attach the 6-inch square inside the first marks, securing it with thin wire or twist ties. Attach the 4-inch square inside the second set of marks, finishing with the 2-inch square inside the third set of marks.

5. Bring the side pieces together to a point at the top, and secure with thin wire or twist ties.

6. Wrap all the individual wires with tape, or reinforce joints with hot glue. Since there are large spaces between wires, use waterproof tape to make crisscrosses before stuffing.

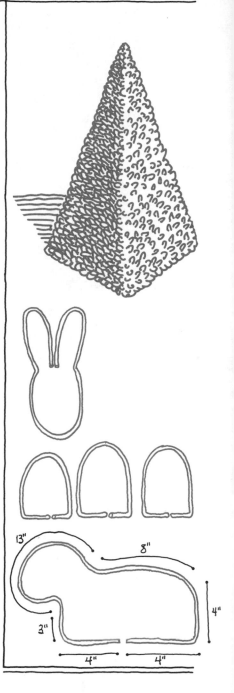

Rabbit

Here's a cute creature to make for Easter or any time of year. Add to its personality by bending the ears. The construction method for this frame is adaptable to many other animals.

You will need:
—wire cutters
—pliers
—one 38-inch piece of wire for the body outline
—one 21-inch piece of wire for the center rib
—two 18½-inch pieces of wire for the outer ribs
—one 34-inch piece of wire for the head and ears
—one 13-inch piece of wire for the head circle
—thin spooled wire or twist ties
—waterproof adhesive tape or a hot glue gun and cartridges

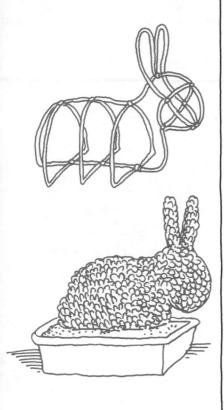

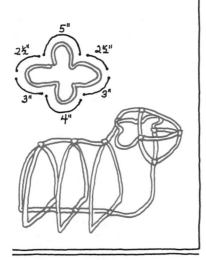

1 Bend the 38-inch wire around to form the body outline as shown, beginning at the middle of the underside and continuing up into the back. Secure the 2-inch overlap with thin wire or twist ties.

2 Bend the 21-inch wire to shape the center rib. Straighten 3½ inches at one end and bend at a right angle. Repeat at the other end. Pull wire ends together to create a smooth arch, overlapping 2 inches. Secure the overlap with thin wire or twist ties. Repeat with the two 18½-inch wires.

3 Attach the smaller ribs inside the body outline near the head and tail as shown, securing with thin wire or twist ties. Repeat with the large rib, placing it at the center of the outline.

4 Use the 34-inch wire to form the head and ears. The ears should be 5 inches tall, with a 1-inch overlap between them. Secure the overlap with thin wire or twist ties. Attach the head piece inside the body outline as shown with thin wire or twist ties. Bend the ears up.

5 Form the 13-inch wire into a circle, securing the 1-inch overlap with thin wire or a twist tie. Insert it into the head as shown, and attach it with thin wire or twist ties.

6 Wrap all the individual wires with tape, or reinforce joints with hot glue.

Lamb

This is a simple variation on the rabbit, substituting a 22-inch piece of wire for the head and ears instead of the 34-inch piece needed to form the larger rabbit ears. Substitute the following directions for Step 4: Use the 22-inch piece of wire to form the head and ears as shown. Secure the 1-inch overlap with thin wire or twist ties. Attach the head piece inside the head outline as shown with thin wire twist ties. Bend the ears down.

Cat

Behold a frisky, long-tailed feline complete with whiskers and luxurious paws.

You will need:
—*wire cutters*
—*pliers*
—*one 36-inch piece of wire for the body outline*
—*one 21-inch piece of wire for the center rib*
—*two 18½-inch pieces of wire for the end ribs*
—*one 22-inch piece of wire for the head and ears*
—*one 13-inch piece of wire for the head circle*
—*one 27-inch piece of wire for the tail*
—*two 16-inch pieces of wire for the front paws*
—*two 8-inch pieces of wire for the whiskers*
—*thin spooled wire or twist ties*
—*waterproof adhesive tape or a hot glue gun and cartridges*

<u>1</u> Bend the 36-inch wire around to form the body outline as shown, beginning at the middle of the underside and working up around the back, through the head, and back down into the belly. Secure the 2-inch overlap with thin wire or twist ties.

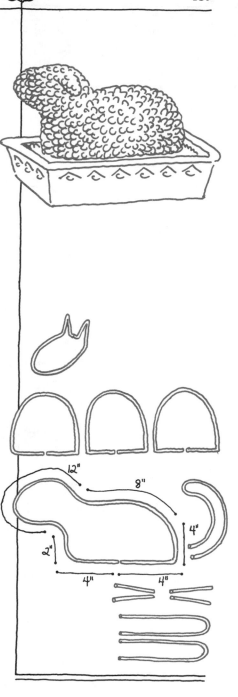

2 Bend the 21-inch wire to shape the center rib. Straighten 3½ inches at one end and bend at a right angle. Repeat at the other end. Pull wire ends together to create a smooth arch, overlapping 2 inches. Secure the overlap with thin wire or twist ties. Repeat with the two 18½-inch wires.

3 Attach the smaller ribs inside the body outline near the head and tail as shown, securing with thin wire or twist ties. Repeat with the large rib, placing it at the center of the outline.

4 Use the 22-inch wire to form the head and ears. The ears should be 2 inches tall, with a 2-inch overlap between them. Secure the overlap with thin wire or twist ties. Attach the head piece inside the body outline as shown with thin wire or twist ties.

5 Form the 13-inch wire into a circle, securing the 1-inch overlap with thin wire or twist ties. Insert it into the head as shown, and attach it with thin wire or twist ties.

6 Bend the 27-inch wire into the tail, and attach with thin wire or twist ties to the base of the center and back ribs.

7 Bend the 16-inch wires into the front paws and attach with thin wire or twist ties at the base of the center and front ribs.

8 Add whiskers by attaching the centers of the two 8-inch wires inside the tip of the nose with thin wire or twist ties.

9 Wrap all the individual wires with tape, or reinforce joints with hot glue. Bend up the ears and the tip of the tail.

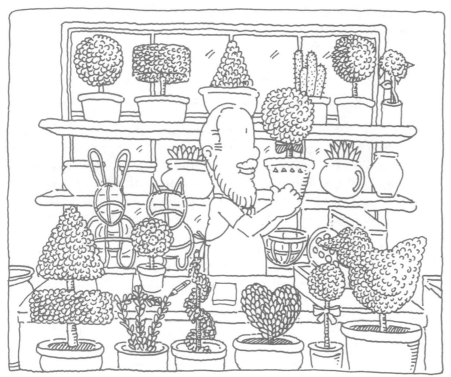

Your workshop can become a display of its own, filled with a profusion of pots, wire frames and completed pieces.

Turtle

This patient reptile is especially cute if you let him slowly make his way among a group of large houseplants.

You will need:
—*wire cutters*
—*pliers*
—*one 48-inch piece of wire for the base of the shell and the legs*
—*one 42-inch piece of wire for the profile of the head, the neck, shell and tail*

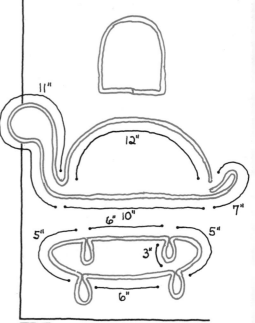

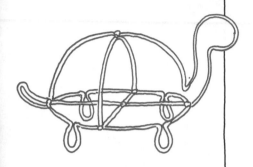

—one 21-inch piece of wire to go across the shell, over the sides, and join underneath
—one 12- by 25-inch piece of chicken wire
—thin spooled wire or twist ties
—waterproof adhesive tape or a hot glue gun and cartridges

1. Bend the 48-inch wire around to form the base of the shell and the legs, starting 2 inches in front of a leg and shaping as shown. The base should be about 10 inches long and 7 inches wide. Secure the 2-inch overlap with thin wire or twist ties. Bend the leg loops down at right angles to the shell outline and adjust until the base stands securely.

2. Use the 42-inch piece of wire to shape the profile, beginning at the tail and forming the shell, neck, head and underside as shown. Attach on top of the base, securing the intersections with thin wire or twist ties.

3. Shape the 21-inch wire into a rib to go through the middle of the shell. Straighten 4½ inches at one end and bend at a right angle. Repeat at the other end. Pull wire ends together to create a smooth arch, overlapping 2 inches. Secure the overlap with thin wire or twist ties.

4. Wrap all the individual wires with tape, or reinforce joints with hot glue.

5. Use chicken wire to wrap under the bottom and up the sides of the shell, securing by twisting the ends around the outline with thin wire or twist ties. Leave the top open for stuffing. Seal afterward by twisting the ends together.

Terrier Dog

Eight pieces of wire add up to a perky canine friend.

You will need:
—*wire cutters*
—*pliers*
—*one 62-inch piece of wire for the base of the body and the legs*
—*one 46-inch piece of wire for the body profile*
—*one 20-inch piece of wire for the middle rib*
—*one 19-inch piece of wire for the back rib*
—*one 19-inch piece of wire for the front rib*
—*one 28-inch piece of wire for the head outline*
—*one 13-inch piece of wire for the head circle*
—*one 13-inch piece of wire for the neck circle*
—*one 8- by 14-inch piece of chicken wire*
—*thin spooled wire or twist ties*
—*waterproof adhesive tape or a hot glue gun and cartridges*

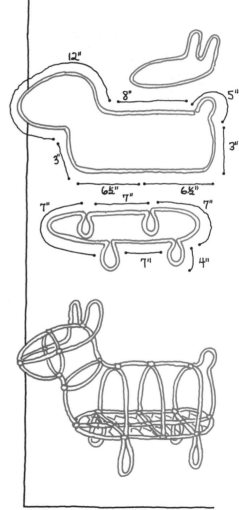

1 Bend the 62-inch wire around to form the base of the body and the legs, starting 2 inches in front of a leg and shaping as shown. The base should be about 12 inches long and 6 inches wide. Secure the 2-inch overlap with thin wire or twist ties. Bend the leg loops down at right angles to the body profile and adjust until the base stands securely.

2 Bend the 46-inch wire around to form the profile, beginning at the center of the bottom of the body and shaping as shown. Secure a 2-inch overlap with thin wire or twist ties. Attach to the base and secure with thin wire or twist ties.

3 Bend the 20-inch wire to shape the center rib. Straighten 4 inches and bend at a right angle. Repeat at the other end. Pull the wire ends together to create a smooth arch, overlapping 2 inches. Secure the overlap with thin wire or twist ties. Repeat with the two 19-inch wires to form the other ribs.

4 Attach the small ribs inside the body profile near the head and the tail, securing with thin wire or twist ties. Repeat with the largest rib, placing it at the center of the outline.

5 Use the 28-inch wire to form the head and ears. The ears should be 2½ inches tall, with a 1-inch overlap between them. Secure the overlap with thin wire or twist ties. Attach the head piece around the body outline as shown with thin wire or twist ties. Bend the ears up.

6 Form each 13-inch wire into a circle, securing the 1-inch overlaps with thin wire or twist ties. Insert into the head and neck as shown, and attach with thin wire or twist ties.

7 Wrap all the individual wires in tape, or reinforce joints with hot glue.

8 Slip the chicken wire over the base of the frame and bend the cut ends around the edges to secure it. This will help to support the stuffing.

Pig

This is a roly-poly green beast, with lower feeding requirements than its animal counterparts. The curly tail could be covered with a single vine growing out from the body.

You will need:
—*wire cutters*
—*pliers*
—*one 54-inch piece of wire for the base of the body and the legs*
—*one 50-inch piece of wire for the body profile*
—*one 26-inch piece of wire for the middle rib*
—*one 24-inch piece of wire for the back rib*
—*one 25-inch piece of wire for the front rib*
—*one 8-inch piece of wire for the front snout circle*

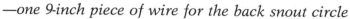

—one 9-inch piece of wire for the back snout circle
—one 33-inch piece of wire for the outline of the head and ears
—one 15-inch piece of wire for the head circle
—one 41-inch piece of wire for the horizontal rib
—one 13-inch piece of wire for the tail
—one 9- by 15-inch piece of chicken wire
—thin spooled wire or twist ties
—waterproof adhesive tape or a hot glue gun and cartridges

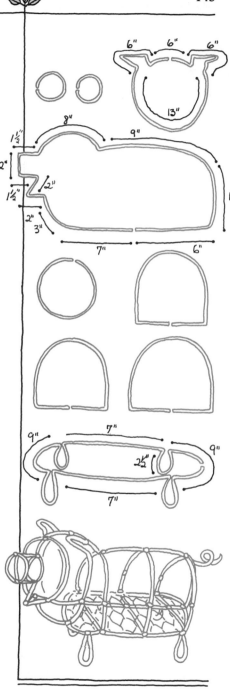

1. Bend the 54-inch wire around to form the base of the body and the legs, starting 2 inches in front of a leg and shaping as shown. The base should be about 13 inches long and 7 inches wide. Secure the 2-inch overlap with thin wire or twist ties. Bend the leg loops down at right angles to the body profile and adjust until the base stands securely.

2. Bend the 50-inch wire around to form the profile, beginning at the center of the body and shaping as shown. Secure the 2-inch overlap with thin wire or twist ties. Attach to the base and secure the intersections with thin wire or twist ties.

3. Bend the 26-inch wire to shape the center rib. Straighten 4½ inches and bend at a right angle. Repeat at the other end. Pull wire ends together to create a smooth arch, overlapping 2 inches. Secure the overlap with thin wire or twist ties. Repeat with the 24-inch and 25-inch wires for the other ribs.

4. Attach the largest rib inside the body profile at the middle of the torso as shown, securing with thin wire or twist ties. Repeat with the smallest rib, placing it near the tail, and with the medium-size rib, placing it at the shoulders.

5. Form the 8-inch wire into a circle, securing the 1-inch overlap with thin wire or twist ties. Insert it around the tip of the snout at a right angle, and attach it with thin wire or twist ties. Repeat with the 9-inch wire, placing it inside the base of the snout.

6 Use the 33-inch wire to form the head and ears as shown, securing the 2-inch overlap with thin wire or twist ties. Attach the head piece around the body outline with thin wire or twist ties. Bend the ears up.

7 Make the 15-inch wire into a circle, securing the 1-inch overlap with thin wire or twist ties. Attach inside the head and at the base of the mouth as shown.

8 Place the 41-inch wire inside the frame about 1½ inches above the base as shown, securing to the vertical ribs, rear profile, head outline, and the lower mouth.

9 Bend the 13-inch wire into an open spiral for the tail. Attach it to the body profile with thin wire or twist ties.

10 Wrap all the individual wires with tape, or reinforce joints with hot glue.

11 Slip the chicken wire over the base of the frame and bend the cut ends around the edges to secure it. This will help to support the stuffing.

Dinosaur

If you are a fan of these gentle prehistoric creatures, bring a leafy brontosaurus to life in your home. If it tends to fall forward, weigh down the tail with a stone while stuffing the frame.

You will need:
—wire cutters
—pliers
—one 54-inch piece of wire for the base and the legs
—one 62-inch piece of wire for the upper body profile

—one 23-inch piece of wire for the lower body profile
—one 20-inch piece of wire for the front rib
—one 23-inch piece of wire for the back rib
—two 11-inch pieces of wire for the tail and neck circles
—one 7-inch piece of wire for the head circle
—one 9- by 13-inch piece of chicken wire
—thin spooled wire or twist ties
—waterproof adhesive tape or a hot glue gun and cartridges

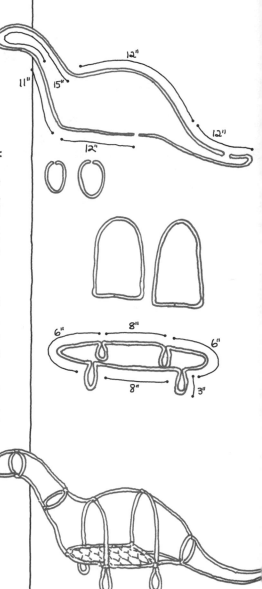

1 Bend the 54-inch wire around to form the base of the body and the legs, starting 2 inches in front of a leg and shaping as shown. The base should be about 11 inches long and 7 inches wide. Secure the 2-inch overlap with thin wire or twist ties. Bend the leg loops down at right angles to the body profile and adjust until the base stands securely.

2 Bend the 62-inch wire around to form the upper profile as shown, beginning at the tip of the tail, and forming the back, neck, head and underside up to the middle of the belly. Allowing for a 2-inch overlap at the belly, bend the 23-inch wire to complete the belly and lower tail, curving around 2 inches to overlap the end of the upper tail. Secure the 2-inch overlaps at the tail and belly with thin wire or twist ties. Attach to the base and secure the intersections with thin wire or twist ties. Adjust the tail until it is level with the legs and helps to stabilize the frame.

3 Bend the 20-inch wire to shape the front rib. Straighten 4½ inches and bend at a right angle. Repeat at the other end. Pull wire ends together to create a smooth arch, overlapping 2 inches. Secure the overlap with thin wire or twist ties. Repeat with the 23-inch wire to form the back rib.

4 Attach the larger rib inside the body profile above the rear legs, securing with thin wire or twist ties. Repeat with the smaller rib, placing it above the front legs.

5 Form the two 11-inch wires into circles, securing the 2-inch overlaps with thin wire or twist ties. Insert the circles at the tail and the middle of the neck as shown, and attach with thin wire or twist ties.

6 Form the 7-inch wire into a circle, securing the 1-inch overlap with thin wire or twist ties. Attach it to the throat as shown, securing the overlap with thin wire or twist ties.

7 Wrap all the individual wires with tape, or reinforce joints with hot glue.

8 Slip the chicken wire over the base of the frame and bend the cut ends around the edges to secure it. This will help to support the stuffing.

Sailboat

This cheerful vessel brings to mind a sunny day at sea, and makes a nice gift for a boat lover. The hull may be stuffed or hollow, and can be filled with flowers for a party.

You will need:
—wire cutters
—pliers
—one 23-inch piece of wire for the lower hull
—one 27-inch piece of wire for the upper hull outline
—one 9-inch piece of wire to go across the hull

—*one 12-inch piece of wire to run the length of the hull*
—*one 27-inch piece of wire for the mast*
—*one 17-inch piece of wire for the mainsail (back sail)*
—*one 13-inch piece of wire for the jib (front sail)*
—*thin spooled wire or twist ties*
—*waterproof adhesive tape or a hot glue gun and cartridges*

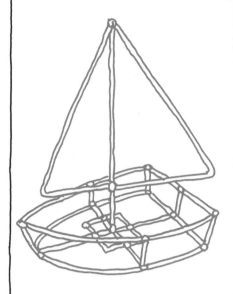

1 Form the lower hull with the 23-inch wire. Straighten 3 inches at one end and bend at a right angle. Repeat at the other end. Pull wire ends together, overlapping 2 inches, to create a curved hull, pointed at the front end. Secure the overlap with thin wire or twist ties.

2 Form the upper hull with the 27-inch wire. It should be exactly the same shape as the other hull but larger, leaving 3½ inches straight at the ends. Secure the 2-inch overlap with thin wire or twist ties.

3 Use the 9-inch wire to make a wide U that holds the two hull outlines 2 inches apart at the sides. Attach across the width of the boat at the intersections with thin wire or twist ties.

4 Use the 12-inch piece to keep the two hull pieces 2 inches apart at the front and back, securing along the length of the boat at the intersections with thin wire or twist ties.

5 Measure 12 inches on the 27-inch wire piece to form a 3-inch-square base for the mast. Bend 1½ inches in to the center, then up at a right angle and straight up into the mast.

6 Attach the mast in the front of the hull, with the back of the square base joining the center support.

7 Form the 17-inch wire into the mainsail and attach it to the back of the mast with thin wire or twist ties. Repeat with the 13-inch wire for the jib, facing it toward the front of the boat.

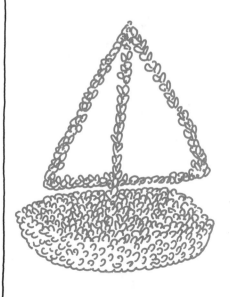

8 Wrap all the individual wires with tape, or reinforce joints with hot glue.

CHICKEN WIRE FORMS

Here are two examples of what can be done with chicken wire. The advantage of these forms is that you don't need many tools and supplies—with a roll of chicken wire, a pair of wire cutters, and perhaps a spool of thin wire, you're ready to go. It is hard on your hands, though, so wear a pair of gloves to avoid scrapes. You can adapt the methods below to a variety of geometric and animal forms, as long as they are simple and not very detailed.

A Quartet of Cones

This is a ridiculously easy and versatile shape that lends itself to dozens of treatments. The 16-inch height is good for dinner table decorations but you can vary it. If you will be covering the cone with cut flowers or training live plants over it, stuff with long-fiber sphagnum moss. If you are using cut branches, newspaper or dry leaves are a long-lasting and less messy filling. You can also add stems to the cones, and set them in a 6-inch pot.

You will need:
—two large paper grocery bags, cut open, or several sheets of
  blank paper
—a pen or pencil
—one 24-inch piece of string
—scissors
—clear tape

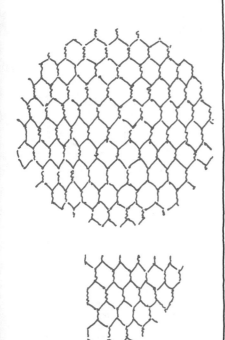

—*thin spooled wire or twist ties*
—*wire cutters*
—*gloves*
—*long-fiber sphagnum moss, dry leaves or crumpled newspaper*
—*two 18- by 36-inch pieces of chicken wire*
—*four 7- by 7-inch squares of chicken wire*
—*(optional) four 24-inch-long branches or dowels*

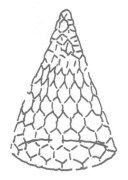

1 Create a 36-inch square piece of paper. Tie string to a pen or pencil so the string is 18 inches long. Use it as a compass to draw a circle on the paper. Fold the paper into equal quarters, unfold, and cut along the fold lines and circle. These pieces will serve as patterns.

2 Place two patterns over an 18- by 36-inch piece of chicken wire. Secure the patterns to the wire in two spots with thin wire or twist ties. Cut the chicken wire along the edges of the patterns. Repeat with the remaining 18- by 36-inch piece of chicken wire and patterns.

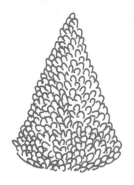

3 Roll one quarter-circle into a cone. Twist the cut ends together. Turn it upside down and stuff with sphagnum, dry leaves or newspaper. Repeat with the other three pieces.

4 Wrap 2 inches of the chicken wire under each cone to form the bottom edge, folding as necessary. Add a 7- by 7-inch square of chicken wire to reinforce the base, bending the cut ends over to secure it.

5 (optional) If you want to set a cone on a stem in a pot, hold a 24-inch branch in one hand, and stick it all the way through the cone. Repeat with the other cones.

Teddy Bear

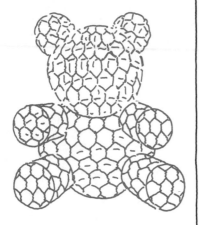

Teddy bears seem to be everybody's favorite animals, and this version is irresistibly huggable. It is easiest to stuff each section individually as you assemble the bear, using either long-fiber sphagnum moss for a live version, or dry leaves or crumpled newspaper for a mock rendition. No two bears made this way will come out exactly alike, so yours will be unique.

You will need:
—*wire cutters*
—*gloves*
—*two 12- by 12-inch squares of chicken wire*
—*one 30- by 12-inch piece of chicken wire*
—*two 9- by 6-inch pieces of chicken wire*
—*two 8- by 5-inch pieces of chicken wire*
—*two 6- by 6-inch squares of chicken wire*
—*thin spooled wire*
—*long-fiber sphagnum moss, dry leaves or crumpled newspaper*

1 Use the 12- by 12-inch square of chicken wire for the base. Shape the bottom about 9 inches across, and fold the sides up to form a shell.

2 Use the 30- by 12-inch piece of chicken wire for the body. Scrunch the piece of chicken wire into the shape of the body, roughly 9 inches high and 9 inches around. Make two folds in the front and two folds in the back to define the tummy and neck.

3 Shape each of the two 9- by 6-inch pieces into a cylinder. Lash them onto the body with thin wire to make the legs. Repeat with the two 8- by 5-inch pieces to form cylinders for the arms.

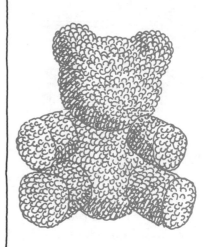

4 Stuff the body cavity, legs and arms tightly with sphagnum, dry leaves or newspaper. Close the ends of the arms and legs by pressing the cut ends of the chicken wire together.

5 Use the second 12- by 12-inch square to form the bear's head, leaving the neck open. Shape the two 6- by 6-inch squares of wire into ears, leaving the bases open. Turn them upside down, stuff them tightly with sphagnum, dry leaves or newspaper, turn right-side up and lash them to the head with thin wire.

6 Turn the head over and stuff tightly with sphagnum, dry leaves or newspaper. Turn the head right-side up and lash it to the body with thin wire.

STANDARD FRAME

A standard is the most popular—and adaptable—topiary shape, a stylized form inspired by the trunk-and-crown silhouette of trees. True standards consist of a woody plant trained and shaped to have a sphere or mushroom-shaped crown of growth on a single vertical stem.

Basket on a Stem

To achieve the elegant look of a standard instantly, make a frame replica, which can easily be made using wire hanging baskets to form the head. These baskets are widely available at garden centers in diameters ranging from 8 to 16 inches.

A single basket turned upside down becomes a mushroom. Or two can be joined at the rim to form a sphere. The shape is completed by nailing the baskets to a trunk made from a dowel, pipe, broom handle, strong wooden stake or tree branch. The trunk can be wrapped in sheet moss—or left bare if the color is attractive and suits your design. Directions here are for a stuffed, portable version, but the frame is also suited to the myriad styles achieved with fresh and dried cut flowers and foliage (see Chapter Three).

You will need:
—*a clay pot with a drainage hole*
—*aluminum foil*
—*plaster of Paris or quick-setting cement*
—*a rigid plastic tube*
—*a sturdy dowel, pipe, broom handle or branch for the trunk*
—*one or two wire hanging baskets, with hangers removed*
—*long-fiber sphagnum moss, or sphagnum moss plus soilless potting mix*
—*sheet moss*
—*thin spooled wire*
—*a large-headed nail*
—*(optional) one large vining plant, or several smaller ones with plenty of long runners; chicken wire*

1 Cover the drainage hole at the bottom of the pot with aluminum foil.

2 Place a rigid plastic tube in your pot so that the ends extend above the rim and through the bottom hole, poking the tube through the foil. This will allow water that drips from the standard to drain through the plaster or cement.

3 Mix the plaster or cement according to package directions.

4 Hold the trunk upright in the pot, and pour in the plaster or cement to an inch below the rim of the pot.

5 Once the base has set, trim the tube ends flush with the plaster surface and the base of the pot.

6 (optional) Remove the vining plant (or plants) from the growing container and put it upside down in the basket, so all the runners protrude through the wires.

7 Line the basket with sheet moss, making a collar where it surrounds the plant.

8 Pack either sphagnum or a mixture of two parts soilless mix plus one part sphagnum around the roots of the plant, filling the basket to the brim. For a sphere, repeat Steps 6 and 7 with a second basket.

9 *For a half-sphere*: Lay a piece of sheet moss over the mix. Cover with a piece of chicken wire, and lash this securely to the basket frame with thin wire. Cover with another layer of sheet moss, and again lash it tightly to the basket with thin wire.
For a ball: Omit the chicken wire. Cover the top of one basket with sheet moss and secure it with wire. Supporting the flat side with your hand, turn the moss-covered basket over and place it on top of the other basket so that the two rims are

flush. Fasten the basket rims together securely with wire. If you have planted the baskets, be careful not to damage the plant runners.

10 Holding the stuffed form with both hands, push it firmly onto the previously anchored stem. Nail the form to the top of the trunk.

11 (optional) Arrange runners and pin to cover the form.

Ivy Training

A VINE ART

Ivy is the impatient topiarist's best friend. Indoors or out, this elegant, adaptable vine can be trained into a myriad of shapes. In your garden, with the help of an underlying support, it is willingly trained into figures, architectural features, patterned ground covers, espalier and other wall ornaments. Ivy is equally amenable to adorning your house, where it can artfully drape walls, windows and doors, grow as a miniature tree, or cover the delightful portable figures described in Chapter One. Virtually every kind of topiary, from small indoor creations to outdoor wall coverings, can be recreated in ivy.

Ivy is evergreen, and therefore always attractive. It withstands northern winters and southern summers. Because it is tolerant of pollution, wind and dense shade, it is the plant to bring topiary cheer to bleak spots and city spaces. English ivy (*Hedera helix*) is the best known of the five species of ivy that belong to the ginseng family. In England, ivy is so widely cherished that it often appears as a decoration on china, fabric and wallpaper. Despite its easygoing nature and widespread popularity, it still conveys an air of British tradition and nobility.

Ivy is a practical plant that has always had symbolic importance. In ancient Egypt it was sacred to Osiris, the god of the underworld, who carried a cane swathed in a garland of ivy. Ancient Egyptian housewives sent ivy wreaths to the dead as a tribute of friendship; preserved examples have been found in archaeological excavations.

Ivy boasts a historic link to festivals and merriment. It was identified with Bacchus, the Greek and Roman god of wine, who is depicted on wall paintings and pottery crowned with a wreath of the vine and holding a staff entwined with an ivy garland. This association with good spirits and liquid cheer continues in England, where the alestake, an ivy-twisted staff, is the symbol for a bar or pub. An ivy topiary will add a festive spirit to your outdoor entertainment and indoor celebrations, dressing up flower arrangements, centerpieces and serving platters.

Evidence at Pompeii reveals that the Romans used ivy to

> **❝***It is well, indeed, in every scheme to allow one colour with its related shades to predominate, and to employ the others as relief agents rather than as features.***❞**
>
> —SHIRLEY HIBBERD
> *The Amateur's Flower Garden*, 1871

adorn columns and train up potted trellises. Although the formal decorative use of ivy is ancient in origin, it was rarely seen in American gardens until Thomas Church, the late San Francisco landscape architect, revived its use in modern gardens. He took his inspiration from the traditional gardens of France and Italy, updating them to accommodate today's smaller spaces and low-maintenance priorities. His talented designs included ivy patterns to relieve the monotony of large gardens and add excitement to small ones. In *Your Private World*, Church extolled ivy's virtues: "... for year-in, year-out green, for either sun or shade and under all conditions from excellent to marginal, there is an ivy for every purpose."

ALL ABOUT IVY

English ivy (*Hedera helix*) is a sporting plant. This refers not to its easygoing nature, but to the fact that branches of the same plant will suddenly show different leaf shape and color. Hence there are so many different kinds—to date the American Ivy Society, which is located in Carrollton, Ohio, recognizes at least 400 varieties. Like dog breeds, some ivies look so much alike that only the expert can tell them apart, while others are as different from each other as a dachshund is from an Old English sheepdog. Even as you read this, new unnamed types are sporting on old plants. The leaves may be tantalizingly pointed, ruffled or curled; in shades of green, white, yellow, red and bronze; ranging in size from the nail on your little finger to the palm of your hand; widely spaced on long trailing stems or closely set on short ones.

Some ivies grow flat, in a refined manner, clinging closely as they climb. These are useful for training on walls or portable topiary. Others grow vigorously and provide fast coverage, but tend to be shaggy and require frequent trimming. A third group grows as compact mounds, making them natural choices for neat

The classic beauty of ivy has graced a wide variety of home furnishings, any of which can be subtly complemented by your ivy topiaries.

> **66Ivy often forms a green and fresh screen across a room, being planted in boxes, and its sprays trained over rustic framework. Ivy often casts its pleasant shadows over a piano, so that the musician may sit before his instrument as within a little bower.99**
>
> —ANNE PRATT
> *Flowering Plants of Great Britain*, 1855

edgings. Foliage colors are ever changing, depending on the age of the leaf and whether the plant is growing in sun or shade. Some turn an attractive bronze or purple in wintertime. When buying ivy plants, look for plants with several stems that are long and well-clothed in leaves. The longer the stems, or runners, on the plant you start with, the less time it will take to cover your ivy project.

Ivy actually has two phases of life: juvenile and adult. Usually ivy is seen in its childhood state, when it climbs upward or crawls over the ground, supporting itself with aerial roots that stick to wood, brick, stone and masonry. It is unable to cling securely to metal or wire, so the gardener must aid it by tying

> **❝The medicinal virtues of Ivy are little regarded nowadays. Its great value is as an ornamental covering for unsightly buildings, and it is said to be the only plant which does not make walls damp. It acts as a curtain, the leaves from the way they fall, forming a sort of armour and holding and absorbing the rain and moisture.❞**
>
> —MRS. M. [MAUD] GRIEVE
> *A Modern Herbal*, 1931

or weaving it onto these materials. In maturity a curious transformation takes place. Suddenly one spring, some of the upper shoots will thicken and grow out like branches, rather than clinging to the support. Aerial roots are no longer produced, and the leaves grow all around the stem instead of in one flat layer on either side of the stem. The leaves on these shoots change shape and increase in size, losing any points or lobes. Loose clusters of green or yellow flowers appear, followed by black

Ivy is a natural partner to any architectural shape. This 17th-century etching shows the shady romance of an ivy-covered bower.

berries. These are signs that the ivy has entered its adult, or arborescent, stage. Over the next few years the change progresses downward, until the entire plant has changed in leaf shape and growth habit.

Any cuttings taken from this plant remain in the arborescent state and are sometimes referred to as tree ivies. They grow in a shrub-like fashion, without support. No one knows what causes ivy to undergo the transformation into adulthood. This change rarely occurs on plants that are constantly trimmed, especially in northern climates where the tips are killed back by winter frosts.

If you want to increase your ivy supply, it's easy to take cuttings from juvenile plants and root them in soil indoors or out. Snip a piece approximately 6 inches long, remove the leaves from the lower 2 inches, and bury this portion in soil. Keep the cutting moist and it will root within a few weeks. It is very difficult to root stems of adult forms, so it is best to purchase established plants if you want more arborescent ivies.

OUTDOOR IVY SCULPTURE

For a fast outdoor topiary in any climate, train ivy over a metal frame. If there are large, open spaces in the frame, wrap it in chicken wire to make it easier for the ivy to climb. Hardware cloth, a sturdy wire mesh, can be bent into a geometric form such as a globe or obelisk. For the most dramatic effect, choose a shape that is fairly large and simple, since ivy tends to obscure small details. Elegant pillars can be achieved by training ivy to cover a wooden post.

Plant the vines, evenly spaced, 8 inches apart around the edge of the frame. At first, you will have to tie the ivy to get it started up and around the shape. As new shoots appear, just tuck and weave them through the wires. Once the frame is covered, snip off stray stems.

Fast he stealeth on, though he wears no wings And a staunch old heart has he. How closely he twineth, how tight he clings, to his friend the huge Oak Tree! And slily he traileth along the ground, And his leaves he gently waves. . . .

—CHARLES DICKENS
from his poem "The Ivy Green," 1837

If you can find adult, arborescent varieties, sometimes called bush ivies, take advantage of their upright habit to create fast, traditional clipped-shrub topiary. Instead of planting around the perimeter of the frame, set them inside it. They will fill out the shape completely. Tie and trim to follow the contours of the frame.

Outdoor sculptures can also be raised in a planter. Choose a container that complements the topiary in shape and style. It should be at least 14 inches high and wide, so that the ivy can safely overwinter. A redwood tub gives a casual flavor to a charming rabbit, while a classic Italian pot is better suited to a peacock. As with sculptures grown in the ground, the ivy for container topiary should be spaced 8 inches apart around the edge of the frame.

Another charming and easy decoration for pots and urns is achieved by swagging them with garlands of ivy. Plant vines about 18 inches apart around the edge of a large planter; train long runners to cascade over the rim. When the stems are long enough to meet their neighbors, tie them together in a graceful fashion. Wrap the two stems around each other until there is about 12 inches of overlap, and then trim off. This gives the bottom of the swag a full appearance. All side stems should be clipped back to about 3 inches for a neat appearance.

IVY AS ARCHITECTURAL ACCENT

Ivy can reinforce the architecture of your garden, creating boundaries or inner divisions. One basic form is a fedge, a solidly vine-covered fence, which simulates a hedge and is often used to disguise a chain link fence. If you train on a post-and-rail fence, keep the openings trimmed to create a windowed effect. See pages 200 to 201 for instructions on constructing a sturdy post-and-wire framework.

Individual lengths of hedge were designed for green amphitheaters, and so came to be known as wing hedges. Take a cue from Thomas Church and erect a series of wing fedges in staggered heights to act as windbreaks, or to add definition within your garden. For year-round drama, cover them in different ivies.

One ancient technique to provide an enclosure involved looping vines between trees. The Babylonians are known to have strung grapevines between trees, a practice still continued today in Italy. The first example of ivy trained for this purpose was in the celebrated garden of Pliny the Younger. His hippodrome, or horse racing track, was enclosed by "plane trees covered with ivy, so that while their heads flourish with their own foliage, their bodies enjoy a borrowed verdure; and thus the ivy, twining round the trunks and branches, spreads from tree to tree and connects them together." A modern adaptation is to create a low garland by sinking 3- to 5-foot posts 18 inches to 2 feet deep, and 4 to 5 feet apart. Hook a heavy chain so it hangs in scallops from post to post; plant ivies at each post, training them up and along the chain. A more humorous arrangement that serves the same purpose would be achieved by joining a group of topiary dogs with ivy leashes.

Arbors and arches are traditionally covered with roses, clematis or wisteria, but ivy is an alternative that has the advantage of being both evergreen and easy to care for. Arch supports may be metal or wooden, rounded, flat-topped or pointed. In a newly planted garden, an arbor covered with ivy quickly creates a serene, established atmosphere, as well as furnishing cool shade over a path or seat, long before trees can grow to fill these nccds. Place arches above a hedge or fedge to heighten a feeling of privacy without sacrificing openness. Potted ivy standards also look lovely set in archways during the summertime.

A stunning and inexpensive freestanding ivy building can be made to resemble a classical gazebo or an Oriental tea house. All you need to create a delightful outdoor room is ivy plants

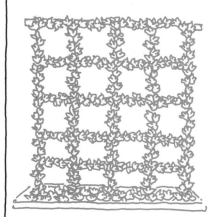

> **66***Vines in Italy are planted at intervals of two feet apart and are usually trained straight upright, without any espalier to hold them until about five or six feet above the ground. Then they have the support of a stout branch from a chestnut, or sometimes a mulberry or willow tree. These trees are usually planted in their midst, and their branches, running out horizontally, form good espaliers for the vines. The trees to which the vines are trained go by the descriptive name of 'Tuteurs.'***99**
>
> —FRANCES GARNET, the Viscountess Wolseley, *Gardens: Their Form and Design*, 1919

A double ivy design decorates both sides of these garden walls. Garlands drape the exterior, while a lattice pattern adds drama to the confined space within.

and a sturdy framework. Use wooden posts and strong wire mesh, such as sheep fencing, to support and guide the ivy up into leafy walls and a roof.

Ivy screens provide shade and privacy for a porch or terrace. String wires from eyebolts screwed into the eaves; secure them vertically or at an angle by attaching to another set of eyebolts in a railroad tie below. A movable screen can be made by training ivies over wire mesh in a rectangular planter. You could have a patterned screen of ivy in a greenhouse, sun porch (ivy will survive an unheated one) or sun room, or as a leafy frame for a bay window or door.

DECORATIONS ON THE GROUND

Ivy can be trained along the ground to create a variety of interesting patterns. Just as the medieval knot gardeners intertwined different herbs for contrasting color and texture, you can weave threads of various ivy varieties, alternating bold and dainty leaves, in shades of green, white and gold. The patterns of herbal knot gardens are usually set off by gravel, turf or flowers, but you could go all-ivy by picking strikingly different varieties to set off your design.

Ground decorations needn't be limited to knot designs. You can use ivy to outline simple geometric patterns—or even an animal. The best types for horizontal training are those that grow in dense, low mounds. 'Lustrous Carpet' could be used for a simple diamond trellis pattern. For any outline design, set the plants about a foot apart. If you are using the ivy as a border around a pattern, set plants at least 6 inches back from the path so they have room to gain in width. Arrange long trailers to grow out on either side and pin them down with bent wire as they grow toward their neighbors, tucking in or snipping off wandering shoots.

You can also use ivy for a solid shape on the ground. 'Dragon Claw' has dramatic, curly leaves. Train a dragon namesake to undulate across your lawn. You could even show menacing flames coming out of his mouth by planting a streak of red begonias. To fill in a solid shape, plant ivy in staggered rows 8 inches apart. Allow the vines to ramble freely over the ground to fill in the space, but tuck in or snip off any stems that extend beyond the edge of the shape.

> **Such borders of Ivy, if employed in the right place, and well kept in order, are a magnificent ornament to the garden. . . . In the large squares, plainly sodded, that are in the gardens of the Louvre and Tuileries, at Paris, there is no other ornament but such borders of broad-leaved Ivy . . . and they make, with the dark green against the lighter turf, a most agreeable contrast.**
>
> —PETER HENDERSON
> *Practical Floriculture,*
> 1897

*Creeping on where
time has been
A rare old plant is
the Ivy green.*

—CHARLES DICKENS
from his poem "The Ivy
Green," 1837

DECORATING WALLS

I f your garden, patio or backyard is enclosed and suffers from a static, confined feeling, an ivy pattern will introduce rhythm and movement. Even if most of your outdoor space is paved, all you need for planting is a narrow strip or patch of soil in front of walls and other vertical surfaces that the shoots can cling to. Ivy can be trained in a variety of ways to dress up your house, adding distinction to a boring facade or enhancing interesting features. If your windows and doors lack ornate moldings, trim them with leafy frames; if a wall of the house is blank, dress it up with an ivy picture.

All sorts of images can be rendered in ivy. Simple patterns of diamonds, squares, zigzags or latticework may be repeated to fill any vertical void. A stunning two-faced design can be made by first training ivy up one side of a fence in any of these patterns. When the ivy reaches the top, allow it to cascade down over the other side and tie the runners together to form garlands. If you have a retaining wall, train festoons of ivy down over it. Suspend a chain from eyebolts embedded in the wall at regularly spaced intervals. Plant ivies at each end and train them along the chain. For artful swags, clip the ivy so that it is wider at the lowest point, gradually tapering as it reaches the top.

Your design can mimic the habits of formal trees: ivy can be clipped to simulate a row of pleached trees, standards or poodles, or to imitate a classic espalier silhouette. For a note of pure whimsy, draw an animal on a wall or fence and outline or shade it in with ivy. Any weather vane shape could be adapted, such as a crowing cock, contented cow or running horse. The owl is a sign of wisdom and nobility—why not add one to the side of your house?

Ivy's sturdy vines can climb rough wood, brick, stone or stucco without help, but must be tied to metal or other smooth surfaces. However, to get a precise shape on any surface you

.do have to guide the vines. Transfer your design to the wall with chalk or charcoal. This will guide you in installing supports, and will eventually wash off. The easiest support to construct for any shape is a pattern of guide wires. You simply tie the ivy along the wires as it grows. Nails or eyebolts are inserted into the wall to follow the outline of your design. Loop the wire around each nail head or through the eyebolt to keep it in place. Ask at your local hardware store for details about securing nails or bolts in wood and masonry. Additional wires aren't necessary if you are growing a simple diagonal pattern on a chain link fence, where you can easily follow the angle in the fencing itself.

Wall ornaments can be enjoyed indoors as well. The Victorians were fond of living architectural features in the house, and sometimes drilled holes in the wall to bring robust ivy stems in from outdoor plants. If you have a lean-to greenhouse or sunroom added to the side of the house, you are probably faced with a large blank wall. Cover it with a favorite pattern for an interesting play of shadows and light. Tack up strips of wire mesh, or hardware cloth, cut out to any shape you desire, as a support for the ivy. On a stationary window or glass door panel, you might outline your shape using transparent plastic suction cups strung together with wire or fishing line.

66[Ivy is] a precious and beautiful climbing plant. . . . [whose] nobility of form and foliage is a desirable accompaniment to good architecture.99

—GERTRUDE JEKYLL AND LAWRENCE WEAVER
Gardens for Small Country Houses, 1912

IVY STANDARDS

Standards are simple, elegant topiaries, with a ball of leaves poised on one tall stem. There are three ways to get this shape with ivies: by pinching; by training on a frame; and by grafting. The first technique entails training a single vine. Tie it so that it grows straight up a stake; once it has reached the desired height, pinch off the tip. Removing the growing tip causes a plant to send out side branches. Leave the side shoots near the top of the plant, which will become the head, and re-

66*The Greek priests presented a wreath of Ivy to newly-married persons, and the Ivy has throughout the ages been regarded as the emblem of fidelity.***99**

—MRS. M. [MAUD] GRIEVE
A Modern Herbal, 1931

move all lower side branches. Pinch each of the remaining side stems so that they, too, develop many side shoots, which will create a full, rounded head. This method requires some patience as you wait for the vine to grow. Because the stem is not very strong, and because of the time factor, ivy standards grown this way should be under 2 feet tall. Depending on the time of year you start the standard and the size of the plant, it will take about six months to get a well-shaped specimen. To speed things up, look for a plant with a very long, thick stem.

The second technique is to train several plants to climb up a lollipop-shaped frame set in a pot. Since the frame provides support, the standard can be taller than the pinched type; the only limit is the time you are willing to wait for the ivy to reach the top. This method is faster than the first—four or five plants

Even if your glass-enclosed sun space isn't as grand as this 19th-century British conservatory, it will still benefit from a trimming of ivy.

with long vines can cover the frame in a few months.

If you're feeling adventurous try the third method, grafting, an ancient gardening art that is also fun, and which results in the most authentic-looking standard. Whereas pinching produces a miniature version, grafting can yield a 5- or 6-foot-tall specimen. Three or four cuttings of English ivy are inserted into a sturdy schefflera or fatshedera trunk; if the two plants are compatible, they'll knit together into one plant in a matter of weeks. Because the graft is high on the plant ivy standards, like rose standards, are vulnerable to freezing damage that can break the graft union. So if you live where winter temperatures reach below freezing, bring the trees indoors until spring.

Making a Grafted Standard

Although few people try grafting, it is easy to do at home. There are many grafting techniques; the one used here, called budding, is simple and works well on ivy. You can use any variety, but to quickly obtain a full crown select a fast-growing ivy with large, ruffled leaves—'Manda's Crested' makes a superb head.

Even indoors, plants grow at different rates at various times of the year. The best time to start your standard is when the ivy is growing actively, usually in late May or early June. The standard will have a head 6 to 8 inches in diameter by December, or in about six months from the time you start the graft.

Schefflera is used to create the central trunk and root system. It is easily found wherever houseplants are sold—look for a straight, sturdy stem that is at least as tall as you want the standard to be, because once the graft is performed, the plant will not increase in height. Use young plants, less than three years old, so it is easy to make an incision in the stem (old plants get tough and woody). If your project is interrupted by a phone call or some other distraction, wrap the ivy buds and the cut surface of the trunk in a damp cloth or paper towel.

> **"Near [Philadelphia], I saw an ivy or Hedera helix, planted against the wall of a stone building which was so covered by the fine green leaves of this plant as almost to conceal the whole. It was doubtless brought over from Europe for I have never perceived it anywhere else in my travels through North America."**
>
> —PETER KALM
> *Travels in North America*, 1748

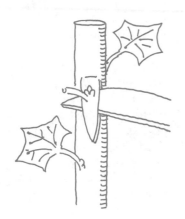

You will need:
—*an ivy plant with young, healthy stems*
—*a schefflera with a straight, sturdy main stem*
—*a paring or pocket knife*
—*raffia or a split rubber band*
—*a gallon-size plastic food storage bag*

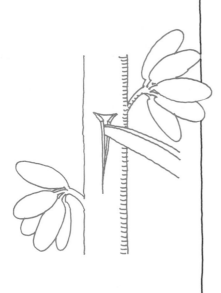

1 Water ivy and schefflera thoroughly before beginning. Work in the shade, so that cut surfaces don't dry out. Choose four ivy buds—the baby shoots that are found in the space between leaf and stem. They should be sufficiently developed so they are easy to handle.

2 Making sure that there are leaves below the cut, cut straight across the schefflera trunk at the desired height. Remove all other main stems from the plant, but leave side branches and leaves along the trunk. Make a T-shaped incision on the side of the trunk near the top, cutting through the outer layer of bark. Carefully pry up the edges from the trunk.

3 Remove one of the selected buds from the ivy by cutting away the leaf joint, retaining a small, pointed portion of the stem below. Remove any developed leaves from the selected bud piece. Cut a strip of the outer skin away from the pointed stem piece, so as to expose the inner tissues to the graft union.

4 Insert the bud in the T-cut on the schefflera, aligning the outer skin of both plants so that the bud is visible above the incision.

5 Repeat Steps 2 through 4 with the three remaining buds, placing them at even intervals around the trunk. Use raffia or a piece of rubber band to wrap the graft unions and hold the buds in place. Be careful not to wrap too tightly, which would cut off circulation to the buds.

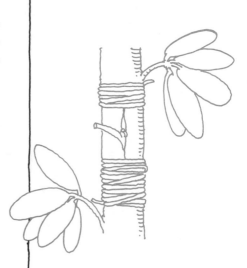

6 Cover the buds and grafts with a plastic bag. Tie loosely onto the trunk with raffia. Grow the standard in a shaded place to prevent overheating inside the bag. If water condenses inside the bag, punch a few small holes.

7 Keep the schefflera well watered. The graft is established once the ivy buds sprout leaves. This should occur within three to six weeks. At this point, the bag can be removed, and the standard should be moved into a brighter growing location.

8 Save the strongest-growing ivy buds and remove any weak or undeveloped ones. The schefflera's leaves will drop off once the ivy leaves are able to feed the standard. As the ivy forms stems, begin pinching to shape the head into a ball or bell.

PORTABLE FIGURES

Ivy is excellent material for indoor topiary. Whether you grow it in a pot and train it upward to outline a hollow frame, or plant it directly in a self-contained stuffed frame, ivy offers a broad palette of shapes, sizes and colors. Experiment with your favorite varieties. In general, choose plants with leaves closely set along the stem that should tend to branch freely.

Tiny tabletop-size portable figures can be created with varieties that have delicate leaves. A squirrel is charming in close-hugging 'Duck Foot.' Or combine several ivies to emphasize the characteristics of your subject. The same little squirrel could also be planted with 'Duck Foot' on the back and head, 'Little Diamond' on the tummy for lighter color, and bushier 'Shamrock' on the tail. On a larger topiary, try white-splashed 'Glacier' to depict a penguin's bib, or a leaf with golden markings such as 'Gold Dust' to highlight a lion's mane. If you want to create a big floor-model indoor topiary, add more drama with large-scale foliage such as 'Manda's Crested' or Canary ivy.

Ivy is a sturdy and reliable houseplant; unlike most of the plants used for stuffed topiary, it can dry out a little between waterings. But in the dry conditions of most winter rooms, it sometimes gets infested with aphids and spider mites. A shower of water from a sink sprayer or misting bottle every few days helps prevent insects and keeps the leaves dust-free and shiny.

A Graceful Spiral

If your appetite for portable topiary has been whetted, but you don't have any frames on hand, don't despair. You can start from scratch and quickly satisfy your desire with a pretty spiral.

You will need:
—a six-foot coil of No. 8 to No. 10 galvanized wire
—wire cutters
—pliers
—a 6- or 7-inch clay pot
—silicone or bathtub caulking; or a hot glue gun and glue
*   cartridges*
—potting soil or soilless growing mix
—several ivy plants with long runners

1 Pull the coil out into a spiral form so that it is broad at the bottom and tapers toward the top. Be sure to leave enough space between each spiral so that the definition won't be lost when it's covered in ivy. The total height should be approximately 2 feet.

2 Measure the depth of the pot and add 6 inches. Mark off the total amount at the wide end of the spiral. Bend the wire at

a right angle, and form a straight section from a piece equal to the depth of the pot. Bend wire at this point into a second right angle, and then into a U-shaped stand to rest on the bottom of the pot. Anchor the spiral by gluing the stand to the bottom of the pot with bathtub sealant or a hot glue gun. A cold caulking bond must cure overnight, but hot glue hardens to a waterproof seal within minutes. (Exercise caution when using a hot glue gun, especially around children, and never leave it unattended.)

3 Fill the pot with soil and plant several ivies with long runners close together around the center of the pot. Tie these to follow the spiral along the outside of the frame. Don't forget to check these ties periodically to make sure they haven't gotten too tight.

TRIMMING

In spite of its reputation as a rambler and a scrambler, ivy's robust growth can be disciplined into any shape. Although it climbs naturally, attaching itself to supports by means of aerial roots, you should tie it initially to establish the pattern you want it to follow.

Each variety grows at a different rate—some are rampant growers and need frequent trimming, while others proceed at a leisurely pace. For fast results, train vines straight upward until they reach the desired height; then pinch back the tip to encourage overall fullness. Screens and fedges can be sheared quickly with hedge trimmers in the spring. Any stragglers that appear during the summer and fall should be clipped off to keep a neat

❝On fedges and walls, once covered, 'the knife, the eye, the hand and the brain must go in harmony to keep the ivy as short as the lawn.'❞

—from the magazine
The Cottage Gardener and Country Gentleman, 1860

PREFERRED ENGLISH IVY VARIETIES FOR TOPIARY

OUTDOOR SCULPTURE

Glacier
Harrison
Tom Boy
238th Street

ARCHITECTURE

Baltica
Dragon Claw
Glacier
Hibernica
Parsley Crested
Pittsburgh

DECORATIONS ON THE GROUND

Dragon Claw
Garland
Gold Heart
Hibernica
Lemon Swirl
Lustrous Carpet
Manda's Crested

appearance—make good use of unwanted stems by rooting them to fill in bare spots or start new projects. Thin out well-established ivy to keep it from becoming too thick and heavy, which could cause the vines to fall away from the support or even bring the support down along with it. It may be necessary to rake out dead leaves and debris, but be careful not to dislodge the healthy vines.

BALTICA

RECOMMENDED IVIES

Following is a list of suggested ivies for all manner of topiary. Unfortunately some varieties have more than one name, and ivies are commonly mislabeled in garden centers and plant shops. If you want to be sure of what you're buying, order your plants from commercial members of the American Ivy Society, who strive to identify varieties correctly. However, feel free to try any ivy that catches your eye. Don't be afraid to experiment until you find the right variety for the shape and location you have chosen. Compared to the cost of other plants, ivy is an inexpensive gamble—though ivy may look aristocratic, it is the cheapest evergreen you can buy. Your guesses will be educated ones if you keep in mind that different types thrive in different conditions. Indoors, variegated varieties prefer more sun, so if you have a dark area pick an all-green leaf. Outdoors, yellow and white markings are more vivid in bright locations, but may scorch in full sun. Ivy planted outside exhibits more compact, denser growth than the same type grown indoors.

THE HARDIEST PLANTS

These varieties have consistently survived harsh winters in test plantings by the American Ivy Society in Ohio, where winter temperatures commonly hover around zero degrees Fahrenheit, and can dip as low as minus twenty along with the added stress of high winds.

'Baltica' is considered by many people to be the toughest of all ivies. It is a vigorous grower that can get shaggy if you don't keep up with trimming. Because it grows so rampantly, it's best used for a large ground pattern or to cover a fedge. The leaf looks like ordinary English ivy, but is slightly smaller, in a dark green shade with contrasting white veins.

'Pittsburgh' has leaves that are similar to 'Baltica,' except that the center lobe is more pronounced, and the color changes to copper in cold weather. It is also a rapid grower.

'Harrison' is one of the ivies recommended by the American Ivy Society for outdoor use. It is ultra-hardy, with smaller leaves that in winter display a prominent white vein against a dark green leaf. It sends out long runners with few side branches, for a dense, flat look in wall patterns.

'Tom Boy' is highly winter-resistant, and equally suited for growing on the ground or vertically. The shiny leaves are unlobed like those of an adult ivy, but the plant retains its juvenile climbing habit so it can only be called a permanent adolescent.

'238th Street' is a truly adult ivy, which grows in an arborescent, or shrub-like, manner. It was named for the street in the Bronx on which it was discovered. The leaves are unlobed and vaguely heart-shaped, and the bushy plants may produce greenish flowers and black berries.

'Lustrous Carpet' is recommended for edging patterns on the ground, where the plant creates a sculptured effect as tufts of growth pop up along the runners. And it's also a nicely behaved indoor plant that might add an interesting texture to portable topiary.

PREFERRED ENGLISH IVY VARIETIES FOR TOPIARY

ESPALIER
Buttercup
Deltoidea
Galaxy
Glacier
Harrison
Hibernica
Lemon Swirl
Minor Marmorata
Parsley Crested
Pedata

STANDARDS
Fiesta
Glacier
Gold Dust
Manda's Crested

PORTABLE
Duck Foot
Fiesta
Galaxy
Garland
Glacier
Itsy Bitsy
Little Diamond
Lustrous Carpet
Minor Marmorata
Pedata
Shamrock

FANCY SHAPES

DELTOIDEA

Until recently, the fancy-leaved types of ivy were believed unable to survive winter outdoors, but test plantings of the past few years have shown that many are quite hardy. In certain parts of the country a plant's ability to tolerate hot sun and drought is more important than its ability to take low temperatures, so this characteristic has also been noted in the descriptions that follow. Some are equally good for growing indoors; see Chapter One for more varieties for indoor topiary.

'Deltoidea,' the sweetheart ivy that florists love for arrangements, is also good for large outdoor patterns. The heart-shaped leaves lie flat and close together along the long runners. Any wall pattern planted in 'Deltoidea' will have a refined espalier look.

'Fiesta' is a ruffled plant, thanks to curly leaves on vigorous stems. It is easy to grow, indoors or out.

'Dragon Claw' has larger, ruffled leaves, best used for edgings or to engulf a chain link fence.

'Garland' has apple green, slightly curled, pointed leaves with veins that stand out and add nice texture. The plants grow as neat mounds, making it ideal for horizontal edging designs or indoor topiary figures.

'Manda's Crested' is a fluffy, wavy-leaved ivy, robust and happy indoors or out. Try it in the garden as a taller edging for patterns, or indoors grafted onto a tall stem for a luxuriant standard.

'Parsley Crested' has a distinctive look due to its dainty, deep green foliage, which is frilled around the edges. It has thrived on chain link fences in Southern California despite sun and drought, so you should try it as a fedge or espalier design in hot, dry locations.

'Galaxy' is a hardy new variety. The leaves look just like five-pointed stars and are born on compact, short branches. It is equally at home lacing a garden wall or an indoor topiary.

'Pedata,' or bird's foot ivy, is a very old variety that looks just as the name describes. The tiny leaves create a delicate look, but the plant has proved quite hardy on walls and fences.

'Itsy Bitsy' is a true miniature, with stems densely covered in tiny, pointed leaves. It is superb for covering small indoor topiary.

'Duck Foot' also has tiny leaves, but they are rounded and slightly lobed. The trailing stems are easily grown indoors.

'Shamrock' has delicately curled leaves that overlap along the stem, giving good, small-scale coverage on indoor topiary.

PEDATA

SPLASHES OF COLOR

Variegated ivies offer a broad palette for topiary. On an animal they define character, lending realistic coloration to a penguin's white bib or a lion's golden mane. They are priceless for brightening a shady corner or a dark surface; the great landscape architects Thomas Church and Russell Page relied on speckled and marbelized ivies to highlight city gardens. In 1962 Mr. Page lavished them with praise in his book *The Education of a Gardener*, observing: "Against a dark wall variegated ivy will give the effect of dappled sunlight."

'Buttercup' is another choice plant if you want a sunny, cheerful effect. The new leaves are greenish-yellow, showing to gorgeous advantage against a dark wall or fence. The color is more striking in sun than shade.

'Lemon Swirl' has slightly curled leaves with luscious golden markings, rather than an overall wash of yellow like 'Buttercup.' The highlights are more obvious in the sun, more subtle in the shade. The compact, well-branched plants do well against walls or on the ground.

'Gold Heart' originated in Italy and is very popular in England. The center of each small leaf wears a golden splotch and the color remains year-round, even in shade. It grows slowly, so

GLACIER

be prepared to be patient unless you are training only a small pattern or indoor display.

'Glacier' is an old favorite with indoor topiarists, who appreciate the silvery-gray markings and an occasional touch of pink on small leaves with red stems.

'Minor Marmorata' is a mouthful to pronounce, but this old-fashioned variety is worth asking for. The small leaves are speckled in many shades of creamy white, gray and green, offset by wine-colored stems. It is super-hardy and retains its bright markings even in the shade. The long, graceful strands are too sparse to use on the ground, but look beautiful on a wall.

'Little Diamond' has small- to medium-size, diamond-shaped leaves in shades of green and pale gray. The dense growth and fine texture are unequalled for portable topiary.

BIG, BOLD LEAVES

Two other species of ivy are also grown outdoors and indoors for their large leaves and splashes of gold, green and white. Canary ivy (*Hedera canariensis*) is not completely hardy, but it's worth trying in the South or in a protected location farther north. The large, shiny leaves are carried on bright red stems. 'Variegata,' also called Gloire-de-Marengo ivy, is a spectacular variety, marked with silver and bordered in white. It is widely planted in Europe and on the West Coast, where it quickly covers walls and fences. It is also striking on large topiary indoors.

Persian ivy (*Hedera colchica*) resembles Canary ivy, but the leaves are even bigger. One sure way to identify it is to crush a leaf—it will smell like celery. It is hardier than Canary ivy, a vigorous grower good for large, upright patterns. 'Dentato-variegata' has toothed leaves splashed with cream and yellow. 'Sulphur Heart' has a splash of yellow on heart-shaped leaves bordered in dark green.

If you want an ultrahardy large-leafed ivy, return to the vast tribe of English ivies and select 'Hibernica,' also called Irish ivy, which will cloak wall or ground in shiny dark green leaves.

AN IVY GARDEN

An unusual, easy-to-care-for garden in the country or city, sun or shade, can be planted entirely in ivy. Border it with a fedge, then plant arches along the outside. At the back your ivy garden could conclude, as Pliny's did, with swags of

Ivy is so versatile that you can use it to create an entire garden. The fast-growing vine is easily shaped into unifying standards, knot gardens, and sculptural and architectural topiary.

IVY IMPOSTERS

All true ivies belong to the genus Hedera. *Although certain plants resembling ivy do not belong to that genus, they are known by the following names:*
- *Devil's ivy (*Epipremnum aureum*)*
- *Kenilworth ivy (*Cymbalaria muralis*)*
- *Poison ivy (*Rhus radicans*)*
- *Swedish ivy (*Plectranthus australis*)*
- *Boston ivy (*Parthenocissus tricuspidata*)*
- *German ivy (*Senecio mikanioides*)*

> **It has been said that vines are to bits of architecture what a dress is to a woman. It may serve to enhance beauty or to cover defects.**
>
> —LORING UNDERWOOD
> *The Garden and Its Accessories,* 1907

ivy looped between full-size trees that naturally retain a neat head. Bradford pear is a good choice since it has a neat, pyramidal top, produces white flowers in the spring, and is as tolerant as ivy of cold and city conditions. Inside the garden, train ivy as an edging to outline knot patterns; accent the center of each with an ivy standard—in cold climates, grow these in pots and bring them into the house to enjoy for the winter. For the middle of your ivy garden, construct a vine-clad pavilion so you can sit in the shade and admire your handiwork.

CARING FOR IVY

Outdoors, ivy is rarely troubled by insects and diseases. An occasional infestation of spider mites during dry weather is just about the only problem. These are too small to see with the naked eye, but their presence is detected by speckled discoloration of the leaves and fine white webs. A good spraying with the hose usually eliminates these bugs. Ivy leaves may develop brown patches in severe winters. Although the spots are unattractive, they don't affect the health of the plant, and the overall look remains evergreen. Spraying with an anti-desiccant such as Wilt-Pruf or Vapor Gard can help prevent winter discoloration. When you plant ivies, they will appreciate the boost of a little ordinary granular fertilizer (such as 10-10-10) and some peat moss mixed into the planting soil.

Inside the house you won't be able to tell if ivy has bugs unless you inspect it closely. An apparently healthy plant can become infested very quickly, so check often, especially for spider mites and aphids. Aphids are black or green insects that appear on the tips of new growth and on the underside of leaves, along with a sticky residue. If leaves begin to brown and fall off, a sign of rot, you are probably overwatering. Let the topiary dry out a bit, and then douse with a fungal drench such as benomyl. Fertilize ivies monthly, as you would any foliage houseplant.

Espalier

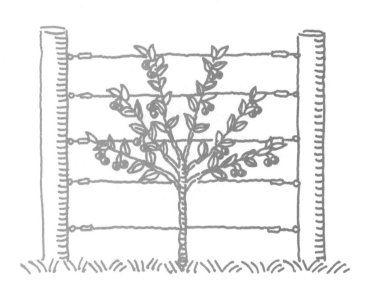

Murals of Tracery, Flowers & Fruit

Espalier is a term used to describe any plant trained into an open, flat pattern, as well as the technique used to achieve this two-dimensional effect. Espaliers are usually trees or shrubs, trained into murals of geometric or abstract design. They give you maximum plant decoration in a restricted space, obscuring or enhancing the side of a building, wall or any vertical surface.

Sometimes espaliers are grown in the open on an independent structure or framework, creating a living fence or screen. They provide a sense of privacy in your yard or entryway without blocking out sunlight and breezes, which dance through the leaves and branches to form lacy shadows on the ground.

With a wide palette to choose from, espaliers offer a four-season display. The decorative tracery of its branches offers filigreed patterns in winter, while spring brings a raiment of blossoms and young leaves. This is followed in summer by the reward of glossy foliage, and in autumn with a spectacular parade of fruits or berries and a curtain of changing foliage.

If you don't have a lot of room, espaliers are a fun way to grow fruit without taking up much space. When dwarf trees are trained in a flat pattern against a wall or used as a fence, you can reap a bounty of luscious, easily harvested fruit. Espaliers are easy to care for—and a good gardening project for people with back problems, since all of the attention the trees require can be given in a standing position. An espaliered fruit tree is a useful, obedient and beautiful creation.

The art of training flat trees was developed in medieval walled towns. The need to remain within fortifications during long states of siege necessitated the harvesting of a great deal of food in a confined area. Space was maximized by growing fruit trees against the inner ramparts. Besides saving space, it was soon discovered that growing plants against a wall had other advantages. Heat emanating from the wall allowed tender varieties to survive in nothern climates, encouraged the trees to bear fruit earlier in the season and improved the size and quality of the fruit. In addition, the espalier technique systematically con-

George Washington is known for his youthful attack on a cherry tree, but he channeled this into a fascination with pruning and grafting in later years. Splendid examples of his artistry with pears and cherries have been recreated at Mount Vernon.

> **66. . . what can be more delightful in spring, in the excursion of the walks, than the charming appearance which the [espalier] trees make when covered with their showy bloom, differing in themselves, in those of different genera, species, and varieties; or in summer, to see the fruit of the different sorts advancing to perfection, and in autumn arrive successively to maturity?99**
>
> —BERNARD MCMAHON
> *McMahon's American Gardener, 1857*

trolled a tree's growth habit, causing it to bear more fruit at a younger age. Espaliered apples bear fruit in 4 to 5 years, compared to the 7- to 8-year period required for an ordinary apple tree. All of these are excellent reasons to grow fruit against a wall, instead of on an ordinary tree.

Espalier is still used extensively in Europe for commercial fruit production, which remains its chief purpose there. In this country, it is a medium through which we have rediscovered our kinship with European master gardeners and early settlers. We have updated our inheritance, revolutionizing the art of espalier by practicing it for the sake of ornamentation with all manner of evergreens and flowering varieties as well as with fruit trees.

Freeform or informal espalier is a modern American version of two-dimensional plant shaping. In contrast to the traditional, symmetrical, geometric European patterns, these creations draw on the Oriental aesthetic of plant training, which stylizes a plant's natural habit. With informal designs training can be more casual than for formal specimens, as you let the growth of the plant direct the development of the design. If you happen to come across a tree or shrub in your garden that suggests a shape to you, you have discovered the beginning of a unique freeform creation.

PLANNING AN ESPALIER

For creating your own espalier, the best plan of attack is as follows: decide on the location, choose a pattern, and then select a plant that suits the site and design. Admittedly, it is not always possible to be so levelheaded in matters of the garden. If your heart is set on a favorite plant, or if a particular design has captured your fancy, by all means stick to it.

You'll find many places around your house just waiting to be dressed up with espalier. Most outdoor spaces are bordered by at least one vertical surface. If your outdoor space is enclosed, train trees along the inner surface as in medieval walled gardens. But don't think that espalier must be limited to antique designs against traditional architecture. If you have a modern house, especially one with maintenance-free stained siding, you have the perfect backdrop for the design of your choice. Think of a freeform blue cedar tree against graying redwood or cedar siding. Where the wall of a house, garage or shed is made of an unattractive material, an espalier will disguise the surface. Planting a two-dimensional pattern against a high retaining wall or fence will break the monotony and add a beautiful view. A small space, such as a condominium yard or hot tub enclosure, benefits from the added color and texture of an espaliered spec-

His ripening fruits
Display
their sweet
temptations
from the wall,
Or gay Espalier.

—ROBERT DODSLEY
Agriculture II, 1754

An espaliered evergreen is a cheering sight to behold through a wintry window, and provides a nice counterpoint to other wintertime creatures.

> **❝Plant your fairest Tulips . . . under Espalier❞**
>
> —JOHN EVELYN
> *Kalendarium Hortense,*
> 1664

imen. If you need a backdrop for a narrow flower bed along a wall, espalier is the answer. If your neighbor erects a fence and you are stuck looking at the back of it, turn an awkward situation into a pretty sight with a geometric pattern of evergreens. A robust grower like forsythia can be trained all the way around your house, gift wrapping it in leaves and flowers.

Where space is too cramped for a hedge, or where a see-through screen is desired, freestanding fruit tree espaliers are a novel solution. They make excellent garden divisions, more exciting than post-and-rail, as the light streams through and fruits appear suspended in leaf-framed windows. Low-growing patterns produce a tasty edging for a path since you can pluck a pear on your way into the house. At Mount Vernon a wonderful gnarled pear is shaped as a low fence around the kitchen garden—this is a custom still seen in France that you might want to try around your own vegetable patch.

The flat silhouettes may also be used to frame three-dimensional works of art, such as a shady kiosk or filigreed summerhouse. Not only can espalier block out unattractive sights and boring surfaces, it can also protect you from inquisitive stares from neighbors. Simple designs can be trained up and then bent at the top as a lean-to against the side of a building to produce a shady covered entrance walk or dining area. Use espalier to devise a pavilion of the classic palmette verrier shape or a leafy gazebo constructed of single U shapes with a fanciful archway at the entrance.

In outdoor areas where they can't be planted in the ground, espaliers can be grown in containers. Potted specimens can be moved around as you desire, and you can raise them indoors in sizes to fit a windowsill or a greenhouse. If you have no garden or only a small space, you can raise dwarf fruit trees in containers. Dwarf fruit trees should be started in a 12-inch pot or 3-gallon tub, as containers this size will stimulate them to bear at a younger age. After two years they can be transplanted into a permanent home, 18 to 24 inches high and wide. The minimum size for any pot, tub or box that will winter outdoors where the temperature will dip below freezing is 16 inches.

For centuries, French professional and amateur gardeners have continued to be enchanted by flattened trees, devising training systems for apples, pears and peaches that still bear the names of their creators. These formal, symmetric patterns can be as wide or tall as the space you want to fill. Some designs can be achieved only with two or more trees, and look best where they can be displayed over a reasonable expanse. Others can be trained from a single tree and are suited to narrow spaces. Of course, the size of the espalier is to some degree determined by the plant you use. As a minimum for most trees and shrubs, figure 6 feet in height for vertical shapes. If the design you choose is horizontal, it can be low as 16 inches, but figure on about 8 feet in width. These dimensions ensure a good crop of flowers, fruit and berries.

Incorporate classic shapes into whimsical ideas. When you have set your tree into a classic pattern, you can add crowning touches. Bend the top of the branches into a two-dimensional heart, bell, finial, circle or fleur-de-lis. This is a pretty way to finish off a living mural and it also curbs the vigorous push upward so your little tree can concentrate its energy on producing lush foliage or a bounty of fruit.

Let your imagination carry you beyond the traditional forms to scenes of your own invention. Wire guidelines can be strung up to outline any design. Maybe you'd like to gaze into the heavens instead of at your garage. Outline crescent moons and stars, then train single-cordon trees to follow the pattern.

You can place one design in front of another for a bas-relief scene such as a fish swimming behind undulating wisps of seaweed. Train a fish outline in forsythia; place a few serpentine cordons of apple or upright yew in front for a seaweed habitat.

Freeform espaliers are generally grown against a solid surface, which sets off their abstract arrangements and permits the random placement of supports. You can be less pre-

In 1769, Maryland Governor Sharpe entertained Lord Baltimore's brother-in-law, and his table shone with the fruits of his own espaliers.

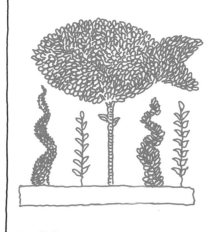

> *Wassaile the trees,*
> *that they may*
> *beare,*
> *You many a*
> *Plum and many*
> *a Peare:*
> *For more or*
> *lesse fruites they*
> *will bring,*
> *As you do give*
> *them Wassailing.*
>
> —ROBERT HERRICK
> from his poem "Cere-
> monies for Christmas"

See-through espaliers can turn an ordinary spot into a special place, height-ening privacy without closing you in. On this front porch, single-cordon trees have been trained on a wire design of moons and stars.

cise in training, but don't let an interesting design degenerate into a wandering mess. This art form needs an eye for the balance of line and mass. Basically, training involves the removal of any branches that either protrude straight out from the wall or cross each other. Use the remaining branches to establish an open, graceful silhouette. As the tree grows, develop the pattern further, removing any branches that obscure the basic design. Ongoing maintenance consists of the periodic removal of weak, diseased, overvigorous or dead branches.

If you are training plants against a wall or fence, the direction in which the wall faces is an important factor. If a profusion of flowers, fruits and berries is your aim, make sure espaliers will receive six or more hours of sunlight each day. South-facing walls are best for heat-loving plants, but are perhaps not ideal in northern climates where the winter sun will cause freeze-thaw cycles. Western exposures may cause the same problem. A surface with an easterly orientation is ideal for most plants, while a northern exposure provides a haven for shade lovers, such as euonymus, Japanese holly and yew.

You should coordinate so that the colors of flowers, fruits and berries don't clash with the background surface. Orange berries don't harmonize well with brick, for instance. And the color of the wall, whether stone, brick, stucco or wood, is of more than just visual importance. White or light-colored surfaces reflect heat, while black or dark materials absorb warmth. Thus the sun bouncing off a light-colored wall can scorch a tree in summer, or cause damaging premature defrosting in winter and spring.

When planting, be sure to leave adequate space between the tree and the wall. The minimum distance for planting in front of all solid walls is 6 inches—for proper air circulation, to prevent disease, to permit spraying and to allow for maintenance of the wall. To protect trees from the reflected heat given off by light-colored or south-facing walls, plant 12 inches away from the base of the wall. Spread the roots away from the wall so they will head for nourishing soil instead of a dead end. If sited against the side of a building, make sure there is a rain gutter overhead to protect the tree from cascading water.

*I*f you simply don't have space for a fruit tree, even one that is espaliered, you can still train fruits against a wall. Blackberries, blueberries, grapes or gooseberries are all handsome and tantalizing small-scale possibilities.

SELECTING PLANTS

O nce you have decided on a design, you are ready to shop for plants. These days the local garden center is likely to offer a good selection; we have listed some mail-order firms in the Source Guide.

Dwarf fruit trees should be purchased for most projects. These miniature versions of standard fruit trees grow only 6 to 12 feet tall when left to their own devices, but their fruit is full size and often larger and of better quality than that of standard trees. At first, most dwarfs grow rapidly, giving you a head start on your espalier, but after a few years they slow down, growing more slowly than "ordinary" trees, so it is easier to keep your espalier the size and shape you want. Standard trees can be used for espalier, but they will require more pruning and a nearly constant battle to keep them 6 to 8 feet tall. Use them only if you are creating a colossal masterpiece as wide as the house and several stories tall.

It may seem like a miracle of modern science that large, luscious fruit can be produced on a miniature tree, but this result is achieved by a centuries-old practice known as grafting. A dwarf tree actually consists of several plants, spliced together into a single specimen. Depending on the type of tree, the graft union may be more or less visible, appearing as a lump or bend in the trunk. The top part, or scion, is taken from a variety selected for its desirable fruit. The bottom part, or rootstock, comes from a naturally dwarf tree; this part of the tree determines its utimate size and rate of growth. Sometimes you will notice two grafts on the same trunk. In this case, a nurseryman has grafted a small section of dwarf tree trunk (to control the size) onto a more vigorous root stock (which makes for a hardier plant).

Espaliered trees flower earlier than those planted in the open, and must be responsible for their own fertilization; so select a self-pollinating variety, plant two trees to cross-pollinate, or graft on a pollinating branch. If you have failed to do any of the preceding, don't despair. As an enticing offering to the bees, create an arrangement of flowering twigs from another variety of the same type of fruit, and place it near your espalier. Use the arrangement afterward as a centerpiece.

Stone fruits of the genus *Prunus*, which includes apricots, cherries, nectarines, peaches and plums, require drastic cutting

Espalier is particularly useful for softening the sense of enclosure in any formally defined space. This etching comes from The Clergyman's Recreation, a British book on "the pleasure and profit of gardening," published in 1715.

66Espalier fruit trees are essentially two-dimensional forms having height and width but (in order to expose the fruit-bearing wood to maximum sun) lacking depth.

Espalier fruit trees are grown on dwarfing rootstock to control the size of the tree. The espalier forms are obtained by bending and pruning limbs to obtain certain pre-determined patterns that enhance fruit bearing.99

—HENRY P. LEUTHARDT
leading grower of espaliered fruit trees

While touring the garden of a certain gentleman, Jonathan Swift realized his host would not offer him the fruit of his trees, and recalled a saying of his dear grandmother: "Always pull a peach, when it is within your reach."

So saying he plucked and ate the nearest luscious example.

back to stimulate a continual supply of new shoots. The best shape for stone fruits is a fan, as this form allows for pruning old limbs and developing replacement lateral branches. Another plus is that most stone fruit varieties are self-pollinating. If you have room for only one espalier, a peach tree is a good choice. The blossoms are quite exquisite and have captivated flower painters for centuries. For flavor, nothing compares to a tree-ripened peach, plum, or apricot.

If visual pleasure is your objective, and you aren't interested in growing fruit, then you can select from a wide range of ornamental plants. Decide which season's appearance is most important to you, taking into consideration a tree's bark color, flowers, fruit, berries and fall color. For a year-round display of foliage, nothing beats the verdance of evergreens.

Rate of growth is also a factor to consider when selecting plants for espalier. Rapid growers will produce quick results, but do demand frequent pruning. Forsythia (*Forsythia × intermedia*) grows quickly with the early cheer of yellow flowers. Consider leaf size, as coarse foliage such as that of magnolias will spoil detail on smaller patterns, but will be striking on a large open design. Some plants, such as yew (*Taxus cuspidata* and *Taxus × media*) or flowering quince (*Chaenomeles speciosa*), have growth habits that make them best suited for informal designs or simple fans.

If you alternate plants within a pattern, you can achieve a mosaic effect. Try a combination of crab apple (any small-fruited species of *Malus*) and firethorn (*Pyracantha coccinea*). For winter the fresh green of the firethorn contrasts with the tracery of the crab apple twigs; crab apple flowers in spring are succeeded by those of the firethorn in summer; and a brilliant show of crimson crab apples and orange berries in the autumn highlights the contrast of foliage colors and textures.

For formal designs, the best purchase is a young, unbranched single-stem tree. This is known in horticultural circles as a whip or maiden. Sometimes a tree without side branches is hard to find; if so, substitute the youngest tree available with an uncut central stem, and cut the side branches back to the main trunk to form a whip. For more informal designs, a finished look may be attained in fewer years if you buy a mature plant that is already flat and resembles the design you have in mind. Bring a sketch of your design along with you to the nursery if you plan to start with an older plant.

Strive for an open and pleasing pattern that showcases the color, texture and branch structure of the plant subject. You don't need to train a plant with accuracy from infancy. Begin with a plant of reasonable size and definite form whose natural shape inspires you. Southern magnolia (*Magnolia grandiflora*) has a pyramidal silhouette, while cotoneaster (*Cotoneaster* in variety) obligingly forms horizontal patterns. Take advantage of plants that have multiple stems emerging from the ground such as forsythia, yew and quince to create informal fans or fountains.

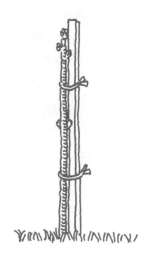

BASIC TRAINING

Medieval fruit tenders discovered that as they restricted and arranged the growth of trees, they yielded more fruit. The more severely a limb bends away from the vertical, the slower it will grow, and as a result its energy will be channeled into the production of flowers and fruits. Therefore, many of the traditional French patterns consist of curved or angled branches. Bending branches downward will stop their growth almost completely. This is sometimes done temporarily to encourage the development of flowering buds or to slow down overvigorous branches that spoil the symmetry of your design. Conversely, if one branch is lagging behind the others, turn its tip up for a few weeks to promote rapid growth.

Knowing these basic principles of growth will help you train a beautiful and bounteous specimen. There are a few types of plant growth that you should recognize in order to establish

> **❝Just as the twig is bent, the tree's inclin'd.❞**
>
> —ALEXANDER POPE,
> *Epistles to Several Persons: To Lord Cobham,* 1734

and perpetuate an espalier. A leader is a stem that is longer and more vigorous than other portions of the tree; it is used to create the skeleton of your shape. Buds are swellings from which shoots, leaves and flowers develop. A scaffold is a major side branch from which secondary growth develops.

Bending is done during the growing season whenever shoots are pencil thick and have grown 12 inches or so beyond the point where they will be curved. If younger they will bruise and break; if older and woody they are likely to snap.

Many designs call for sharp angles in the branches. If the branches become too stiff, it may be necessary to accomplish this bending gradually, being sure to tie the branch to a support

Post-and-wire frameworks can be made into charming fence designs, as well as supports for your espaliers.

in more than one place to prevent pressure points. Once the desired angle has been attained, the branch must be tied gently but securely into place until the tree settles into its new posture.

The art of espalier calls for some ruthlessness on your part. Remove any branches that don't contribute to the pattern. Even informal designs require the elimination of growth that detracts from a graceful effect. Pruning is not senselessly cruel—rather, it stimulates the sprouting of buds into healthy leaves and flowers. New growth may be removed while still in the bud stage by rubbing or pinching off with a fingernail; older stems and branches are cut off with pruning shears. Deciding which buds to remove or retain is easy if you bear in mind that shoots will grow in the same direction the bud is facing. Slant the cut away from the bud so that the resulting shoot can grow in the right direction. Winter pruning is done while the tree is dormant in order to stimulate the formation of new wood; summer pruning is performed while the plant is in active growth during spring and early summer, and brings about more flower buds. Summer pruning is not essential, but if you're fond enough of your tree to give it this attention, you will have more fruit and a more distinct silhouette throughout the summer. For best results, perform the trimming at least twice a summer. But don't prune in the late summer in cold climates, because the tender new shoots will be killed by autumn frost.

Where side shoots are desired, cut the leader back 3 to 4 inches below the horizontal guide on which side branches will be trained. Shoots will sprout near the cut and can be bent up and onto the wire.

> **❝There can, however, scarcely be a more beautiful display of the art of the horticulturist, than a fine row of trained trees, their branches arranged with the utmost symmetry and regularity, and covered, in the fruit season, with large and richly coloured fruit.❞**
>
> —ANDREW JACKSON DOWNING
> *Fruits and Fruit Trees of America*, 1845

SUPPORTS

The word espalier derives from *spalliera*, an Old Italian word meaning "something to lean against," thus, a support. Frenchmen later called the trellising used to train trees against a wall *espalier*. Because they are essentially two-dimensional, all espalier must be grown on some kind of support. If you are training an espalier against a wall or a solid fence, you have a ready-made support. If, on the other hand, you decide to grow a freestanding espalier, or plant one in a container, it is necessary to construct an independent framework.

Initially, each young tree should be tied to a stake to ensure the development of a strong, straight trunk. Where the espalier is trained against a solid surface, all you need to add is a network of guides to aid you in shaping the plant. Various devices, known as wall aids, hold the branches in place a few inches away from the surface—this permits air circulation for the tree and allows you to paint the wall. You may use long, heavy-duty nails, lead wall nails, long-shanked eyebolts or even antenna guides, depending on the type of wall. Your local hardware store can advise you on the best hardware for wood, brick, stone, concrete or metal. Use paint or a marking pen to outline the exact shape on the surface. Attach wall aids along this outline as needed to lay out the pattern, tying the branches to them as the tree grows.

Many people prefer to train the tree along a system of wires in order to reduce wear and tear on the wall, as well as to facilitate maintenance. Wire is secured to the wall with brackets, angle irons, nails, eyebolts, or antenna guides. The best sort of wire is vinyl covered, since it is both long lasting and gentle to tender stems. Use a color that blends with the wall, or a dark color if the espalier is freestanding, If you are unable to find coated wire, galvanized wire may be substituted. Wires should be installed with turnbuckles for tightening, since they will sag with the weight of the maturing plant. Unscrew turnbuckles as far as possible before attaching them to the wires. This allows you to tighten them in the future as the wires sag. Additional horizontal, vertical, and diagonal support for young trees can be provided by bamboo stakes or wood lath attached between the wires. The stakes or lath may be removed when sturdy trunks develop, and the trees secured directly to the wires.

For tying the branches to wires or wall aids, use a soft material that is strong but will give. This will save you from the constant worry that the tie will girdle or chafe branches as they grow. You must still check periodically, however, as no material has infinite stretch and strength. Limbs never recover from severe girdling injuries, although it may take years for a branch to die. Good ties include old stockings, twine, osier or basket willow, and notched garbage bag closures.

Frames for small, container grown espalier are easy to devise (see the discussion of indoor espalier on page 216). Freestanding supports for trees should be sturdy but unobtrusive; the framework must be planned and put in place before planting. One solution is to use a sturdy wooden trellis. This is the best method for espaliers in planters, and you could make use of ready-made trellises. On a large scale, however, the latticework tends to distract the eye from the espalier itself, unless the trellis is custom-made to duplicate the pattern. A better system for larger, freestanding designs, which will showcase the espalier itself as a living fence, is one where wires are strung between upright supports. Choose a material for the uprights that is long lasting, attractive, and either unobtrusive or in keeping with other architectural details on your property. Possibilities include rustic posts (generally the most attractive); 4-by-4s of redwood, cedar or locust; metal poles; or fence uprights. Beware of wooden posts that have been treated with preservatives that are toxic to plants. For added stability on windy sites you may wish to set the posts in concrete. If you are planning a long row of espalier, or if you want to mix patterns, be sure to position your posts so that they act as vertical supports for the trees but don't break the lines of your display.

To construct a freestanding support for fruit trees or ornamental shrubs and trees, you will need a thicker wire than is used against a solid surface, since it will be the only means of support for the tree and will be subject to the added stress of the wind. If you can't get vinyl-coated cable, galvanized wire rope or telephone wire may be substituted. Since all of these are

66 *Whenever I write about gardening, I am struck by the amount of physical labor I seem to be describing. On paper it sounds overwhelming—but that is the nature of written directions. The reality is not so onerous.* **99**

—ELEANOR PERÉNYI
Green Thoughts: A Writer in the Garden, 1981

66No fencing, however, for a kitchen-garden where intended to have wall trees, especially in the more northerly parts of the Union, is equal to brick walls, which are considerably stronger, warmer, and more durable than paling fences; and their natural warmth, together with their reflection of the sun's heat, is the most effectual for the growth and ripening of the latest and more delicate kinds of fruit.99

—BERNARD MCMAHON
McMahon's American Gardener, 1857

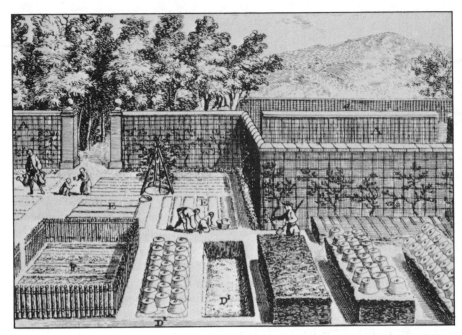

Wall-trained espaliers were originally developed for their remarkable ability to bear fruit in gardens of limited space, as depicted in this 18th-century etching.

very thick, ask the hardware store to cut the wire into the necessary lengths, figuring 2 feet extra per wire for attaching it to posts and turnbuckles.

To secure each wire cable between posts, you will need two eyebolts, one turnbuckle, two wire rope thimbles, and two wire rope clips. Attaching the cable with the fasteners only sounds complicated; once you have the hardware in front of you, it is quite simple—and the best way to assemble a strong support system. Screw one eyebolt into each post. Open the wire rope thimble with pliers, slip it through one of the eyebolts, and close it with pliers. The next step is to thread the cable through the eyebolt and around the outside of the thimble, bringing the end back along the cable. Unscrew the wire rope clip and clamp it over the doubled cable; slip it up behind the thimble and screw down tightly. Use the second thimble and wire rope clip to se-cure the other end of the cable to the closed end of the turnbuck-le, leaving the clip slightly loose. Unscrew the turnbuckle as far as possible, and hook it onto the eyebolt. Finally, pull the tail of the cable through the clip until the wire is taut, and screw the clip down tightly against the thimble.

HOW TO MAKE CLASSIC SHAPES

Once you have shopped for your tree, and a few supplies, you are ready to embark on an espalier project. Though training must be performed with precision, it really doesn't require a lot of time. But it is important to check your little charge frequently, so that bending is accomplished while the branches are pliable—if necessary, bend sharp angles grad-ually over a two-week period. With pruning shears and ties in hand stroll out to inspect your tree, which will soon reveal its personality and become a good friend. By the second season, most shapes will be established, rewarding your efforts with a living mural.

Instructions given are for traditional French shapes, plus a few novelties. The dimensions given are appropriate for apple, pear and other dwarf fruit trees, but may be varied for plants of different size and habit. In creating formal shapes you must plan ahead, figuring the design precisely before you start plant-ing and training. If you want to vary the size from the dimen-sions in the following instructions, map out the new pattern on graph paper before you lay it out on a wall.

For most designs, the simplest way to train a tree is on five horizontal rows of wall aids or wires. The lowest row or wire should be 15 to 20 inches from the ground, with successive parallel rows placed at 12- to 18-inch intervals. This will result

66. . . even to this day, in some parts of England, the antique custom of saluting the apple trees in the or-chards, in the hope of obtaining a good crop the next year, still lingers among the farmers of portions of Devonshire and Here-fordshire. This odd ceremony consists of saluting the tree with a portion of the con-tents of a wassail bowl of cider, with a toast in it, by pouring a lit-tle of the cider about the roots, and even hanging a bit of the toast on the branches of the most barren, the farmer and his men dancing in a circle round the tree, and singing rude songs. . . .99

—ANDREW JACKSON DOWNING
Fruits and Fruit Trees of America, 1845

> **Pinching is an indispensable operation in the management of trees trained as dwarfs, pyramids, or espaliers. Most trees have a natural tendency to grow most vigorously towards the top and at the extremity of the branches; this should be kept in continual check, for if one portion be permitted but for a short time to grow more vigorously than the others, the balance is destroyed, and much time and severe measures are required to restore it.**
>
> —BERNARD MCMAHON
> *McMahon's American Gardener*, 1857

in a 6- to 7½-foot-tall espalier. If your pattern consists mainly of diagonals, use wall aids to exactly outline the branches, stretch wires on an angle, or add stakes to the horizontal wires. All shapes begin with an untrimmed, single-stem whip planted a few inches in front of the wall and tied securely to a stake.

For All Espalier Designs

You will need:
—*one or more unbranched, single-stem dwarf fruit tree whips*
—*bamboo or wooden stakes (see each design for lengths and quantity needed)*
—*vinyl-coated wire, galvanized wire or wall aids to guide branches*
—*old stockings, basket willow, notched garbage bag closures, or twine to tie branches to guides*
—*pruning shears*
—*a tape measure or yardstick*
—*waterproof adhesive tape or a waterproof marking pen*

Vertical Cordons

The simplest espalier shape is a cordon. The word derives from the French *cordon* meaning "ribbon" or "cord." All other traditional designs derive from this versatile, single-stemmed shape, which may be vertical, diagonal or serpentine, and which can be repeated in multiples to simulate a fence. Dimensions can be adjusted for leaf size and plant habit. Vertical cordons can be repeated 2 feet apart in a row, used as end posts, or alternated with other patterns. This form is easily trained with stakes; a system of guide wires or nails is unnecessary for shaping. A vertical cordon must be at least 6 feet tall in order to bear a good crop of fruit. For each cordon, you will need a stake 8 feet tall.

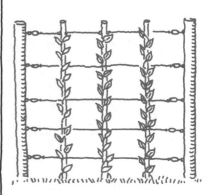

1   For each cordon, sink an 8-foot stake 2 feet into the ground and a few inches in front of the wall. Use wall aids and wire to attach the stake to the wall. This will hold it steady as it supports the weight of the growing plant.

2   Shorten side shoots to the first set of leaves or bud. Do *not* prune the central leader.

3   Tie the leader to the stake at 6-inch or proportionally frequent intervals. Lop off the central stem when it reaches the desired height. If you have a row of vertical cordons, an alternate way to finish the design is to bend the leaders when they reach the desired height, and train them horizontally along the wall. After a few years, the stakes may be removed, and the cordon can be secured directly to the wall.

4   As the plant grows upward, prune back any new side shoots, as well as old ones, encouraging the development of short, compact growth along the central stem.

Diagonal Cordon Variation

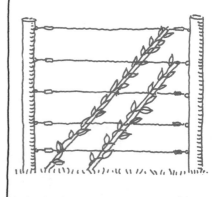

This is a simple variation on the vertical cordon. But because the branches are trained at an angle, growth is slower than vertical cordons, and more energy is channeled into fruiting. If alternate plants are angled in the opposite direction, a latticework effect will be obtained. Sink stakes on a 45-degree angle and secure them to a wall. Plant whips in front of the stakes at the same angle. If the plants are grafted, place the knob of the graft union on top. As the plant grows, prune back any new side shoots, as well as old ones, encouraging the development of short, compact growth along the central stem.

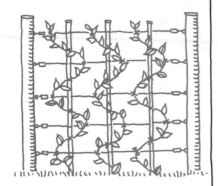

Serpentine Cordon Variation

This is another variation on the vertical cordon, but the leader is trained in an undulating fashion. When the top is reached, the cordon may be either cut or allowed to grow up and then bent down to form a serpent's head. You will need a network of horizontal wires or wall aids, spaced 16 inches apart, starting 8 inches from the ground, to create this pattern.

Position vertical stakes 2½ feet apart. Mark 6 inches on either side of each stake on the horizontal wires or wall, as well as the halfway mark between the wires along the stakes. Plant whips and tie to stakes. Tie the leader along the vertical stake to the first wire, then gently bend the whip to the left until it forms a curve out to the mark on the second wire. Tie securely to the second wire and curve the whip to the right, crossing and attaching to the stake halfway between the wires. Continue training the cordon in an S fashion until the top wire is reached. Check the tree frequently so you can bend the leader before it becomes too woody. As the plant grows, prune back any new side shoots, as well as old ones, encouraging the development of short, compact growth along the central stem.

Horizontal Cordon

The horizontal cordon is formed from two leaders trained in opposite directions from a central stem. To save a year of training, two whips may be bent in opposite directions if you want to create a single tier. Two or more tiers of cordons may be trained from a single plant, depending on how tall you want the espalier. This pattern looks best with a single tree where you have a wall space at least 8 feet wide, or with several trees as a freestanding fence. If you are making a fence, space trees 8 feet apart; for a more unusual effect, vary the distance between the arms.

1 Make the basic guidelines of rows of wall aids or horizontal wires, spacing them at 16-inch intervals. Sink a stake into the ground a few inches in front of the wall, making sure it is stable. Use wall aids and wire to attach the stake to the wall. This will reinforce it as it supports the weight of the growing plant. For single cordons, you need only one wire or row of wall aids plus a short stake. For double or multiple cordons, construct a horizontal guide for each arm, and use a stake as tall as the top arm.

2 Plant a whip, tie it to the stake and cut the leader 3 to 4 inches below the first horizontal guide.

3 Allow two shoots to form, and tie in opposite directions along the lowest row of wall aids or wire. If multiple arms are desired, retain a third bud to create a central leader.

4 The next spring, nip the leader 3 or 4 inches below the second row of wall aids or wire. Train new shoots as in Step 3. Repeat these steps for multiple arms.

5 When the top level has been reached, retain only side branches to form the final cordon.

6 As horizontal cordons reach the length you prefer, cut off or bend tips downward to encourage the development of side branches. Regularly prune back wayward growth to maintain the design.

Natives of Siberia have devised a way to raise fruit in their harsh climate by growing "creeper trees." Apple trees are planted in rows, and when they reach a height of 3 feet, the branches are bent over and interwined so that a blanket of snow protects them in winter.

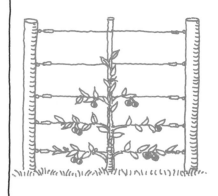

Louis Verrier, head gardener at the Salieu School of Agriculture in France during the 19th century, taught the art of espalier and preached the superiority of the shape that now bears his name.

Palmette Verrier

This is the best known and perhaps most elegant of all espalier designs. Once established, the shape is easily maintained and results in a very balanced tree. It is basically a triple horizontal cordon with the arms turned up in a candelabrum. Modified palmette verrier may be created from double cordons for a four-armed design. This adapted form is better for spaces narrower than 8 feet. You will need seven 8-foot stakes for this design.

1 Make five horizontal guidelines of wall aids or wire, spaced 16 inches apart. Sink one 8-foot stake 2 feet into the ground, a few inches in front of the wall in the center of the horizontal guides. Use wall aids and wire to attach the stake to the wall. This will hold it steady as it supports the weight of the growing plant. Sink six additional stakes 2 feet into the ground: two stakes 8 inches on either side of the central stake; another pair 24 inches from the central stake; and the two outermost stakes at 40 inches from the center.

2 Plant a whip in front of the central stake. Cut 3 to 4 inches below the first horizontal guide.

3 Allow three shoots to form; tie the two outer ones in opposite directions along the lowest guideline, and train the middle shoot to create a central leader.

4 The next spring, nip the leader 3 to 4 inches below the second horizontal guide. Allow three shoots to form: two to form a second pair of horizontal cordons, and the third to continue the vertical leader. Allow the two lower cordons to grow 12 inches beyond the outermost stakes. Bend upward gently and tie so that these branches rest on the inside surface of the outer stakes.

5 During the summer cut the leader off when it is just below the third guide. Select two outside shoots (pruning off any

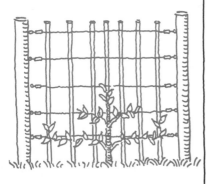

others), and train along the third horizontal guide to form the final tier. Allow the second cordon to grow about 36 inches out from the central stem, and bend upward on the stakes that were placed 24 inches from the central stake.

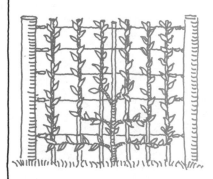

6 The following year, begin training the third cordon up the stakes 8 inches on either side of the center.

7 When the six vertical arms reach the top guide, cut them to retain the candelabrum shape and to stimulate the formation of flowering and fruiting side shoots. After a few years, the stakes may be removed, and the cordons can be secured directly to the wall. To preserve the design and encourage the development of compact growth along the main branches, remove wayward growth and prune side shoots regularly.

Single U-Shape

This simple form is admirably suited to the decoration of narrow areas, and has all the maintenance advantages of a palmette verrier. You will need one 3-foot and two 8-foot stakes for this pattern.

1 Sink the 3-foot stake 1 foot into the ground, a few inches in front of the wall, where you want the center of your design. Sink the 8-foot stakes 2 feet into the ground, 16 inches on either side of the short one, using wall aids and wire to attach the tall stakes to the wall. This will hold them steady as they support the weight of the growing plant. Add a row of wall aids or wire 16 inches above the ground, extending between the outermost stakes.

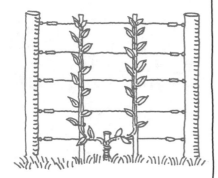

2 Plant a whip at the center stake and prune 3 to 4 inches below the horizontal guide.

3 Select the two strongest shoots, one on each side of the trunk, and train in opposite directions, tying along the wall guides or horizontal wire.

4 The next year, allow the two cordons to grow 12 inches beyond the outer stakes (28 inches out from the trunk). Bend upward along the inside surface of the outer stakes and fasten securely.

5 Continue vertical growth to desired height, and cut off. After a few years, the stakes may be removed, and the cordons can be secured directly to the wall. Periodically remove wayward growth and prune back side shoots. This will preserve the design and encourage the development of compact growth along the main branches.

Palmette Oblique

This is essentially a four-tiered horizontal cordon, in which the pairs of arms have been bent at 45-degree rather than 90-degree angles from the trunk. You need a space at least 8 feet wide for this shape, and one 8-foot stake.

1 Sink the 8-foot stake 2 feet into the ground, a few inches in front of the wall in the center of the space. Use wall aids and wire to secure the stake to the wall. This will hold it steady as it supports the weight of the growing tree.

2 Attach eight guidelines of wire or wall aids to the wall at a 45-degree angle, starting at the center stake and extending up and out on either side, following these measurements: at a point 16 inches high on the stake, attach two diagonal guides 5½ feet long to points 5 feet 1 inch up on the wall; at 32 inches high on the stake, attach a pair of guides 5½ feet long to points 6 feet 5 inches up the wall; for the third set of arms, at 48 inches high on the stake, attach two diagonal guides 3 feet 10 inches long to points 6 feet 8 inches up on the wall; for the uppermost diagonals, at a point 5 feet 4 inches high on the stake, attach guides 1 foot 10 inches in length to points 6 feet 8 inches up on the wall.

3 Plant the whip and snip it off just below the first pair of diagonal guides. Keep the three strongest shoots and cut off all others. Train the outer two along the lowest pair of diagonals, and use the center shoot to form the vertical leader.

4 The following summer prune the vertical leader just below the second pair of diagonal guides. Train the three best shoots as in Step 3 to form the second pair of arms.

5 Repeat Step 4 the following year to obtain the third pair of diagonal arms.

6 Cut the leader off below the fourth set of guides, saving only a pair of strong shoots to form the final angled arms. Cut off all diagonals when they reach the end of their respective guides. Once a sturdy trunk develops, the stake may be removed, and the trunk can be secured directly to the wall. Regularly remove wayward growth and prune back side shoots in order to preserve the design and encourage the development of compact growth along the main branches.

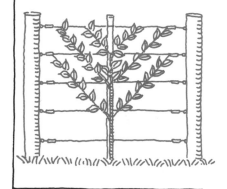

> **❝For the placing of your trees in this Orchard, first for the wals: Those sides that lye open to the South & Southwest Sunne, are fittest to bee planted with your tenderest and earliest fruits, as Apricockes, Peaches, Nectarius, and May or early Cherries: the East, North and West, for Plums and Quinces, as you shall like best to place them.❞**
>
> —JOHN PARKINSON
> *Paradisi in Sole,*
> *Paradisus Terrestris,*
> 1629

Belgian Fence

Multiple plants are needed to establish this pattern. Each tree is trained into a Y so that its arms cross those of its neighbor at a 45-degree angle, creating a lattice effect. Five or more trees are recommended, planted 2 feet apart, but the more trees you use, the more effective it will be. You might train a Belgian fence to camouflage an unattractive wall surface or to make a stunning freestanding screen. The most attractive support for a freestanding Belgian fence would be a wooden trellis or a wire network constructed so that the framework exactly follows the lines of the oblique branches. For each tree in the pattern, you will need a 3-foot stake. The following directions are for five trees.

1 Sink five 3-foot stakes 1 foot into the ground, at 2-foot intervals and several inches in front of the wall or freestanding framework. Attach two guidelines of wire or wall aids to the wall at a 45-degree angle, starting at the top of the center stake and extending up and out on either side to a height of 7 feet. Repeat with the two stakes on either side of the center one. On the outermost stakes, construct one guide to angle in at a 45-degree angle to the height of 7 feet, and the second to continue vertically, in order to establish the edge of the pattern. The guides will cross each other to form a diamond.

2 Plant five whips, one in front of each stake. Top off each tree just below the top of the stake and tie securely.

3 Keep two buds on each tree, removing all others. For the center three trees: develop a pair of buds into shoots extending along the diagonal supports. For the end trees: train the inner shoot along a diagonal, but grow the outer branch as a vertical cordon along the upright guide to form the pattern edge. To fill in the pattern, side shoots of the two end trees can be trained to angle in at 3 feet 4½ inches high and 5 feet 4½ inches high along the vertical cordons.

4 Once the ultimate height is reached, main branches may be either cut off or bent and trained horizontally along the top of the design. Once a sturdy trunk develops, the stake may be removed, and the trunk can be secured directly to the wall or wire framework. Regularly prune back side shoots to preserve the design.

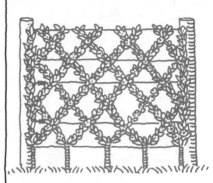

Braided Trees

At first glance, this resembles a horizontal cordon. Closer inspection shows it to be a more fanciful confection of two trees plaited together. When interlacing the two stems, feel free to vary the space between them. A more open weave will remain dramatic even after the branches have thickened. The pattern of a tight braid will be lost with time as the branches knit together. For this design, look for a pair of young, pliable specimens to facilitate training. The length of the horizontal cordons can be extended to whatever length you desire, or each successive tier may be shortened for a triangular outline. A row of braided trees is an impressive freestanding fence. For each braided pair, you will need two 3-foot stakes, one 8-foot stake and waterproof adhesive tape or a waterproof marking pen.

1 Use wall aids or wire to make five horizontal guides 16 inches apart. Sink the central 8-foot stake 2 feet into the ground and a few inches in front of the wall, using wall aids and wire to secure the stake to the wall. This will hold it steady as it supports the weight of the growing tree. For initial support of the trunks, add two 3-foot stakes, 16 inches high, placed 6 inches on either side of the taller stake. Mark the halfway point between the guides on the center stake. This is where

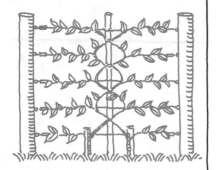

the leaders will cross. Mark 6 inches out from the center stake along each horizontal guide. These will be the widest points of the braid.

2 Plant one whip in front of each short stake and tie securely. Bend each of them gradually down along the lowest horizontal guide in opposite directions. Permit one vertical side shoot to develop at the top of the bend on each tree. Remove all others.

3 Later in the summer, cross the new stems at the first mark on the center stake. Tie together and to the stake loosely but securely.

4 When leaders reach the second guide, tie them at the marks on the center stake. Once again, gradually bend them down and train horizontally along the second guide wire to form another tier of cordons. Allow a shoot to form at the top of each bend and remove all others.

5 Repeat Steps 3 and 4 until the fifth guide is reached. At this level train the leaders along the top to finish the pattern. Once sturdy trunks develop, the stake may be removed, and the trunks can be secured directly to the wall. Regularly prune back wayward growth to preserve the design.

Fan

This is not so rigidly formal as the other classic designs; it results in a graceful wall decoration, allowing you to work with the natural curves of the branches. This shape is very successful with stone fruits as well as many ornamental trees and shrubs, which aren't as easy to bend as apple and pear. This particular fan requires a space 8 feet wide, but you can alter the design to suit the width you desire. In addition to wall aids or wire, you will need a 4-foot stake, a piece of string about 5 feet long, and waterproof adhesive tape or a waterproof marking pen.

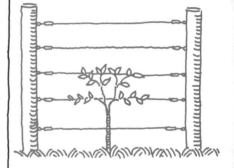

1 Use wall aids or wire to center a horizontal guide 8 feet long and 32 inches off the ground. Sink the 4-foot stake 1 foot into the ground in the center of the horizontal guide a few inches in front of the wall. Use wall aids or wire to secure the stake to the wall and to hold it steady as it supports the weight of the growing tree.

2 Tie the piece of string to the top of the stake and cut it so it is exactly 4 feet long. Move it in an arc from one side of the horizontal guide to the other, marking the outline of the fan with the pen.

3 Plant the tree and tie it to the central stake. Cut it off a few inches below the guide, just above four closely spaced buds. Allow them to develop into lateral branches.

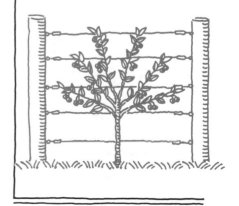

4 The following winter, prune each of the four side branches back to two buds. Allow these to develop into lateral branches. Train the outermost two in opposite directions as horizontal cordons along the horizontal guide. Train the remaining six laterals at regular intervals to describe the ribs of the fan; add wall aids as neccessary to guide the branches in a graceful manner toward the outline marks.

<u>5</u> Cut the horizontal branches and six ribs when they reach the outline marks on the wall. Once a sturdy trunk develops, the stake may be removed, and the trunk can be secured directly to the wall. Periodically remove wayward growth and prune back side shoots. This will maintain the design and encourage compact growth along the outer branches.

MURAL MAINTENANCE

To keep an espalier impressive, be patient yet attentive to its needs. Half the fun is participating in its maturation, enjoying and influencing it at all stages of development. Most patterns take a few years to establish, but from planting time on they are striking accents. Inspect your handiwork regularly, removing any vegetative buds or shoots that protrude straight out from the two-dimensional plane. These spoil the effect and rob vigor from the framework of your design. Check the ties frequently for constriction around branches and stems; this can girdle and strangle the tree by cutting off the flow of water and nutrients. If a branch dies from disease or girdling, you can rescue your pattern by grafting on a new one.

When espaliers are young, they benefit from special attention. Protect them from the intense summer heat produced by background surfaces by shading with annual vines such as morning glory or thunbergia. Once established, the flattened tree's own foliage will be thick enough to shade it. The same wall or fence that scorches in hot weather can cause freeze-thaw cycles during cold periods. Place neatly bundled straw between the tree and the wall to prevent winter damage. If gnawing rodents are a problem in your area, treat espalier as you would any young specimens and wrap the trunks with plastic guards.

PRUNING FOR FLOWERS, FRUIT AND BERRIES

T o have an espalier clothed with blossoms and pendant with fruit, you must understand the habits of the plant you have chosen. Some trees flower on the branches they produced the previous year, while others bloom on the growth of the current season. For instance, pyracantha bears its berries only on branches that are a year old or more, while American holly forms berries on new growth.

Cherries, plums, and most varieties of apples and pears bear fruit on specialized structures known as spurs. These are short twigs with a gnarled appearance that live for many years, elongating slowly. They should be removed when they peter out and produce smaller, inferior fruits. Nectarines, peaches and a few apples and pears bear only on the previous year's growth; no branch produces fruit two years running. Always cut back these fruits to encourage two new shoots—one for fruit, and the other to start off the next year's harvest. Apricots bear both ways. Part of the crop is on short-lived spurs that bear for about three years, while the rest grows along the previous year's branches.

Although it's hard to pull off cute little baby fruits, thinning them assures that the ones left to mature will be of superior size and quality, and that the tree will have the energy to produce a crop the following season. Few people realize how much effort a tree expends to produce fruit—for example, one apple is fed by the energy of 50 leaves. The fewer the fruits on a peach family tree, the greater the flesh-to-pit ratio. Space between young fruit should be as follows: apples and pears, 6 to 8 inches; peaches and nectarines, 4 to 5 inches; large plums and apricots, 3 to 4 inches. Small plums, cherries, quinces and nuts need no thinning.

The ancient gardener shook his head:
"You dasn't hurry 'em, he said.
"Unless you lets 'em take their time,
You'll never see 'em in their prime. . . .

—REGINALD ARKELL
from the poem "In God's Good Time"

*Always untouch'd
the chiefest
Branches save,
From whom you
hope a future
Race to have.
Now if the Season
proves reciprocal
You may behold
your Fruit upon
the Wall
Your Gardens
Riches then will
make you
glad. . . .*

—PERE RAPIN
from *Librus IV*

INDOOR ESPALIER

Perhaps you long to grow tropical fruits such as citrus or pomegranate (*Punica granatum*), or other tender plants such as hibiscus (*Hibiscus rosa-sinensis*) or rosemary (*Rosmarinus officinalis*), but you don't live in a cooperative climate. Satisfy your craving by growing portable espaliers in containers. Try a graceful palmette verrier kumquat (*Fortunella margarita*), which produces tiny, orange-like, edible fruits. You can summer them outdoors, sinking the pots into the garden to use the plants as seasonal accents.

Windowsill-size espalier may be devised with herbs and houseplants. Orange mint (*Mentha aquatica* 'Citrata') is especially good for hoops, as it is fast growing but short lived.

Frames for potted espalier may be purchased or constructed. Interesting shapes can be improvised from ready-to-use objects, including peony hoops, wreath frames and antique rug beaters.

If you have a simple shape in mind, you can train and support the plant with wooden stakes inserted into the soil or attached to the outside of the pot. Another alternative is to lash twigs together with raffia or twine for a rustic Adirondack look. Any small plant can be trained into a classic shape on a support made from ¼-inch wire mesh, or hardware cloth. Use a permanent marker to draw the espalier shape on a rectangle of mesh. Using wire cutters, remove a line three squares wide where the branches will be. Cut two vertical slits in the bottom of the mesh so that it fits over the rim of the pot. Tie the plant to the wires with raffia or soft string. Periodically turn the pot 180 degrees so that foliage develops on both sides of the design. Rosemary (*Rosmarinus officinalis*), myrtle (*Myrtus communis*), Jerusalem cherry (*Solanum pseudocapsicum*) and mistletoe fig (*Ficus deltoidea*) are good varieties to train in this manner.

Knot Gardens

Twined Between the Old and the New

Plant designs that carpet the ground are often referred to as knot gardens. These are composed of low, level beds and ornamented with a pattern of intertwining lines made of dwarf hedges or clipped herbs. They give your garden a formal layout, partitioning the area into various sections where you can experiment with different plants and color schemes. Knot gardens, like rugs, range from simple to elaborate, and may be of any size.

Unlike other outdoor topiary forms, plants quickly grow to a suitable height, so the beauty of the design is immediately appreciable. And if you use evergreens, the surface of the garden will be interesting year-round. While the patterns look difficult to maintain, once planted they provide maximum ornamentation with a minimum of care.

Decorations on the ground aren't limited to knot patterns. With flat topiary you can use plants to illustrate anything that captures your fancy. Spell out a message or draw an animal; outline the shape in clipped evergreens or fill it in with a solid mass of plants. Use these horizontal designs to transform the entire space, or to accent a particular spot. If you've grown tired of the usual lawn ringed by boring flowerbeds or shrub borders, why not enliven your property with a knot garden or other form of flat topiary?

KNOT GARDENS

Knot gardens evolved from medieval kitchen gardens, where separate beds contained medicinal and cooking herbs to prevent confusion. They traditionally consisted of four square compartments within a larger square, with different patterns inside each compartment. In the 16th century, knot motifs became enormously popular for woodcarving, plasterwork and stained glass, as well as garden patterns. Virtually every English gardening book of the time included designs for

The first designs for garden knots appeared in 1499, in Venetian monk Francesco Colonna's book The Strife of Love in a Dream. *Influenced by detailed Venetian lacework, he designed intricate herbal schemes. Colonna gave astrological significance to geometric shapes; the square represented earth and its elements, while the circle stood for the heavens.*

The Duke of Buckingham paid his gardener three shillings and four pence in 1520 "for diligence in making knottes in the Duke's garden."

66And the plainer Parterres are, the more Grandeur, for when they are fluff'd up with so many Small Ornaments, they break the Rays of Sight, and the whole appears a Confusion.99

—BATTY LANGLEY
New Principles of Gardening, 1728

Today's town house gardens can take a clue from orderly and efficient medieval kitchen gardens. Ornamental plants, herbs, fruits and vegetables are neatly combined in trim geometric arrangements.

garden knots, just as today's magazine racks are crammed with pattern books for needlework projects. Perhaps the interlocking designs offered a feeling of security that was especially valued in these first gardens to venture outside castle walls or monastery cloisters after years of siege. The Elizabethan love of puzzles also inspired maze designs. But since the plants used were kept at a height of a foot or two, they were intended purely to delight the eye—rather than to confuse the feet, as did the full-height mazes of later times.

Some designs were practical, with each ribbon about 18 inches wide at the base and the tops clipped absolutely level to provide an outdoor table for drying linens. Purely ornamental arrangements were placed so they could be appreciated from the upper story windows of the privy rooms that were the owner's private quarters.

To give these plans a third dimension, the corners or center of each knot might be ornamentally dotted with topiary cones or globes. Often, the intimacy was increased by a surrounding hedge or wall. Espaliered fruit trees were frequently trained up the inside of the walls, treasured as much for their spring flowers as for their fruit.

Originally, the lines were formed with several kinds of herbs trimmed into dwarf hedges, whose contrasting gray and green tones made it easy to trace the different threads in the design. At the end of the 16th century boxwood, often referred to simply as box, became the favorite material for knots with the development by the Dutch of a dwarf or edging variety. Boxwood is a dependable dark green regardless of the season, and sparkles against a blanket of snow. This slow-growing material remains the most popular plant for knots.

In early gardens the patterns contained inner beds for herbs, vegetables or flowers. Later on, when gardens became purely ornamental, the hedges themselves became the design focus and the spaces between them were filled with earth, sand, brick or coal dust to enhance the pattern. This style is easy to maintain and looks attractive all year round, making it a wonderful idea for a low-maintenance garden.

Gradually, the intricate interweavings were replaced by new designs incorporating fluid arabesques, open scrolls and fleurs-de-lis, called parterres. The name derives from the French *par terre*, meaning "on the ground." At the end of the 16th and start of the 17th centuries, the French enlarged the formal part of the garden, from a small area surrounding the house to an expansive panorama covered in interesting patterns of clipped boxwood, flowers, grass and stone that imitated embroidery. Although it is unlikely that you will want to reproduce parterres on their original scale, there is no reason not to adapt the grace-

PARTERRES

By the early 1700s, three distinct types of parterres evolved:

PARTERRES DE BRODERIE
Boxwood edgings and colored earth imitating embroidery

PARTERRES À L'ANGLAISE
Turf cut into patterns and edged in clipped boxwood

PARTERRES OF CUT WORK
Boxwood outlines filled with flowering plants

ful French curves to a smaller scheme of clipped evergreens, gravel and flowers that fits into your own garden.

FLAT TOPIARY

While Elizabethan books referred to all low patterns of clipped herbs and boxwood as knots, many designs were pictures rather than geometric patterns. Traditional subjects included names, dates, animals and coats of arms. You can choose an emblem of your own hobby or special interest, and depict it in neatly trimmed plants. For example, if you play cards, clip the four suits. If fishing is your line, put a leaping trout or a flat flounder in your garden. If you are an animal lover, try cats, horses or your favorite dog. An eagle or the Liberty Bell is appropriate if your house is Early American. As a symbol of welcome you could plant a cricket or pineapple. The only limit is your imagination, for any emblem that appeals to you can be depicted in flat topiary.

In the first century A.D., Pliny the Younger proudly displayed low hedges that spelled out his name as well as that of the gardener. You have probably seen examples of topiary spelling, since many towns and corporations display their names and initials in clipped mini-hedges. Why not monogram your own property?

Sundial faces were favored subjects for flat topiary. The gnomons, or hands, of sundials were made of a small tree, upright piece of topiary or carved piece of wood, which cast a time-telling shadow on the flat topiary numerals. The Edwardians were fond of topiary sundials—a 19th-century example can be seen at Ascott, the English former estate of Leopold de Rothschild. At the turn of the century Lady Warwick wrote proudly of hers, "Never was such a perfect timekeeper as my sundial, and the figures which record the hours are all cut out and trimmed in box."

In 1617, William Lawson published The Country House-Wife's Garden, *encouraging women to create attractive and functional gardens. He included plans for nine "choice, new forms" of knots, but urged them to concoct their own patterns since, "for special forms in squares, there are as many, as there are devices in Gardeners brains."*

As for the making of knots . . . they be but toys: you may see as good sights many times in tarts.

—SIR FRANCIS BACON
Of Gardens, 1625

All kinds of images can be incorporated into a sundial pattern. Many sundial faces are encircled by the signs of the zodiac, but you could personalize yours with your favorite things. Instead of numerals, use a sun face with 12 rays or a radiating circle of fish or dachshunds.

As shown in this view of a 17th-century garden, a series of elaborate beds dresses up a flat stretch of ground, while multi-tiered poodles provide contrast.

Wyth flora paynted and wrought curyously
In divers knottes of marvaylous gretenes
Rampande lyons stode up wonderfly,
Made of all herbes with dulcet sweetenes,
Wyth many dragons of marvaylos likenes,
Of dyvers flowres made ful craftely,
By Flora coloured with colours sundry.

—STEPHEN HAWES
from "The Pastime of Pleasure," 1554

VICTORIAN REVIVAL

T he Victorians developed elaborate ideas and simple techniques for flat topiary that have been sadly overlooked. The most unique style was carpet bedding, in which patterns were formed of annual flowers, succulents, coleus and other plants with gaily colored foliage, instead of herbs or boxwood.

If you are one of the people caught up in a new love for Victorian furnishings and houses, it's fun and easy to carry the style out to the garden. In the 19th century, virtually every path of suburban lawn and public park was transformed into carpet bedding: mosaics of paisleys, ovals, circles and stars were cut out of the turf and filled with tender annual bedding plants. Garden authors fed the fashion for carpet bedding as eagerly as the Tudors had the passion for knots, with a wealth of patterns that were inspired by old parterre arrangements or current fabric and wallpaper designs. One ingenious and popular idea was to create working clocks, where mechanical hands swept over a face of flowers.

Annual plants are still popular for bedding today, bought anew each spring and ready to be set out in the garden. Instead of planting them hodgepodge, let your imagination follow the Victorians, and set them out in a glittering picture inspired by old illustrations or in a configuration of your own invention.

CREATING A KNOT

K nots, flat topiary and carpet bedding are perfectly suited to today's smaller gardens and more casual lifestyles. Filled with gravel or crushed stone instead of bedding plants, a knot will require minimal care. And if you use slow-growing plants for the lines, the task of clipping will be limited to once annually.

The first step is to choose a location. Unless you are doing a design in shade-tolerant annuals such as coleus, select a sunny location. Otherwise plants grow sparse and leggy, spoiling the pattern. You don't really need a lot of space. The early Tudor knot gardens were a cozy 10- to 12-feet-square, and this is a useful size in many contemporary situations. Traditional patterns are also easily adapted to fit any site. The late California landscape architect Thomas Church used knot and parterre elements to add excitement to tiny gardens and divide larger ones into areas for entertainment. Try cultivating a slender strip of elegant parterre around your patio or alongside a path. A small, wedge-shaped bed is a charming way to soften corners and add decoration to your garden without sacrificing living space.

Even where outdoor space is at a premium, there are many places to tuck in little flourishes. Knots look well in the enclosed areas of condominium entries, backyards and courtyards. Use different colored flowers each year for a change of scene. Place knots and flat topiary just outside a picture or bay window, so they may be enjoyed from indoors. For the best effect in a small space, choose a simple design.

If you have more space, you can experiment freely with ground decorations. Place them on a hill or at the base of a slope for better viewing. An herbal knot outside your kitchen door is a handy and beautiful addition to any property. Flank a swimming pool with patterned borders, so you have something interesting to gaze at while you sunbathe. If you pick a clock or sundial, you will be able to relax outdoors and still keep track of time.

Many vegetables have a tidy, compact habit and interesting foliage that makes them decorative as well as useful. If you arrange them in a knot pattern, you'll have a vegetable patch you don't have to hide. One square could be filled with leaf vegetables, contrasting dark green spinach with light green and red lettuces. In another, feature root vegetables: burgundy-veined beet greens and feathery radish, carrot and parsnip tops make a pretty combination.

CARPET BEDDING

Many new flowering plants were introduced to Europe and the United States after 1834, when a special case for shipping plants was invented, and parterres became favorite places for displaying the tantalizing flood of exotic arrivals.

"In carpet bedding, plants of all the same height were planted in very intricate designs. Some resemble mosaics, others the webbing on a butterfly's wing, and one's imagination could really run wild."

—RUDY FAVRETTI
For Every Home a Garden, 1977

American colonists brought with them the custom of knot gardens, perhaps as a reassuring symbol of civilized order between the house and the untamed wilderness that surrounded their settlements. Thomas Jefferson grew up with a splendid acre-size knot of ovals and concentric circles at his father's Tuckahoe plantation. The boxwood hedging that makes up the knot would extend for one and a half miles if laid out in a straight line.

Flat topiary is the perfect way to make a plain lawn into a personal statement. Your initials or the likeness of a family pet serves proud notice to passersby, while traditional motifs can accent the style of your house.

Inspiring modern examples based on early knot designs can be seen at the Brooklyn Botanic Garden in New York City, the National Herb Garden in Washington, D.C., Filoli near San Francisco, and the Denver Botanic Garden. Gardening writer Rosemary Verey has recreated a 17-century design at Barnsley House, her English home and garden showplace.

Colonial Williamsburg in Virginia and Tryon Palace in New Bern, North Carolina, have several separate gardens devoted to parterres. A more whimsical combination, incorporating topiary sculptures, can be seen at Ladew Topiary Gardens in Monkton,

Maryland, or at Green Animals in Portsmouth, Rhode Island, where elephants, camels and giraffes wander among flower-filled patterns.

Some examples of carpet bedding are on view for inspiration at the Smithsonian Institution in Washington, D.C., Sonnenberg Gardens in Canandaigua, New York, and at Disney World in Lake Buena Vista, Florida, but Europe seems to have more affection for Victorian gardens. Many cities have colorful mottoes, and there is a superb flower clock in Geneva, Switzerland.

BOXWOOD

Boxwood (*Buxus sempervirens*) is unsurpassed for clipping into velvety edgings and designs. Its magnificent bright green appearance is different from any other evergreen. Although grown mostly in the Middle Atlantic states and southern New England, boxwood will grow in other regions, so check with a local nursery to see if it will succeed in your area. In some southern states it can't withstand extreme summer heat and dryness; dwarf yaupon (*Ilex vomitoria* 'Nana'), a native drought-tolerant holly that resembles boxwood, is used as a beautiful substitute.

One complaint is that, slow growing as it is, boxwood inevitably outgrows the pattern in width and height. This can be prevented by planting dwarf varieties. These forms grow slowly and can be easily kept at a height ranging from 6 to 36 inches. The original dwarf or Dutch edging box (*Buxus sempervirens* 'Suffruticosa') won't always survive winters north of Zone 6, but there are new varieties such as Vardar Valley (*Buxus sempervirens* 'Vardar Valley'), Korean boxwood (*Buxus microphylla* 'Koreana') and Kingsville Dwarf (*Buxus microphylla* 'Compacta') that are equally slow-growing and hardier.

Dwarf box grows at a rate of 1 to 4 inches a year, so it can be kept at the desired height with just an annual clipping. This

In the 17th century, the poet René Rapin wove a charming tale about the origin of boxwood in the garden. He wrote that the goddess Flora's hair hung in disarray until a nymph took pity on her, arranging her tresses and securing them with a wreath of boxwood. Her beauty was so transformed that boxwood has been used ever since to trimly edge beds "where flowers disordered once at random grew."

> **66***They walked over the crackling leaves in the garden, between the lines of Box, breathing its fragrance of eternity; for this is one of the odors which carry us out of time into the abysses of the unbeginning past; if we ever lived on another ball of stone than this, it must be that there was Box growing on it.***99**
>
> —ELSIE VENNER
> *Oliver Wendell Holmes,*
> 1861

is best done in the spring before hot, dry weather sets in, so the new growth has a chance to harden before the first frost. Some authorities recommend clipping just after a rainfall to help prevent discoloration of the leaves.

The roots of boxwood are notorious for robbing the surrounding soil of moisture and nutrients. If your design is purely of boxwood and gravel, this isn't a problem. However, if you decide to fill in the pattern with flowers, be aware that their root systems are no competition for greedy box. In order to produce a successful show of blossoms, sever the boxwood's roots on the inner edge of beds with a sharp spade.

A knot or parterre comprised solely of boxwood and grass or gravel is a restful study in shades of green, but perhaps you would prefer to look at a more varied four-season display. There are variegated types of edging box to add a touch of yellow and white to the picture, or you can combine green boxwood with the many tones of different herbs. Boxwood plants are expensive, but it is possible to start your design without spending a lot of money. If you can find someone with established plants who will allow you to take some cuttings, they can be easily rooted in your own garden. Cut branches 8 to 12 inches long, and remove all side branches and leaves except for three or four twigs at the top. Bury the cuttings in your garden, all the way up to just below the tuft of leaves. Once the branches have sent out new rootlets, the top will grow into a nice beginning for your design.

Boxwood has been used since ancient times for clipping into shapes, and by Pliny's time it was a garden plant of long standing. He writes that it was traditionally watered with wine. Stories are told about the boxwood's ability to conjure up visions of the past, evoked by its pungent, bitter odor. Many people recall its perfume with affection; some can detect only a faint aroma, no stronger than that of a freshly mown lawn; while others never even notice the smell. Soon after taking the throne, Queen Anne, disgusted by the smell of boxwood, ordered that many of her predecessor's hedges and topiaries at Hampton Court be cut down.

HERBS

Herbs are wonderful in knot gardens. The contrasting tones and textures of their different foliage make each ribbon in the design delightfully easy to trace. Elizabethans were fond of sweet-smelling herbs for knots, because the clippings could be used for cooking, perfumery or strewing on the floors inside. Most herbs require little upkeep—for a trim appearance, they should be lightly sheared every two weeks from the end of May to the end of July. Established plants that have reached the desired dimensions should be pruned back in March or April.

Thyme, santolina, lavender, rosemary and hyssop are aromatic herbs used in knot patterns since the 15th century. Common thyme (*Thymus vulgaris*) is available in a bewildering assortment of gold, silver and lemon-scented varieties; be sure to pick an upright rather than a spreading type to include in your pattern. Winter savory (*Satureja montana*) resembles thyme in appearance and flavor. It has shiny, pointed leaves, lavender flowers, and is useful for cooking.

Santolina (*Santolina chamaecyparissus*) is also called lavender cotton; by any name, its delicate, aromatic gray foliage is distinctive for clipping into smoky lines or filling in beds.

Lavender (*Lavandula angustifolia angustifolia*) is well loved, both for its aromatic foliage and its spikes of flowers used for perfumes and potpourri. The name derives from the Latin *lavare*, "to wash," because its flowers were used to perfume washwater. Lavender symbolizes purity and is said to derive its odors from the Holy Infant's clothes. Munstead Dwarf (*Lavandula angustifolia* 'Munstead') is a smaller, more compact grower. In order to enjoy lavender's blooms, refrain from clipping until it finishes flowering in June or July. You could plant a colorful knot purely of lavender by combining the common blue-flowering plant with varieties such as white 'Jean Davis' and deep purple 'Munstead' or 'Hidcote.'

> **❝ . . . scores of unmeaning flowerbeds, disfiguring the lawn in shapes of kidneys, and tadpoles and sausages, and leeches, and commas. ❞**
>
> —T. JAMES, architect, protesting the excess of fancy bedding in 1839

A garden sweet, enclosed with walles strong, Embanked with benches to sytt and take my rest; The knotts so enknotted, it cannot be exprest, With arbors and ayles so pleasant and so dulce, The pestylent ayers with flavors to repulse.

—GEORGE CAVENDISH
1557

Hyssop (*Hyssopus officinalis*) is frequently recommended by Elizabethan garden authors. Unlike most herbs, it will grow in partial shade. In addition to the usual lavender-like purple flowers against narrow dark green foliage, hyssop can show white or pink blooms. The bitter leaves can be used as a flavoring for strong-tasting fish or game.

Rosemary responds well to clipping, forming a dense, low hedge of dark green needle-like leaves. Sprigs are wonderful in potpourri and invaluable in cooking lamb. Sadly, rosemary doesn't do well wherever winter temperatures fall way below freezing.

A graceful scroll becomes striking when repeated in a pattern to fill a large area of your garden, creating a sense of grandeur. A single scroll can be tucked into a corner of the yard for a more subtle accent.

A few herbal members of the artemisia family have silvery, aromatic leaves and compact growth. Wormwood (*Artemisia absinthium*) is best known for its use as an ingredient in the infamous liqueur absinthe. Roman wormwood (*Artemisia pontica*), and southernwood or old man (*Artemisia abrotanum*) can't claim such heady uses, but the finely divided, pungent-smelling leaves are pleasing. Dwarf sage (*Salvia officinalis* 'Compacta') is another aromatic gray-green plant with a tidy habit.

Rue (*Ruta graveolens*), also called Herb of Grace, has distinctive blue leaves that contrast well with other herbs. It naturally maintains a mounded shape about 2 feet tall. Some people are sensitive to the leaves and develop blisters from contact with the plant in hot sun, so you might want to test a leaf on a patch of skin before adding rue to your garden.

Germander (*Teucrium chamaedrys*) is an antique herb, lacking in fragrance but exceptionally neat, that can be kept at a height of 6 to 12 inches. Thrift (*Armeria maritima*) is another traditional plant you might include in your knot. This herb is valued for its tidy upright growth and showy pink flowers.

> **❝Germander is hot and dry and excellent against the Kings-evill, Obstructions of the Spleene and hardnesse of urine. It is an harde hearbe and will prosper in any ground. . . . It is most comely for the setting forth of knots in Gardens.❞**
>
> —GERVASE MARKHAM
> *The Whole Art of Husbandrie,* 1631

DWARF SHRUBS

Today, many dwarf evergreen shrubs are available that were unknown to earlier gardeners. These can be planted instead of—or in combination with—herbs and boxwood for a colorful year-round display.

Candytuft (*Iberis sempervirens*) is easily maintained as a low edging. It is covered in spring with white flowers; shear back after flowering, so plants keep a neat dark green appearance all season. Sometimes bloom is repeated in the fall.

Heller's Japanese holly (*Ilex crenata* 'Helleri') is an excellent substitute for boxwood, especially in cities, where it thrives despite soot and air pollution. It will tolerate some shade. The

> **A parterre is the first thing that should present itself to sight. . . . The sides of a parterre should be furnished with such works as may improve it and set it off; for this being low, and flat, necessarily requires something raised, as groves and hedges.**
>
> —DEZALLIER D'ARGENVILLE
> *The Theory and Practice of Gardening,* 1712

small, rounded shiny leaves glow in the sun, and stand out against a background of snow when other plants have lost their summer luster. It is appropriate to use where the pattern will be 1 to 2 feet high.

Crimson Pygmy Japanese barberry (*Berberis thunbergii* 'Crimson Pygmy') is always clothed in small red leaves that bring a striking contrast to any design. Barberry is good for low designs, since it can be kept as short as 6 inches in height. Its sharp thorns deter cats or dogs from uprooting your plantings.

Any small-leaved variety of wintercreeper (*Euonymus fortunei*) could be included in a knot or parterre, although if you use it for ribbons, rather than for filling in, it will need frequent trimming. Many varieties have gold-and-green or white-and-green foliage.

Arborvitae (*Thuja occidentalis*) is well known as a large bush or tree, but dwarf varieties like 'Tiny Tim' and 'Hetz Midget' are perfect for pygmy hedges.

ANNUAL HERBS AND BEDDING PLANTS

There are several reasons for planting a knot or parterre with annuals. If you are contemplating a pattern, try it out for one season before you invest in costly perennial herbs or shrubs. Maybe you have only a tiny space for gardening and want to enjoy something different every year. Whatever the reason, patterns set out in annuals are an inexpensive and fast way to add style. Annual herbs will give your knot a traditional look, as well as provide useful sprigs. Shear annual herbs and flowers with grass trimmers several times during the summer to keep them low and compact.

Fresh parsley (*Petroselinum crispum*) is always welcome in the kitchen, and you can create interesting textures in your pattern with the gay curly leaved or flat Italian varieties.

Chives (*Allium schoenoprasum*) are really hardy perennials, but fast-growing and affordable enough to be grown as annuals. Their spiky leaves are distinctive in any design. Thin and harvest them by removing the whole blade at the base of the plant. Puffy flowers add to the show in midsummer. Garlic chives (*Allium tuberosum*) are close cousins, with wider blades, white flowers and a subtle garlic flavor.

Little-leaved or dwarf basil (*Ocimum basilicum* 'Minimum') must be clipped often to maintain it as a rounded hedge 1 foot tall, but the tasty trimmings are unlikely to be wasted. A few varieties are care free, naturally keeping a low, mounded shape. Look for 'Green Globe' or bronze-tinged 'Ball Basil.'

Flowers add brilliant color to permanent knots and parterres, and can be used alone to create shimmering Victorian carpet bedding schemes. In either case, select compact, low-growing, and free-flowering types. Sweet alyssum, marigolds, ageratum, red salvia, geraniums and lobelia were 19th-century favorites, and are good choices for sunny locations. In shadier spots, try impatiens and vinca.

Colorful foliage plants are an authentic part of carpet bedding; their reds, greens, pinks and purples make any design resemble a jewel-toned mosaic. Coleus comes in a rainbow of colors that brighten dark, shady spots. Bloodleaf (*Iresine herbstii*), Joseph's coat (*Alternanthera* in variety) and succulents come in many shades—browse through a seed catalog to familiarize yourself with the wide selection.

LAYING OUT THE PATTERN

Since the plants are closely spaced within the patterns, competing for nutrients and water, they need optimum conditions to thrive. Before you lay out the design, it is well worth the effort to prepare the entire bed thoroughly. Re-

> **❝An old Jersey farmer and his wife . . . who, happening to be driving [on the grounds of a Mr. Hoey, who was noted for his carpet bedding] one day when a shower came up, drove up to Mr. Hoey's residence and told the servants to get in the carpets, as they were getting ruined by the rain!❞**
>
> —PETER HENDERSON
> *Gardening for Pleasure,*
> 1907

> **❝Of all the best Ornaments used in our English gardens, Knots and Mazes are the most ancient.❞**
>
> —GERVASE MARKHAM
> *The Countrey Farme,*
> 1616

move turf, stones and weeds, and loosen the soil with a fork or spade. Incorporate as much peat moss or compost as necessary for a rich, well-drained mixture. In return for this extra initial work, you will have a knot garden with healthier plants and fewer weeds.

Many fancy-looking knot patterns are actually composed of simple squares, circles and semicircles. These are easily laid out in the garden by marking out the four corners and center with string and stakes, and taking all subsequent measurements from these points. Less geometric designs are drawn out first on graph paper. The ground is then divided into an equal number of squares with string and stakes, so each element can be enlarged proportionately. Once the guidelines have been marked out, the design is traced in the garden with ground limestone or white sand.

If you wish to fill in between your plant lines with gravel or crushed stone rather than other plants, lay down sheets of heavy black plastic in these areas before adding the gravel. You can also use heavyweight trash bags. This eliminates the need to weed, and also cuts down on watering as the plastic conserves soil moisture.

PLANTING

Whatever the pattern or size of your design, you will need a lot of plants. Each line is, in effect, a miniature hedge. Plant in a single row along the strings, limestone or sand guidelines. Space the plants closer together than is generally recommended for the particular type of plant, so your design fills in rapidly. If you have selected a knot design, you should plant it so as to create the illusion that the lines intertwine, since one kind of plant can't actually be planted on top of another. Decide which line will appear to go over the others, and plant it as one continuous row, including the intersections. Then plant the remaining lines, leaving out a plant at the points where the lines cross. Whether you use herbs, dwarf shrubs, annual bedding plants or vegetables, they should be trimmed back to encourage compact growth.

Once the row has filled in, trim the lines. They can be either flat topped and straight sided, or rounded; for more contrast, use both silhouettes within the design. The width of each line should be in proportion to the overall size of the design. The height is determined both by the scale of the design and the habit of the individual plant. Boxwood, for instance, can be kept at a height of 6 inches; but if your pattern is very large, you would want to keep it as tall as 2 feet. Some herbs, such as thyme, can be maintained in delicate lines only a few inches tall. To heighten the effect of knot patterns, you can sculpt the lines that will cross underneath so that they appear to go down and under the continuous one crossing over.

If you wish to adapt any of the patterns to carpet bedding, don't plant the lines, but rather use them as guides to mark the divisions between masses of different-colored plants. The plants should be equally spaced within each area, and kept trimmed so the edges of the design don't get fuzzy.

Basic Outline

This design is made up of straight lines and right angles, so it is simple to lay out. Directions here are for a 10-foot square, but the knot can be any size you wish. You can use this design as is for a simple knot, or use the basic dimensions as a guide for creating more complex patterns.

You will need:
—four short (12- to 18-inch) stakes
—a ball of sturdy twine

> **In planting the parterre it is as easy to make mistakes as in designing it, and the most frequent errors are the employment of primary colours in excessive quantity and strength, and the neglect of neutral tints to soften it, and of brilliant edgings to define it. The stereotyped repetition of scarlet geraniums and yellow calceolarias is in the last degree vulgar and tasteless, and the common dispositions of red, white, and blue are better adapted to delight savages, than represent the artistic status of a civilized people.**
>
> —SHIRLEY HIBBERD
> *The Amateur's Flower Garden,* 1871

> **❝I think it should certainly be a regular geometric figure, and planted in masses, each bed containing flowers of one kind, so as to produce something of the effect of a Turkey carpet when looked down upon from the windows of the house.❞**
>
> —JANE LOUDON
> writing of flower beds
> in *The Lady's Country Companion*, 1845

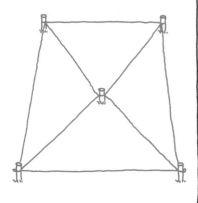

1. Set one stake to mark the first corner. Tie twine to it and measure out from the stake 10 feet. Stretch twine taut and drive a stake into the ground at that point. Tie twine to the second stake. You have now established the first side, from which all subsequent measurements are taken.

2. Measure out the second side and the third side in the same manner.

3. Measure out the last side as above. You will have to adjust the second and third sides until they form perfect right angles.

4. Prepare the soil within the square as described on page 233 (Laying Out the Pattern).

5. Mark out a diagonal line crossing from one corner of the square to another.

6. Measure out the remaining diagonal. The intersection of both diagonals marks the center point.

7. Plant as instructed on page 234 (Planting), or use this outline as the basis for the Elizabethan knot (below).

Elizabethan Knot

This comes from *The Gardener's Labyrinth* by Didymus Mountain (Thomas Hill), which was first printed in 1577. The pattern looks most spectacular when planted in three different kinds of herbs, so your eye can trace the lines over and under. Dozens of combinations can be used for a contrast of colors and textures, but try thyme for the circle, lavender for the square and santolina for the semicircles. You could also plant the lines in annuals—dwarf yellow and orange marigolds with white sweet alyssum would make a sunny picture.

You will need:
—nine short (12- to 18-inch) stakes
—a ball of sturdy twine
—a small-mouthed bottle filled with ground limestone or sand
—plants to create the design

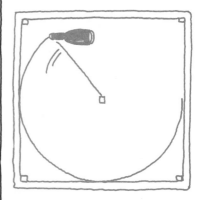

1 Lay out the basic outline pattern (page 235) following Steps 1 through 6.

2 Mark the center point with a stake and remove the diagonal strings. Tie a string to the center stake. Measure out 5 feet and tie a lime-filled bottle to the other end. Use the string and bottle as a compass to describe a circle within the square, sprinkling lime to mark the line.

3 Mark the halfway point on each side of the square with a stake.

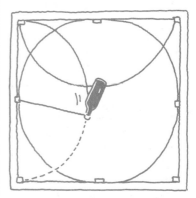

4 Tie the compass string to the halfway point on one side. Measure to one corner. Draw the semicircular curves from one corner to the other. Repeat to form four arcs.

5 Connect the four halfway stakes with string to create a square within the square.

6 Plant as desired along the string and limestone or sand guidelines, as described on page 234 (Planting).

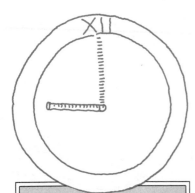

Sundial

The basic outline and the Elizabethan knot designs fit within a square bed and are suited to filling in with flowers. The sundial, however, calls for a circular bed and looks best filled with light-colored gravel so the hand's shadow can be clearly seen. You could cut each numeral out of turf rather than preparing an entire bed, but be prepared for some tricky mowing. If you want to mark each hour with numerals, your dial should be at least 15 feet in diameter; but if you simply mark the time with a line your face can be much smaller. Boxwood is the classic plant for sundials, and makes an elegant composition in dark green, although in the South yaupon is often a more successful plant. If you are a Northern gardener, a similar effect can be achieved with Japanese holly. A yew planted in the center and clipped into a triangular gnomon is a spectacular finishing touch; a wooden fence or iron hitching post is an attractive alternative; for an amusing look, use a pink flamingo.

In order to construct an accurate, as well as ornamental, sundial, you must set aside two days for this project.

You will need:
—a tall (6-foot) stake
—a ball of sturdy twine
—a small-mouthed bottle filled with ground limestone or sand
—eighteen short (12- to 18-inch) stakes
—extra limestone or sand to outline the numerals
—plants to complete the design

1 Use a tall stake to mark the central point for your gnomon. Tie a string the length of the desired radius of your sundial to the stake, and attach a sand- or lime-filled bottle to the other end. Using it as a compass, mark the circumference. This will be the perimeter of the bed. Prepare the soil within the circle as described on page 233 (Laying Out the Pattern).

Shorten the string by 1½ to 2 feet and reattach the bottle. Mark a smaller circle within the first one as a guide for the inner edge of the numerals.

2 At noon (or one o'clock Daylight Savings Time), mark where the shadow is cast. This will be the number twelve.

3 That same afternoon, with a string tied to a short stake at the perimeter, mark where the shadow of the gnomon falls when one, two, three, and each proceeding hour elapses after noon. The following morning, mark the hours before noon. Sundials are traditionally marked from 5:00 A.M. to 7:00 P.M.; mark all of these hours, or only those that are important to you.

4 Using the stakes as a center point and the circles as a size gauge, lay out each numeral. Roman numerals are the classic indicators, but you may prefer Arabic numbers—or whimsical configurations such as the fish numerals illustrated.

5 Plant the numerals along the limestone or sand guidelines, as instructed on page 234 (Planting).

Flat Topiary

By using a grid any design may be transferred and enlarged to fit the space you desire in your garden. Create your own pattern on graph paper, or try the graceful design shown. The outline of the shape itself defines the bed that you will prepare.

You will need:
—graph paper

SUNDIAL MOTTOES

Many sundials have mottoes around the face, and you may wish to spell one out on yours. Traditional phrases include: "I Count Only Sunny Hours"; "Grow Old Along With Me The Best Is Yet To Be"; "Tempus Fugit" (Time Flies); and "Lumen Me Regit" (Light Rules Me).

—*a pencil*
—*short (12- to 18-inch) stakes*
—*a ball of sturdy twine*
—*ground limestone or sand*
—*plants to complete the design*

1 Prepare the soil as described on page 233 (Laying Out the Pattern).

2 Trace the design you've chosen for your ground decoration onto graph paper.

3 Transfer a grid of the same number of squares onto the ground with stakes and string.

4 Use ground limestone or sand to trace the pattern square by square.

5 Form an outline of evergreens and fill in with seasonal flowers; or plant a solid mass of low-growing evergreens or flowering perennials within the outline.

> **❝And all these [flowers] by the skill of your Gardiner, so comelily and orderly placed in your borders and squares, and so intermingled, that one looking thereon, cannot but wonder to see, what Nature, corrected by Art, can do.❞**
>
> —WILLIAM LAWSON
> *A New Orchard and Garden,* 1618

Verdant Sculpture

ORNAMENTAL SHAPING OF TREES AND SHRUBS

It is when topiary enters the realm of sculpture that it most exploits the potential of both plants and the human imagination. Any image, no matter how plain, gains great vitality when rendered in living plants. The sculpture of shrubs and trees involves an ongoing relationship—each clipping session will add detail and refinement to your jade statuary and increase your sense of pride. Long-term topiary is interesting at all stages of growth, and there is great satisfaction in participating in the metamorphosis of a common bush into a unique sculpture.

You don't have to be a professional to exercise your imagination in outdoor topiary, as the late Harvey Ladew clearly proved. In 1929 he bought a Maryland farm that has become one of the most spectacular topiary gardens in America. Although Ladew had no formal training, he dreamed up 22 acres of theme gardens, and for many years clipped all the topiary himself. There are examples of every style of plant sculpture, from a contemplative evergreen Buddha to playful yew dogs.

This art is a most acceptable outlet for eccentricity. People who in other aspects of their lives are quite reserved have been known to unleash their wildest ideas in leafy splendor. Gus Yearicks, a retired utility company employee from Cape May, New Jersey, remembers that on his way to chop down an overgrown hedge, "a voice came in me mind and said don't cut it down—make a boat out of it." He didn't even know what to call his art form in 1928 when he transformed that old hedge into the H.M.S. *Queen Mary.* So began the sculpting of more than a hundred figures that eventually filled his yard of a few acres.

Even if your visions aren't as dramatic, your own imagination can still guide the way. Sometimes bushes will tell you what they ought to be. Look at them from all angles to see what forms they naturally suggest, just as a sculptor perceives his statue in rough marble. In *The English Scene* Eric Parker recounts that for years his yew "stood in its corner and would tell me nothing. . . . And then one day I saw, or it told me, it

> **❝I had always loved gardening, and, therefore, I decided that, though I would certainly make many mistakes, I would do the whole thing, including the landscaping, myself.❞**
>
> —HARVEY LADEW
> *Random Recollections*

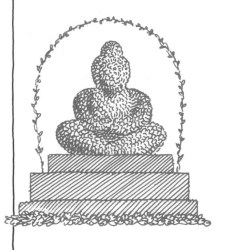

> **"I had never been particularly interested in Topiary until one day, about forty years ago, when I was hunting with the Beaufort Hounds. Hacking to an early meet, I rode along beside a very tall yew hedge bounding a large estate. As I looked up, I was astonished to see a most amazing sight. Along the top of the hedge was a realistic Topiary fox hunt: a fox closely pursued by a pack of hounds. I instantly decided to try to meet the owners and to ask them if they thought I could possibly reproduce this marvelous piece of living sculpture in America."**
>
> —HARVEY LADEW
> *Random Recollections*

was a dolphin of a shape the most classic, with open mouth, dorsal and pectoral fins all proper, and a superb tail."

Whatever shape you decide to try, it should be one that absolutely delights you since you will be spending a lot of time tending to it and it will be a long-term feature of your landscape. Generally, the shape should be broader at the bottom and taper toward the top, so that light reaches all parts and so that heavy loads of snow won't accumulate and cause breakage.

THE TRADITIONAL REPERTOIRE

As different cultures have made topiary part of their own garden style, many shapes have developed. Some of these became classics, recreated for centuries in European gardens. Today, these enduring and endearing forms are a wonderful addition to the garden; you can become a part of history by fashioning your own versions of traditional shapes.

The Dutch are historically the most skilled practitioners of the garden craft of "bush-barbering." The high winds in Holland precluded the existence of stately old trees, whose root systems failed to find secure anchorage in the watery ground. To this day this flat, treeless landscape demands manmade focal points—so the Dutch joyfully enliven their prim, tidy gardens with toy-like topiary features such as jugs, coffeepots, spirals, birds and chairs.

The English have an even greater fondness for whimsy, which they have exhibited enthusiastically since Dutch-bred monarchs made topiary the height of garden fashion. An abundance of figures filled the large manicured gardens of Jacobean England. Levens Hall is a rare survivor from the period. A lion, a judge's wig, and a giant umbrella dating from the late

You can select topiary styles to complement the exterior of your house, evoking the charm of an English cottage.

17th century sprout out of the flower parterres, joined by a crown created in 1977 for the Queen's Silver Jubilee.

Oblivious to prevailing fashion, the English cottager has been a devoted curator of carved evergreens, sheltering them from the waves of disfavor that swept grander gardens clean. Virtually every image that has ever been attempted in yew or boxwood can be found in the dooryards of village dwellings, pubs and inns, rising from a jumbled profusion of flowers and vegetables. Often colossal Alice in Wonderland shapes tower above the thatched roofs.

Just as the nude has been a favorite image in sculpture since the Greeks, so the peacock has been a universal favorite in the realm of topiary. The royal bird itself was a highly prized Oriental import, costly and difficult to obtain and keep alive

LADEW TOPIARY GARDENS

Harvey Ladew was lucky enough to be able to vent his imagination and eccentricity in topiary, creating his plant statues for almost 50 years until his death in 1976. The spectacular Ladew Topiary Gardens was started in 1929, when superior hunting lured Ladew from Long Island to a farmhouse in Monkton, Maryland. He brought with him a cakestand topped with a peacock, an auspicious first addition to a property whose planting had been confined to a scraggly lilac bush. Other figures include a giraffe, assorted fowl, and various chess pieces. The Japanese-style iris garden is highlighted by a privet junk afloat in a pool and a contemplative yew Buddha.

GREEN ANIMALS

A dromedary, giraffe and elephant, along with many other shrub animals, live in this seaside garden, created around 1900 by industrialist Thomas Brayton and his gardener Jose Carreiro. On Brayton's death, Green Animals was adopted by his daughter Alice and cared for by Carreiro's son-in-law George Mendonca. The menagerie was toasted by Newport society at garden galas. Green Animals shares with Ladew Topiary Gardens in Maryland the distinction of being the finest topiary gardens in America.

on European estates. Noblemen traditionally swore oaths on these rare birds and honored them with evergreen replicas that dotted the grounds. The estate gardeners of England returned up the lane to their more humble abodes determined that they, too, would own a shrub imitation.

The mathematical bent of the French led them to create a style of gardening whose beauty lies in its measurability. In the vast, elegant creations of 17th-century landscape designer André Le Nôtre, clipped legions of holly and boxwood were trained into armies of cones, obelisks and spheres. Figurative plant sculptures can be found in French gardens, but geometric shapes are the rule. Abstract shapes also prevail in historic Spanish gardens, where tastes were influenced by Moorish precedents. Since the Islamic faith prohibited representational sculpture and portraiture, the cypress, boxwood and myrtle of palace courtyards were trimmed into serene, rounded shapes.

THE AMERICAN STYLE

The aesthetics of many cultures mix in America's gardens, just as plants from many continents thrive here side by side. In addition to the traditional European topiary subjects, a new style has developed in this country, drawing on the Oriental flair for stylized, natural shapes and symbolic forms. Plants are shaped to contrast qualities of airiness and density. This is sometimes called cloud or pompom pruning.

Animals are favorite subjects for topiary, adding a humorous note to even the most formal gardens. The earliest recorded appearance of a bush bear was in Renaissance Italy. Since Teddy Roosevelt spared a cub while hunting, teddy bears have been dear to the hearts of many a child and grown-up around the world. There's probably nothing about a bush that would make you want to embrace it, but an evergreen cut into a bear is

eminently huggable. Rhode Island's Green Animals is home to a seated yew bear with outstretched arms. This beast has proved irresistible to scores of visiting children, as evidenced by the bare patch of ground between his legs. Instructions for creating an adorable teddy can be found on page 258.

The African giraffe has become an American topiary classic—examples abound, not only in places such as Ladew Topiary Gardens, Green Animals and Disney World, but also in backyards and motel parking lots. When the privet giraffe at Green Animals suffered a tragic decapitation in a hurricane, the gardener cut a few feet off the neck and reshaped the head. Visitors are laughingly told that Rhode Island giraffes have short necks. Standing 20 feet high it remains a most respectable specimen.

The oldest piece in the repertoire may be the ship. Pliny the Elder records "fleets of ships" hewn from cypress on Roman country estates. Ships are a perennial choice of the topiarist, offering landlocked seafarers a living tribute to their vessels. Harvey Ladew created a privet junk afloat in the pool of his Oriental iris garden. Gus Yearicks began his fleet of boats with an homage to the British *Queen Mary*, but then made a patriotic switch to Yankee models. Boats ranging from clipper ships to modern luxury liners, some as large as 28 feet long, have floated on Yearicks' lawn to the delight of thousands of summer visitors.

Geometric shapes range from strict mathematical figures to inventive variations, and can be just as exciting as birds, beasts and boats. Longwood Gardens in Kennett Square, Pennsylvania, one of the nation's best known topiary gardens, doesn't focus on animals—the majority of its pieces are geometric variations on cones, cylinders, cubes and spirals. Though the individual pieces are fairly simple, they are quite large and arranged so as to create an atmosphere of mystery, splendor and strength.

Shapes that combine the appeal of geometry and whimsy, a common sight in England, also appear at Longwood. Peacocks and other birds roost on pyramids, columns and cones. Often a tree or bush is cut into a series of disks, decreasing in diameter as they ascend the trunk. These tiered forms have the unlikely

> **66***Even the topiary works of the Renaissance, the green ships and helmets, giants, dragons and centaurs, had something of reason to recommend them, for by their very strangeness they would be likely to compel attention, to stir imagination, to strengthen memory, to banish the consciousness of self and all trivial or obsessing thoughts.***99**
>
> —SIR GEORGE SITWELL
> *On the Making of Gardens*, 1909

> **❝The effect, especially by moonlight, of the lake seen through the balustrades of the parapet, and among the vases and statues which surmount it—with the splashing of the fountain, and the very unique features, at least in this country, of the formally clipped trees and topiary work, quite lead us to suppose we are on the lake of Como.❞**
>
> —H. W. SARGENT describing Hunnewell's Italian Garden in his revision of A.J. Downing's *The Theory and Practice of Landscape Gardening*, 1858

The Italian Garden at the Walter Hunnewell Pinetum, planted in 1851, contains some of America's oldest geometric topiary. This engraving, from Sargent's 1858 book, shows the garden in its early years.

moniker of cakestand.

Topiarists around the world have favored the hunt as a subject—it has been portrayed in literature and engravings since ancient Roman times. Instead of being limited to isolated pieces of plant sculpture, the topiarist has the opportunity to create an entire scene. Prints show one such display, no longer in existence at Versailles, where boxwood men and dogs chased a stag. Harvey Ladew's hunt is alive and well, and perhaps the most photographed topiary scene in the world. On the fringe of the garden a horse and rider jump a white gate, following on the heels of a stream of hounds, who themselves are in hot pursuit of a fox racing for his life across a stretch of lawn.

Many topiarists have delighted in monogramming their creations. Pliny the Younger ornamented his garden with his initials, as well as those of his esteemed gardener. Monsieur Guillaume Beaumont, designer of England's topiary showplace Levens Hall, saw to it that a big letter B stood among the other pieces. Harvey Ladew celebrated the end of World War II by turning one of his stateliest bushes into Churchill's V for victory.

DISPLAYING GREEN SCULPTURE

T aking a cue from the lively little gardens of the Netherlands, you can use plant sculpture to provide detail in an otherwise simple garden. Just one topiary ornament will make an ordinary garden unique. Place the figure wherever punctuation is needed, or to provide a focal point. When the 16th-century Dutch lacked enough good ground for large topiary, they displayed smaller versions in pots or wooden tubs. If you are short on space, or want to decorate a paved area, house your plant sculpture in an attractive container.

Sculpted evergreens are beautiful all year and at any time of day; because of this, they deserve to be placed where you can see them from indoors. They're sparklingly attractive in the winter, when no flowers compete for attention, and when the sheen of their lustrous green coats is heightened by a contrasting blanket of snow.

Many topiary artists are enchanted by their shrub sculptures in the moonlight: the forms blacken against the sky, taking on a haunting quality. If you want a reliable evening show, lights can be concealed within your topiary. Harvey Ladew's Florida residence featured a walk flanked by evergreen whales. The whales had electrified eyes, which cast beams of light to sparkle on their water spouts. This extravagant display also served to illuminate the path, a stunning but practical idea you might

66. . . the box is interposed into groups, and cut into a thousand different forms; sometimes into letters, expressing the name of the master, or again that of the artificer, whilst here and there little obelisks rise intermixed alternately with fruit-trees. 99

—PLINY THE YOUNGER describing his Tuscan villa, 1st century A.D.

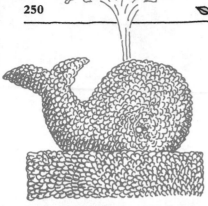

LONGWOOD GARDENS

The area of Longwood Gardens that is now the Topiary Garden was begun by Pierre Du Pont in the thirties as a formal space centered around a sundial, originally known as the Yew Garden. Although Du Pont shunned faunal forms, he was captivated by the geometric pieces at Ladew and tried to buy two of them. Harvey Ladew wouldn't sell, so Du Pont contented himself with some cones that are now almost 70 years old. In 1958, after his death, the garden was enhanced by an exceptional collection of geometric topiary pieces transplanted from Long Island.

adopt on a smaller scale for your garden.

Shrubs planted around the foundation of a house too often become shaggy disguises that hide the distinction of the house and cast an indiscriminate, gloomy shade. One or more topiary ornaments nestled around the home will instead offer an elegant complement to the architecture, with the added benefit of pretty shadows.

There is a special appeal to plants trained in pairs—one on either side of the path to your door is a welcoming sight. Doves so placed are a traditional English symbol of domestic tranquillity. Use a set of topiary to frame a view, or to dress up a glimpse into another part of your garden, inviting people to venture forth. Birds and other designs look best in these situations when they are formed from the top of a bush whose base has first been clipped into a pedestal. The base could be a column, pyramid, cone or some combination of these shapes. The figures don't have to match exactly—after forming two identical bases, you can fashion different top designs and still achieve the effect of a pair.

Groupings can be arranged to define areas of the garden, or to accentuate or preserve a vista. To enhance his panorama of Lake Waban in Wellesley, Massachusetts, Horatio Hollis Hunnewell sculpted native trees on the steep, terraced bank into open cakestands, leaving wide spaces between the disks. As one moves around the garden, changing views of the water are brought into focus through these apertures.

Sober geometric shapes march in rows to add drama and definition to the vast layout at Versailles. Smaller troops will do the same for your scheme. For the pure fun of it, stage a scene to be enacted by plant sculptures. Choose the classic hunt, or invent a new scenario: Gus Yearicks paid tribute to Babe Ruth by placing him at bat in a privet baseball game.

While individual topiary is best displayed elevated on a pedestal, collections may be trained on top of a continuous hedge for better viewing. You can crown the crest with an assortment of shapes, or repeat the same motif. A stag hunt, in which the poor creature tries to outrun the Devil, streams along the top of a cypress hedge at Mount Stewart, in Ireland. At Ladew, swans float on an undulating row of yew; you could achieve a similar effect with classic peacocks or casual chickens.

Two practical considerations must be kept in mind when making aesthetic decisions. The first factor is sunlight. Any successful topiary depends on lush, healthy growth. If the sculpture will be visible from all sides, choose an open spot where it will receive good light to develop evenly all around. Topiary can, of course, be placed against the house, but the side facing the wall will have the weakest growth. In these situations, clip that side flat, or plant some distance away from the wall so that light can reach the back of the figure. The second consideration is space. Be sure your living statue has room to grow. "Plants don't just sit around," observes Dave Thompson, Longwood horticulturist. Even with close clipping they increase gradually in breadth and height, as each year a bit of new growth must be retained. Narrow spaces won't be a problem, however, if you use a vertical shape.

SELECTING PLANT MATERIAL

It is easier to train a plant if its natural growth habit is related to the shape you are working to achieve. A giraffe or slender obelisk is quickly developed from an upright plant. If you are planning on a squat frog, sphere or cube, start with a bush that has a more spreading habit, with many stems arising at or near the ground. For detailed shapes, choose a plant with compact, finely textured foliage. Fast-growing plants will shorten the time it takes to obtain a completed figure, but the sculpture will require frequent trimming in order to be identifiable.

I threw my window open wide;
(It was the mystic hour of Dawn)
And just below me I espied
Two peacocks sitting on the lawn:
The largest I had ever seen;
And both of them were coloured green!
"This is the aftermath," I said,
"Of hours convivially spent.
So this is why I've such a head;
So that was where the whisky went.
If I start seeing things like this,
I'd better give the stuff a miss."
And then at breakfast-time, my host,
Between the marmalade and tea,
Spoke of his one especial boast,
His triumph of topiary;
His pride, his joy—his Peacock Hedge!
So now I needn't sign the pledge.

—REGINALD ARKELL
"Green Peacocks"

> 66. . . [privet] is so apt, that no other can be like unto it, to bee cut, lead and drawne into what forme one will, either of beasts, birds or men armed, or otherwise.99
>
> —JOHN PARKINSON
> *Paradisi in Sole,*
> *Paradisus Terrestris,*
> 1629

Sculpting can be practiced on many plants, but the best for your first venture, and perhaps any project, is yew. As with people, plants vary in their responsiveness to instruction; yew is a good and obedient pupil. Some of the figures at Levens Hall have withstood continuous shearing for more than two hundred years. But docile though yew may be, it doesn't lack for personality. Frances Garnet, the Viscountess Wolseley, rhapsodized in her 1919 book *Gardens: Their Form and Design* that "there are few trees that bear round them more glamour of romance than our English oaks and yews." The yew has a fine, dense texture that lends detail and character to sculpted forms. And the light green of the new needles gives a fresh look to any piece.

Yew has the perfect rate of growth—not so rapid that frequent shearing is necessary, nor so slow that many years go by before the figure is finished. Topiary formed on a frame assumes the desired shape quite effectively in two or three years and has the appearance of an heirloom in five. In many cases, established pieces can be maintained with one annual pruning. English yew (*Taxus baccata*), the species native to the British Isles and trained there for centuries with great success, is not dependably hardy in many areas of the United States. Japanese yew (*Taxus cuspidata*) and the hybrids between English and Japanese yew (*Taxus × media*) are the best for American topiarists. Nearly all the pieces at Ladew are Japanese yew, which Harvey Ladew called "the best shrub for topiary." There are upright and spreading varieties for sculpting a range of forms, and they can be combined in one piece. For example, a sitting dog might have an upright yew planted at each paw to start the front portion, while a spreading variety might be employed to create the hindquarters and tail. Try to obtain a female specimen, so red and black berries will decorate your plant sculpture (nurserymen refer to this as a "pistillate" plant). And be sure there is a male yew ("staminate" plant) nearby for pollination.

In warm climates where yew is not grown, cypress is an excellent material for detailed work. In Ecuador, the Arizona cypress (*Cupressus arizonica*) in the Tulcan Topiary Garden and

Topiary styles can go far beyond the formal European tradition. The intricately detailed figures at the Tulcan Topiary Garden and Cemetery in Ecuador were all designed, created and trimmed by one man.

TULCAN, ECUADOR

This remote town is home to one of the world's most impressive collections of topiary statues. Since 1936 the park manager has filled this three-acre site, which is now a national monument, with enormous cypress figures. Using book illustrations to guide him, Don Azael Franco Guerrero carved bushes into Egyptian pyramids, French geometric shapes and Indian elephants. The most remarkable pieces, however, are the Inca heads, birds and mythical beasts created in his native style.

Cemetery have been modeled into a showcase of velvet emerald statues whose surfaces are engraved with complex decorations. Eugenia (*Eugenia uniflora* and *Syzygium paniculatum*), yaupon (*Ilex vomitoria*) and southern yew (*Podocarpus macrophyllus*) are good choices for less intricate designs. Many examples can be seen at Disney World, where a podocarpus sea serpent appears half submerged in an ocean of turf.

Privet (*Ligustrum* in variety) is another top choice for plant sculptures. It's inexpensive, easy to obtain, and grows quickly and contentedly in a wide variety of growing conditions. Privet beasts can be found from Rhode Island to Florida

to California. It is well known for its ability to grow near the ocean; the plants at Green Animals thrive despite salt spray from Narragansett Bay. Privet is not evergreen, but the bare skeleton is handsome when set off against a background of snow. The stark winter appearance is soon followed by a flush of new leaves and fragrant, tiny white flowers. Privet is good for practicing topiary skills, since it recovers quickly from any accidental disfigurement. A new supply of plants can be readily started by rooting cuttings from older bushes. It is not as structurally strong as yew, however, and must be trimmed several times during the growing season. But while you await the maturity of slower-growing sculptures, you can content yourself with a privet form.

Experienced topiarists concur that boxwood (*Buxus sempervirens*) is best suited for gently rounded, simple shapes, and not usually successful for designs that have acute angles—although some have managed to coax boxwood into beautiful chessmen, peacocks, dolphins and penguins. With age, boxwood takes on a romantic, billowy appearance.

Fine-textured juniper (*Juniperus* in variety) is another good choice. The gray color creates an interesting contrast in a collection of other shrubs and creates an illusion of fur on animals. It is best used for designs that call for a certain amount of bare stem, as many varieties tend to lose their lower foliage. This would include birds on two legs, animals on four slender limbs, or something in an open Oriental style such as pom poms. Juniper is also a rewarding plant for the standards, spirals and poodles described in Chapter Two.

Feel free to try other trees and shrubs. All of Gus Yearicks' creations were privet — until one day he discovered four wild cherry saplings in a corner of his yard that reminded him of a giraffe. When H. H. Hunnewell began his garden, large specimens of European topiary plants and Japanese yew were unavailable, so he successfully experimented with native trees such as spruce, eastern white pine, hemlock, juniper, and arborvitae, which had never before been used for topiary.

Yew, privet, euonymus and arborvitae come in variegated varieties splashed with yellow or white, which can add interest to plant sculptures. Harvey Ladew's giraffe is an authentic color because he made use of golden privet. Flowering plants seasonally dress a sculpture in new shades. Try forsythia for a splendid golden spring chicken, or azalea for a startling pink flamingo. Pruning time affects blooming, so check your local nursery for the best time to trim without sacrificing flowers.

Combine different plants in one piece of sculpture for contrasts of color and texture. At Disney World, a green privet frog sits on a toadstool clipped from a silver variety of the same plant; a seal of yaupon (*Ilex vomitoria*) balances a red

TOPIARY WORK AT LEVENS HALL : WESTMORELAND

Levens Hall, laid out in 1701, is England's most elaborate topiary garden. It is shown here in all its grandeur, as depicted in Sir Reginald Blomfield's The Formal Garden in England.

> **66***It somewhat resembles those racks, long out of fashion, which carried a series of plates bearing elaborate cakes and bread and butter, thin as wafers, which were a necessary adjunct to the flimsy, polite tea table.***99**
>
> —MILES HADFIELD describing a topiary cakestand in *Topiary and Ornamental Hedges,* 1971

66*It was after a visit to Elvaston . . . that I conceived the idea of making a collection of trees for topiary work in imitation of what I had witnessed at that celebrated estate. As suitable trees for that purpose could not be obtained at the nurseries in this country, and as the English Yew is not reliable in our New England climate, I was obliged to [select] from such trees as had proved hardy here—the Pines, Spruces, Hemlocks, Junipers, Arbor-vitae, Cedars and Japanese Retinosporas. The trees were all very small, and for the first twenty years their growth was shortened twice annually, causing them to take a close and compact habit, comparing favorably in that respect with the Yew.***99**

—HORATIO HOLLIS
HUNNEWELL
c. 1900

azalea ball on his nose, while a yaupon Mary Poppins totes a pink bougainvillea umbrella.

Whatever plants you decide to try, you should buy the largest, healthiest specimens you can afford. There is no sense in investing time in a sickly plant that won't respond to your attention. And the closer the new purchase is to the planned size of your figure, the sooner it will be complete. Large pieces can be formed quickly by employing several plants. Use one at each paw of a four-legged beast. For tall figures that rise from a wider base, place three or four small bushes around a larger, central specimen. An obelisk, for example, can be made in this way. Careful planting and attention to young candidates for sculpture is essential to prepare the plant for the rigors of frequent pruning. Take care that the shrub is planted at the correct depth. Don't bury the stem—if you leave the plant a little high, it will settle into the ground at the correct level, leaving room for mulch. Water regularly the first year.

If you already own old, overgrown plants, they can be prepared for topiary by a program of drastic cutting. This is best performed in early spring, pruning the bush or tree into a rough cone shape. Don't be afraid to go almost as far back as the main stems—fresh growth will emerge over the season. Cut the branches back to at least 6 inches smaller than the projected dimensions of the sculpture. Once the plant has filled out with young shoots, usually by the following year, you can begin training it to the desired shape.

TRADING THE CHISEL FOR THE SHEARS

I t is a good idea to keep a record of each topiary, noting when it was begun, and accompanied by a sketch of the shape you're working toward. In subsequent years, jot down when clipping was done, and any new details you are adding to the figure. Refine what you invent in your mind's eye with pictures. Phil Krach, head gardener at Ladew, keeps several close-up photos of horses with him when he is clipping the hunt scene, so that he can create the proper lines of a horse's legs and capture the feeling of the animal in motion.

Until you get used to clipping, take off a little at a time. Sometimes it's tempting to get carried away with shears in hand, but don't remove any branches until you are sure they can't contribute to the development of the figure. Remember, whatever is cut can't be put back. If you are unsure about the potential of certain branches, leave them for another day's clipping session. There are two ways to sculpt plants: by freehand carving, or by training with a frame. Each one is appropriate for certain shapes; once you are familiar with the basics of each, you will be able to choose the best method for your design.

Freehand carving, the closet cousin to chiseling stone, is the oldest of plant sculpting techniques. Walk up to your plant and, starting from the bottom of the bush, cut a rough approximation of the shape. A vague likeness will emerge after this initial shaping. Keep in mind that a plant's natural tendency is to go up. When a portion of the shape has to be developed sideways or downward, you will need the assistance of stakes and twine to force the branches in the desired direction. Freehand carving is best used to create simple shapes, and also to etch detail into the surface of any design.

If your abilities fall short of Michelangelo, enlist the aid of a metal frame. Training time is considerably shorter than

> **66In Scotland Privet is called Primprint. Primet and Primprivet were other old names. Box was called Primpe. These were all derivative of prim, meaning precise.99**
>
> —ALICE MORSE EARLE
> *Old Time Gardens*, 1901

with the freehand method, and the frame itself serves as a decoration while the plant is small. First tie branches in bundles to form a rough layout, and to make it easier to slip the frame over the bush. Reluctant branches are then bent and tied to the frame, and more willing twigs are tucked in. Once the frame is filled, any protruding branches can be clipped away.

Frames can either be purchased from the suppliers listed in the Source Guide, or fashioned from wire. Sometimes a simple outline is a sufficient guide. For more complex shapes, make a three-dimensional framework by adding circular ribs to the basic outline. To prolong the life of the frame, and to make it unobtrusive, paint it dark green or black.

CREATING A SCULPTURE

These classic designs are made with time-honored, dependable yew. The shapes may be executed in other plant materials, however, adapting dimensions as appropriate for the habit of the plant. The techniques can be applied to any shape you desire. The bear, alphabet, and cakestand are made using the freehand method, while the peacock instructions demonstrate training with a frame. Training can be started anytime except winter, when frozen boughs snap too easily if bent.

A Seated Teddy Bear

The size given for the upright yew bush (3½ to 4 feet) is a minimum, and will result in a 4½- to 5-foot bear. If you want a bigger bear, start with a larger bush.

You will need:
—one upright yew bush, 3½ to 4 feet tall
—one 5-foot stake

—*a ball of twine or other soft, sturdy tying material*
—*two 3-foot stakes*
—*four short (12- to 18-inch) stakes*
—*two 2-foot stakes*
—*pruning shears*

1 Before you begin, study the bush to determine which branches can be used to form the limbs. Select two strong branches near the ground for the legs, and two higher up and growing out from the same level for the arms.

2 Tie the central stem (there may be more than one) to the long stake, which has been sunk firmly into the ground. The stake is also helpful in securing the branches that make up the appendages.

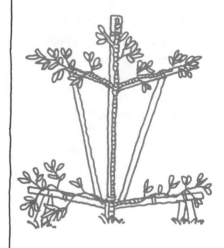

3 Tie a 3-foot stake along the underside of one leg branch. Being careful to avoid damaging the branch, bend it until it is parallel with the ground. Secure it in place by setting two 12- to 18-inch stakes on either side of the leg and tying the branch to them. Repeat with the other leg. The legs should be spread apart so that they will be well defined even after the yew has filled out.

4 Tie each arm to a 2-foot stake. Hold them in a horizontal position by tying to the 5-foot vertical stake.

5 Trim back growth along the bear's limbs. Clip in above the arms to form the neck. Clip back the growth all over the bush to encourage fullness, but do not cut the leader, as this must increase in height to start the head the second year.

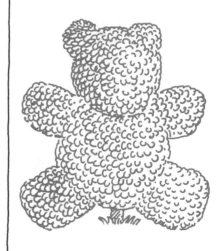

6 The following year, cut off the tips of the limbs if they are the desired length so they will thicken. When deciding on the length of the legs, keep in mind that the body will fill out. If the bush has reached its ultimate height, shear the top into

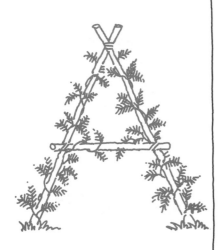

a ball. Allow three tufts to emerge, two for the ears and one to start the snout.

7 In subsequent years, maintain the shape by shearing. Check ties to be sure that they are not girdling the branches. Within a few years, the limbs will harden into place and the stakes can be removed.

Alphabet

Specific instructions follow for the letters A and B; the same procedures can be adapted to produce your own initials or any other letters. Numbers, such as your street address, may also be formed in this manner.

For the letter A you will need:
—two 5-foot yew, cypress or hemlock trees
—two 8½-foot bamboo or wooden stakes
—a ball of twine or other soft, sturdy tying material
—a 3-foot bamboo or wooden stake
—pruning shears

1 Plant the two trees 5 feet apart. Sink the 8½-foot stakes 18 inches into the ground on the inner side of each tree at an angle so that the tops of the stakes meet. Tie the tops of the stakes together. For each tree, train the leading shoot up the stake to form the outside of the letter A, tying it along the stake.

2 Select a side branch on each tree to form the cross bar. Approximately 3 feet up from the ground, tie the 3-foot stake horizontally between the two side stakes to form a horizontal line. Tie the side branches along the horizontal stake.

3 When the leading shoots reach the point where the stakes meet, tie the tops together.

4 Trim the tree regularly to define the letter A. In subsequent years, maintain the shape by shearing. Check ties to be sure that they are not girdling the branches. Within a few years, the limbs will harden into place and the stakes can be removed.

For the letter B you will need:
—one 5-foot tree with a single stem that branches halfway up into
 three leaders (one will be used for each part of the letter)
—one 8½-foot stake
—a ball of twine or other soft, sturdy tying material
—pruning shears

1 Use the sturdiest, most upright leader to make the straight side, tying it to the 8½-foot stake.

2 Choose the leader with the most upward inclination to form the top half of the B. Bend it upward and tie it securely to the stake.

3 Repeat Step 2 with the third leader, curving it downward to form the lower portion of the letter B.

4 Trim the tree regularly to define the letter B. In subsequent years, maintain the shape by shearing. Check ties to be sure

that they are not girdling the branches. Within a few years, the limbs will harden into place and the stakes can be removed.

Peacock

You can either purchase a peacock frame (see the Source Guide) or make one yourself by following the directions in Chapter Four and using heavy-gauge wire.

You will need:
—a spreading yew bush
—a wire peacock frame
—a 3-foot piece of wire if your frame lacks a spike
—twine or other soft, sturdy tying material
—pruning shears

1 Study the bush to determine which branches can be used to form the head and tail. Separate branches into two appropriate bunches and tie with twine.

2 Wiggle the frame down over the bush, pushing the spike into the ground. If necessary, bend the 3-foot piece of wire into a U and use it to steady the frame.

3 Untie the bush. Bend, tie and tuck branches to fill out the frame. As the plant grows, clip off any stems that stray outside the wire.

4 In future seasons, shear to maintain the shape. Allow the bush to grow out an inch or two beyond the frame so it will be concealed.

Cakestand

Raise your royal peacock on this handsome pedestal. Many other shapes can be easily trained from the top growth of cakestands, or it can be left as a simple geometric piece. Double your pleasure and start a pair. If you want a large cakestand, consider using a white pine (*Pinus strobus*).

You will need:
—a 5- to 6-foot upright yew, with a strong, uncut central stem
—pruning shears

1 The location of the branches along the trunk will probably suggest where each tier should be formed. Be sure to leave enough space between them so that the upper surfaces aren't shaded.

2 Cut out the branches between tiers. Clip the outer edge of each disk. The tiers may be of equal size, or you can decrease the diameter of each successive one.

3 As the tree increases in height, add successive tiers. Maintain the shape of the disks by shearing.

> **66What's a noble-man's garden without peacocks?99**
>
> —BENJAMIN DISRAELI

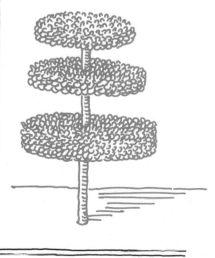

CARING FOR SCULPTED TREES AND SHRUBS

Beautiful topiary depends on a healthy root system. Remember to look down when you model your figures—take a few minutes to keep the underlying ground mulched and cleared of weeds and turf. Young pieces grow vigorously and must be trimmed often to promote fullness. As with all living things, older plants slow down and need less frequent clipping. Since winter appearance is important, if you can trim only once do so in August or September. Cosmetic surgery for smooth contours can be done throughout the growing season, as the plant dictates and your time permits. Skim off foliage gradually until you reach a darker layer, which is the previous year's growth. After shearing, shake or rake the bush to see if curled shoots pop up, and cut these back.

Periodically, older established shapes need more than a quick haircut. The extra attention is well repaid, because it takes less time and expense to refurbish your creation than to start again. To thicken a thin coat, you must clean out the middle of the topiary. Remove dead wood so that light penetrates to dormant buds inside the bush, which will sprout for a denser layer of growth.

If you inherit neglected topiary, or have been too lenient in your pruning, you will find yourself with a sculpture that has lost its form or outgrown its spot. There are two ways to recover the proper shape and size. The simplest solution is to cut it back to the desired dimensions all at once. This is most appropriate for plants like yew that readily regenerate new foliage from old wood. Such severe pruning should be performed in February or March. The second method ensures that the figure will always look good, but it does take more time and effort. In this scenario, gradually move the green layer back with each successive pruning.

Hedgecraft

BUILDING HALLS AND WALLS
OF GREEN

Architectural topiary bridges the gap between the house and the garden by combining the forces of architecture and nature to form breathtaking outdoor structures—living walls, halls and rooms of green. These elegant edifices hail from the great gardens of Europe, but their creation is well within the range of any modern gardener. With characteristic ingenuity, American gardeners have updated the classic designs in keeping with the smaller proportions and lower maintenance requirements of today's gardens. Architectural topiary is functional as well as ornamental, but it doesn't have to be serious—there's plenty of room for whimsical self-expression.

The hedge, a row of trees or shrubs planted and trimmed into a solid line, is the basic building block of verdant architecture. Many gardens, whether old or modern, vast or tiny, are defined by hedges. Instead of starting an architectural project from scratch, you can work with existing hedges to turn an ordinary garden element into a permanent but ever-changing feature. Dress up a plain hedge with windows, garlands and other embellishments.

If you do start from scratch, though, you will have the opportunity to select from a broad repertoire of architectural forms. The utilitarian hedge becomes a magic presence if you arrange it in a maze design. Or add an air of gracious fantasy with a topiary archway, tunnel or garden house. A variety of shapes and styles have developed as different gardening traditions borrowed from the realm of architecture. Patience is required, since it takes several years for these structures to reach their ultimate dimensions. However, it is well worth the time and effort because you will end up with a living heirloom that will be treasured for many years to come. The form is interesting to look at even in the early stages, and it's exciting to see how it changes and develops each time you prune and train the plants. In 1870, Frank J. Scott advised the sculpturing of evergreens for small properties in *The Art of Beautifying Suburban Home Grounds*: ". . . they will also afford most pleasing labor from the beginning; and the infantile graces of the trees, which are year

> **A hedge is a line of trees or shrubs formalized in semblance to a wall or fence, and usually serves to define the limits of a given area.**
>
> —NORMAN TAYLOR
> *The Garden Dictionary*, 1936

by year to be developed into verdant arches, will probably afford quite as much pleasure in their early growth as in their perfected forms."

HEDGES

Hedges are the backbone of the garden, the main ingredient vital for a finished garden picture. On the practical side, they serve many functions: increasing privacy, reducing wind and noise, guiding vision and directing feet. They may be planted in curved or serpentine lines as well as in straight rows. For a complete sense of enclosure they should be taller than eye level, although they don't have to be monumental. Waist-high hedges are also valuable, defining parts of your garden or bordering paths without blocking the view.

No matter how severely they are clipped, hedges will always give the garden a more romantic, natural feeling than could be achieved with a fence or a wall. And hedges keep the whole garden from being discoverable at a glance—they introduce an element of surprise. Use them as inner divisions as well as boundaries: you can create quiet, peaceful areas within a small garden, or separate a large garden into a more intimate series of spaces. The famous garden at Hidcote in England is partitioned by green walls into a series of twenty-four "rooms," each with a different type of flower or color scheme.

"Hedge" has its root in the Old English *hag*, an enclosed pasture whose boundaries were composed of shrubs and trees grown in impenetrable rows. When livestock nibbled on the young shoots, they inadvertently pruned the rough growth into a regular outline. The prickly field boundaries were adapted as man-made security hedges for medieval pleasure gardens located beyond the castle walls. These "quicksette hegges" of hawthorn and sweetbrier were made by a technique know as pleaching or plashing, which involves planting flexible thorn

Even on a city rooftop, a bit of hedge will increase privacy and enhance the view.

66*[French architects] Le Corbusier and Pierre Jeanneret devised what is probably the ultimate use of movable screens in their 1931 design of the De Beistegui penthouse roof garden. Clipped hedges were set into electrically operated sliding boxes. One had only to flip a switch for complete privacy or a fabulous view of Paris.***99**

—SUSAN CHAMBERLIN
Hedges, Screens and Espaliers, 1983

cuttings in a ditch, and then bending and weaving the shoots together into a solid mass. Their dense, thorny growth is still a convincing deterrent to trespassers; and though prickly to touch, they are pretty to look at, with their attractive flowers and brightly colored ornamental fruits.

The Romans used cypress and boxwood clipped in imitation of masonry to structure their gardens, but the skill was neglected during the Dark Ages. With the rediscovery of Roman garden art in the Italian Renaissance, the functional boundary hedge attained its present status as a practical and decorative element, usually made from evergreens rather than

> **❝You have heard that the first need-full thing for a Garden is water. The next to this is enclosure, that it be well inclosed, both from unruly folks and theeves, and likewise from beasts: lest lying in waite for your herbes and your fruits, they may both bereave you of your paines, and your pleasure. . . .❞**
>
> —GERVASE MARKHAM
> *The Whole Art of Husbandrie*, 1631

the hawthorn of medieval gardens.

Hedges offer several advantages for today's smaller gardens. They occupy less of your valuable garden area than an untrimmed row of trees or shrubs, and because you control the dimensions, they won't outgrow their allotted space. By training buttresses out from a hedge and filling the space between with flower beds, you can squeeze color and interest into a narrow side yard or town house garden. Fanciful hedges can be placed anywhere if they are potted in rectangular planters on wheels. Use them on a terrace or patio to hide your barbecue, gas tanks or workbench. Rearrange them for a party room—you can even roll them into the house.

You could selectively create openings in your hedge, so that desirable views are highlighted while privacy is maintained. In this way, your own garden picture can be enhanced by tantalizing views of your neighbor's handiwork or of the surrounding woods and fields. Realizing that the best formal gardens don't shut out the nearby countryside, Italians frequently pierced windows in their hedges to incorporate the surrounding views. At the Villa Gambraia, peaked windows frame pictures of Florence and the hills of Tuscany. And in Maryland, the changing colors of the seasons can be seen through windows in hemlock hedges at the Ladew Topiary Gardens.

Once the height has been established, plain hedges can be embellished by carving bas-relief decorations in the sides of tall hedges or along the top surface of short ones. Any decoration used on walls can be reproduced on your hedge: garlands, geometric or floral motifs—even the mythical birds and beasts that often appear on gothic buildings. Sometimes a new way to dress up a hedge comes as a sudden inspiration. While clipping his waist-high privet one Saturday, a man in Ocean City, New Jersey, decided to carve out his last name and Masonic symbol.

Another way to add decoration to your hedge is to train the tufts of growth that appear at the top into topiary sculptures. Finials, turrets, scalloping or other architectural details make a simple but striking finish. Turn-of-the-century garden designer Frances Garnet, the Viscountess Wolseley, referred to hedge ornamentation as "a touch of childishness here and there"; in this spirit, hedges can be topped off with any whimsical touch you desire. A couple in Newmarket, England, topped their hedges with Scottish terriers and a pair of cats. At the Ladew Topiary Gardens, an elegant effect is achieved with a flock of swans swimming across the top of a tall, wavy hedge.

With clever layouts, uncomplicated hedge shapes can produce a stunning effect. Green renditions of the Roman amphitheater are constructed by planting a series of wing hedges and training them in staggered heights. At the Villa Garzoni in Tuscany and the neighboring Villa Reale, there are two beautiful examples, complete with little boxwood globes to represent footlights. A theater layout can be used in your garden for informal occasions, or for staging special events such as parties, weddings and graduations.

Verdant architecture reached its peak in 17th-century France, adding ornament and refinement to earlier Italian artistry. Hedges appeared in elaborate variations known as palissades. The sheer size of these edifices was staggering. These days, their magnificent designs have been scaled down in size and complexity, bringing them into the realm of possibility for modern gardens. For unequalled drama, it is well worth adding a palissade to your garden.

The stilt hedge, or pole hedge, is one version of the classic palissade. The shape consists of a square-cut head raised on smooth trunks. This noble design has many practical advantages. A stilt hedge allows you to add greenery without giving up ground, and keeps trees in proportion to limited surroundings. If you want to raise your level of privacy, use a stilt hedge to add height beyond the top of a wall or fence. This is especially helpful where building codes or zoning regulations prohibit constructing walls or fences above a certain height—which is often too low for total privacy.

> **The garden is best to be square, encompassed on all the four sides with a stately arched hedge. . . . Over every arch, a little turnet, with a belly enough to receive a cage of birds. . . .**
>
> —FRANCIS BACON
> "Of Gardens," 1625

TOPIARY MAZE

A topiary maze is a fun project for your backyard—and it's not as confusing to create as it is to find your way around it the first time. Sometimes called a puzzlehedge, it is a network of paths framed by hedges to make a life-size game. The correct path leads to a central goal, such as a sculpture, seat, topiary feature or garden house. Although it takes several years for the hedges to grow taller than eye level, a maze will instantly become an interesting visual element in your garden. And once the green walls are waist-high, they'll be tall enough to make the maze fun for children. Planting a maze doesn't have to be expensive. The maze at Deerfield, in Rydal, Pennsylvania, was started with 6-inch boxwood plants purchased by the lot from a local nursery. And if you shop around for faster growing yew at a quantity discount, it won't be long before you lose yourself on your own property.

The ancient and mysterious lore of the labyrinth dates back to the one that housed the Cretan Minotaur, around 1600 B.C. Its circular form was adopted as a Christian symbol, decorating the floors of cathedrals as an emblem of the pilgrims' path to Jerusalem. The maze took on a playful aspect in lavish Renaissance and baroque garden schemes. The idea was, as British garden authority Penelope Hobhouse puts it, to elicit "amusement through confusion." Mazes were enjoyed in the same spirit as the water games, or *jeu d'eau*, that were concealed about the grounds to drench unwary visitors. The maze at Villa Garzoni was unrelenting in its good-natured abuse: water jets could be turned on to douse already perplexed guests. Some mazes were placed near the house so that derisive remarks could be shouted from the windows at trapped victims.

One of the best known mazes, and the oldest in Britain (replanted in 1690 from an earlier design), is at Hampton Court. The design has become a classic, reproduced many times in England and elsewhere, most notably in Williamsburg, Virginia, with American holly. The irregular trapezoidal shape of the Hampton Court maze was planned to fit into an existing garden layout, but you can adapt the perimeter of any maze design to suit your available space. The Victorians created many notable mazes, some rich in topiary detail, to attract the increasing ranks of tourists to public parks and commercial pleasure grounds. Many of these have disappeared, but we have included some mazes whose puzzles you can still tread in Gardens to Visit.

Mysterious topiary mazes are actually nothing more than a network of hedges. This life-size puzzle has been dressed up with a potted poodle at the center and a dramatic palissade backdrop.

Capability Brown (1716-1783), an ardent creator of naturalistic gardens who uprooted many formal garden features, lived next to the Hampton Court maze during his 20-year tenure as Royal Gardener—and was commanded not to alter it. Over the centuries, impatient visitors would crash through the hedges; to discourage this, the maze was patched up with thornier plants. Eventually it fell into such dishevelment that it was replanted in sturdy yew.

*All weave on high
a verdant roof
That keeps the
very sun aloof,
Making a twilight
soft and green,
Within the
column-vaulted
scene.*

—ALFRED B. STREET

ARCHES, TUNNELS AND HOUSES

There is no better front door to the garden than the leafy gateway of a graceful arch. It can be freestanding or incorporated into hedges where an opening has been left for a path. Even the most meticulously cared-for hedge sometimes develops holes; often, it turns out that these have been made by children or dogs who have found a convenient shortcut. You can turn these unsightly gaps into enticing elements of green architecture. Perhaps you're lucky enough to have a pair of trees on your property that can be trained into an attractive archway. If you have mature bushes or trees close to the house

As this 19th-century etching shows, colossal topiary is no problem as long as you are flexible. Here the tallest portions are simply allowed to form a more natural arch.

that are outgrowing their space and blocking your windows, train them to frame your front door or a bay window.

As with hedges, arches may be clipped in imitation of classical architecture or modeled into a more humorous form—one giant arch over a driveway has been fashioned into a topiary elephant. Arches can also be used to shelter a seat or to add punctuation along paths.

A group of trees trained and clipped into a radiating circle of arches to form an open pavilion is known as a glorieta. A simplified version consists of two arches that cross each other. The glorieta originated as a Spanish garden feature, usually planted at the intersection of paths or water channels.

A connected series of arches can form a sheltering passageway. Strolling through this tunnel of greenery, also called an allée or a covert alley, you can enjoy the garden in hot sun, sharp wind or rain. And the shadows it casts, whether in the solid shapes of evergreen forms or the dappled patterns of deciduous trees, themselves become a decorative element.

There are two kinds of tree tunnels: those with the casual flavor of soft architecture, and those of formal design. The first type, simply constructed by interlacing the overhead branches in a double row of trees, is known as a pleached alley or charmille; the latter is derived from the French word for hornbeam, a favorite tree for this purpose.

Arbors are the second type of tree tunnel, and these are usually trained on an underlying framework to help define more precise contours. Often the wood or metal structure is decorative in its own right, a distinct advantage while you are waiting for the trees to cover the form. Arbors, also called berceaux, were a favorite element in Dutch schemes, sometimes running the entire perimeter of the garden. A fine replica can be seen at Colonial Williamsburg in Virginia.

Topiary buildings can be spacious or snug, rustic or fancy. Charming little structures can be made from trees by weaving together the branches to create a leafy roof. They aren't complicated to construct; most are actually composed

> *Every branche and leaf must grow by measure Pleine as a bord, of an height by and by.*
>
> —GEOFFREY CHAUCER

of a simple series of arches. The invention of garden houses grew out of a need for privacy that was unavailable in the large communal rooms of villas and châteaux. Gardens solved the need for seclusion by modeling green pavilions, gazebos, tea houses and banquet rooms—the Dutch would walk to theirs after dinner for an evening of music, drinks and games. If you have the space and the patience, you can create a similar place for summer fun, perhaps connecting it to your house with an alley.

PLANTS

Although many plants lend themselves to architectural treatment, your selection will be narrowed by the specific shape and style you want to achieve. Any design that calls for weaving, or pleaching, requires a plant with supple branches. If you want to create detailed shapes in the French manner, use a plant with small leaves—yew, hemlock, and cypress all have a smooth, velvety texture that allows you to create detailed adornments. Less formal arches, tunnels and garden houses may be formed with foliage of any size. If you are in a hurry, pick a fast-growing plant, but be aware that you will have to clip it more often. Price may also be a consideration if you are planning a structure that requires many plants.

Dark green yew (*Taxus baccata, Taxus cuspidata* and *Taxus × media*) is the classic evergreen for hedges, adding an air of traditional dignity and elegance to any setting. Despite its aristocratic appearance, it is a tough plant that grows happily in a range of conditions. Yew is able to survive in poor or dry soil by greedy feeding, robbing the surrounding soil of nutrients. Because of its appetite, leave some space between yew hedges or arbors and flower beds. It can be trained into virtually any form; and if trimming is neglected, overgrown shapes can be restored to their former dimensions and density

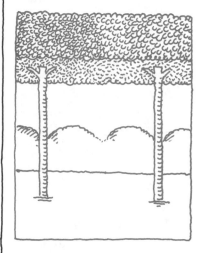

with a severe haircut. Select pyramid-shaped plants about 3 feet tall—smaller plants need more time to reach a good height, and larger ones grow more slowly and don't always survive transplanting. Aurescens (*Taxus cuspidata* 'Aurescens') is a golden yew that makes striking finials at the end of a green hedge.

Hemlock, or Canadian hemlock (*Tsuga canadensis*) as it is sometimes known, is inexpensive and easy to obtain. Hemlock is the plant best suited to constructing large-scale hedges, arches and garden houses. It has a fine texture and a good growth rate, maintaining flexible main branches that are easily bent and tied. Unlike most plants, which naturally reach for the light, hemlock shoots have a peculiar habit of bending in toward the center. Before trimming, it is necessary to pull out the inwardly curled growth.

Arborvitae or white cedar (*Thuja occidentalis*) is another American plant that has proved itself for simple hedges, as it naturally maintains a uniformly full shape. You could try it for archways instead of hemlock.

In warm climates, cypress (*Cupressus* in variety) is a good choice instead of hemlock. It is traditionally used in Spanish glorietas. But beware of Monterey cypress (*Cupressus macrocarpa*), which eventually becomes bare at the base. Arizona cypress (*Cupressus arizonica*) or Leyland cypress (× *Cupressocyparis leylandii*) are more successful choices.

Another good shrub for mild areas is eugenia (*Eugenia uniflora* or *Syzygium paniculatum*). The small new leaves are almost red in full sun, and the shrub is further adorned with puffy white flowers and purple fruits. It fares well with close clipping.

Boxwood (*Buxus sempervirens*) has a noble history in the realm of topiary, and a unique appearance, but it grows too slowly for most people trying to establish large, architectural shapes. Its best use is in the low-growing lines of knot gardens and other flat topiary, unless you live where tree box (*Buxus sempervirens* 'Arborescens') thrives.

❝Yew and box, beech and hornbeam are plants for hedges, and when I draw out my first tentative lines on paper to represent the general organization of a garden, its boundaries and volumes will, as likely as not, be limited by hedges.❞

—RUSSELL PAGE
The Education of a Gardener, 1962

❝Your Gardner can frame your lesser wood to the shape of men armed in the field, ready to give battle; of swift-running Grey-hounds, or of well-sented and true-running Hounds to chase the Deer, or hunt the Hare. This king of hunting shall not waste your Corn, nor much your coyn.❞

—WILLIAM LAWSON
A New Orchard and Garden, 1618

Japanese holly (*Ilex crenata*) has a similar texture to boxwood but is of more rapid and hardy growth. Very few plants can match the glow of its brilliant shiny leaves on a sunny winter's day.

Holly (*Ilex* in variety) has been used for centuries, admired for its ease of shaping, shiny leaves and attractive berries. There are variegated varieties for added interest. Buy a male to place among females to insure a crop of berries.

Coarse-textured evergreens make good large-scale topiary hedges and garden houses. Norway spruce (*Picea abies*) and Colorado blue spruce (*Picea pungens*) are dense enough that they can be allowed to reach the ultimate dimensions before shaping. White pine (*Pinus strobus*) tends to drop its lower limbs—but you can take advantage of this habit to form palissades or bowers with a flat tabletop of foliage and bare-trunked columns.

With deciduous plants you can enjoy a fresh green canopy in summer, cherish the changing colors in autumn, treasure the contrast of twig patterns in winter, and grow early spring flowers underneath, which will flourish before the structure leafs out once again.

Linden (*Tilia* in variety) is the traditional tree for alleys, tunnels and palissades in England, where it is called lime, although it bears no relation to the fruit. The flexible branches are easily trained and have fragrant flowers in the spring. The small fruits are inedible, but leaves and flowers can be used in salads and teas. Linden is well suited to city gardens because it is resistant to air pollution. Hornbeam (*Carpinus betulus*) is another deciduous plant, commonly used for architectural forms in Europe, that deserves to be used more frequently in this country. It doesn't have the bare look of most deciduous trees in the winter, because the leaves turn dark brown and stay on the tree until spring. Green and copper beeches (*Fagus sylvatica* 'Purpurea' and 'Riversii') are widely grown as shade trees, and can be used for large designs.

Privet (*Ligustrum* in variety) is an old standby in America

This towering tree house, known as the Maple of Ratibor, was a popular early-19th-century attraction in northern Italy. Its two stories easily accommodated 20 people.

❝Its docility to shaping into wall, niche, arch and column is so complete and convenient that it comes first among growing things as a means of expression in that domain of design that lies between architecture and gardening.❞

—GERTRUDE JEKYLL AND LAWRENCE WEAVER
writing of the yew in *Gardens for Small Country Houses*, 1911

HIDCOTE MANOR GARDEN

Hidcote Manor Garden in Gloucestershire, England, was laid out in 1907 by an American named Lawrence Johnston. The central walk is bordered on either side by a monumental yew hedge, which opens at intervals into archways that lead to a series of enclosed gardens. The total separation allows each garden to be treated as a furnished "room" with a different color scheme. The White Garden is resplendent with low, scrolled hedges that surround beds filled with white flowers. Perched in the beds are sculptural topiaries in the form of four fat peacocks. Perhaps the most famous room is the Stilt Garden, where pleached hornbeams frame sky-ceilinged hallways.

for hedges, and is certainly a dependable plant, but you might try hawthorn (*Crataegus laevigata*), the "quick-set hedge" of the English countryside, which offers more unusual leaves, attractive foliage, flowers and fall color highlighted by red berries.

The same form that adds structure to your garden can also provide food. Currants (*Ribes sativum*) can be trained as low hedges, but don't grow them near white pine as they are host to the white pine blister-rust disease. Train filbert or hazelnut trees (*Corylus americana, Corylus avellana* and hybrids) into admirable small tunnels and arches. Plant at least two different varieties for cross pollination in order to insure a crop of nuts. Apples (*Malus* in variety) and pears (*Pyrus* in variety) are often trained into spring flowering tunnels—for more on shaping these plants, see Chapter Six.

Different plants can be combined in one form for varied height, color and texture. Several hedges can be planted alongside each other for a stepped effect; or you can mix plants in one hedge for a tapestry effect. At the Hidcote Manor Garden in England, the fuchsia garden is enclosed within a multicolored assortment of plain and variegated holly, yew, box and copper beech.

TECHNIQUES

The basis of the fanciful recipes that follow—and any architectural form you dream up—lies in the fundamental techniques of hedge-making and pleaching. Once you understand these methods, adding the embellishments is merely a matter of invention and patience.

A well-made hedge is the foundation of many topiary designs. There's an old saying that a hedge should be "horse high, pig tight and bull strong." Start with the largest, fullest plants you can afford, remembering that beyond a reasonable size transplanting is risky. For most hedges, this would mean 3-foot-tall, bushy specimens. Trim lightly after replanting for a dense end result. If expense is more of a concern than time, start with younger plants, pruning severely after replanting. This assures that shoots will sprout at the base so the hedge develops fullness at the bottom. Down the road, it is harder to restore a good base than to add height. Do *not* remove the leader on needled evergreens.

The spacing of plants will vary with the particular design and material you have chosen. Use the following distances as a guide: for plants over 6 feet tall, space 3 feet apart; for plants 5 to 6 feet tall, space 2 feet apart; for plants 3 to 4 feet tall, space 12 to 18 inches apart. Stretch a string between two stakes to mark a straight line. For closely spaced hedges, the simplest planting method is to dig a trench the length of the row; but if plants are far apart, it's less work to dig individual holes. After preparing the trench or holes, mark each planting spot exactly. If you plan to have openings or use the trunks to form a colonnade, plan your spacing accordingly.

When planting, position trees or shrubs slightly higher than ground level to allow for settling of the soil. Water well, and provide a mulch while the plants are young in order to retain moisture and keep down weeds. In the early years before the spaces between the plants have filled in, it is especially important to keep after weeds.

Begin shaping your hedge so that it is wider at the bottom than at the top. This shape ensures that light will reach the lower portions and also gives developing hedges a solid, established appearance. Angled sides, referred to in architectural parlance as "batter," should decrease in width 2 to 4 inches for every foot of height. Once the hedge has developed, there are a variety of possible profiles, ranging from flat vertical to curved surfaces. The top may be flat, rounded or trimmed into any fanciful shape. For a contrast in texture, clip the top and one side smooth, leaving the soft feathering of new growth on the opposite side.

What's won is done—joy's soul lies in the doing.
—WILLIAM SHAKESPEARE

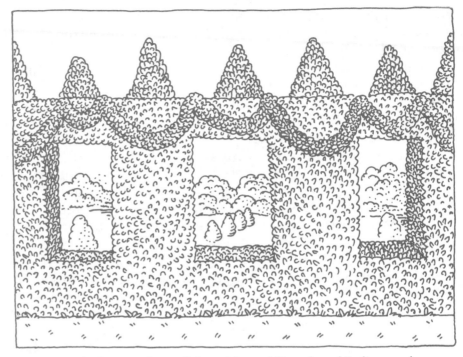

Windowed hedges, in the tradition of formal French and Italian gardens, are perfect embellishments to the American landscape.

Pleaching is a method used to create many forms of architectural topiary, ranging from a rustic tunnel to the formal palissade. Deriving from the Old French *plessier*, "to twist" or "to plait," it is a technique whereby branches are woven together to form a solid wall or canopy. Initially, support may be necessary, but eventually some of the intertwined branches will grow together, forming natural grafts that strengthen the structure of the arch or roof. A rustic pleached tunnel is made by planting a row of saplings on either side of a pathway and tying the tops together. For a formal alley, the trees are fastened to a series of arch-shaped supports and the outside surface is clipped into a fancy contour. Once the shape is set, pleached shapes will only need pruning every year or two.

In many instances, architectural topiary is formed without a frame or other means of support. Detailed shapes, however, are more easily accomplished on an underlying structure. This can be an unobtrusive system of natural wood, pipe or wire that becomes invisible once the shape fills out. Or the framework itself can be enjoyed as a decorative feature; in this case a more attractive framework is used. It may be unpainted and left to weather naturally, or painted. Green and white are the colors most often featured, but consider painting it a hue that harmonizes with your landscape and house for an integrated garden picture. Gates in European gardens are sometimes painted blue or plum, and they blend surprisingly well with their surroundings.

The long, flat blade of hedge trimmers is often a sufficient guide when clipping simple or well-established shapes. But to create and maintain really clean edges, angles and corners, you should set up temporary guidelines when you are shaping. The simplest method is to use a network of stakes and garden twine to establish height and width. Follow the string with your pruners or hedge trimmers. You may have to enlist additional aids to ensure perfection on shapes with many changes in height and thickness, especially on sloping ground. For level surfaces, sink stakes into the middle of the hedge at the exact desired height. Balance a thin board on top of them, and set on it a carpenter's level, adjusting the stakes until the board is level. Precise vertical surfaces are assured by using a plumb line. This consists of heavy twine with a heavy object such as a large fishing weight suspended from one end.

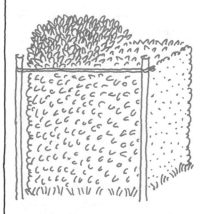

"A clipped hedge is just as natural as the cut grass of a lawn, and is closely akin to it."

—ALICE MORSE EARLE
Old Time Gardens, 1901

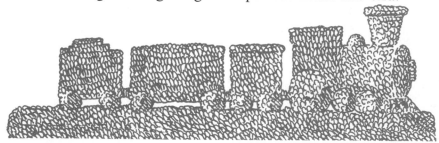

DRESSING UP HEDGES

Before you dress up your hedges, they must be dense, healthy and nearly full grown. If your hedges need work, you can get them into shape with the remedies offered on page 296 (Preservation and Renovation). Then all sorts of interesting details can be added. You might want to begin with windows, which are easy to cut. Once you have had some practice at artful pruning, and you've gained confidence in your skills, you can move on to more intricate details. When the hedge has grown to its ultimate height, finish it off with shapely toppings.

Windows

As soon as a hedge has reached the size you want, you can cut out windows. Create one window in a short length of hedge for a glimpse beyond your yard, or repeat them in a longer row for a series of scenic pictures. The windows should be placed so that they are about halfway between the trunks of the trees or shrubs that make up the hedge, otherwise you will end up killing the plants.

After deciding what you want the window to reveal, and what shape it will be, you are ready to start clipping. Ordinary objects can be used as a template to guide your carving. If you decide on round windows, a trash can lid is a perfect guide; if you prefer rectangular or square openings, use a window screen of the desired size.

You will need:
—a well-grown hedge
—a trash can lid or window screen for a template
—pruning shears

1. Hold the template up to the side of the hedge and, with pruning shears, nick out an outline of the window.

2. Remove the template. Starting in the center, cut away the hedge a little at a time until you reach the nicked outline. This may require cutting back through the bare, woody part of the hedge, but new growth will soon appear.

3. In future seasons, trim the windows whenever you prune the hedge.

For All Bas-Relief Decorations

A finishing touch is given to architectural topiary by carving the top or side surface with decorative forms. These embellishments can be added to any size hedge. Hemlock, yew and cypress are three evergreens that have the fine texture necessary for this kind of detail. Start on bas-relief decorations when your hedge is clearly in need of a trim, with at least 6 inches of new growth, by cutting away the new growth around the design. The techniques described can be adapted to any design. To save time and end up with a smooth surface, do most of the clipping with electric trimmers or manual hedge shears. Then go around the edge of your decoration with hand clippers for clean details.

You will need:
—a well-grown hedge
—twine or string for a guideline
—electric hedge trimmers or manual hedge shears
—hand pruners
—(optional) cardboard plus a knife or scissors; bamboo or wooden stakes 1 foot longer than the height of the hedge; a plumb line, depending on the design you choose

The Oxford English Dictionary defines the word hedge as "a row of bushes or low trees (e.g. hawthorn, or privet) planted closely to form a boundary between pieces of land or at the sides of a road: the usual form of fence in England."

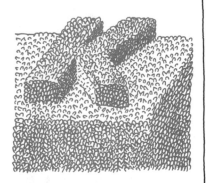

Garlands

It is simple to festoon the side of your own hedge with graceful garlands like those on the hemlock hedge at Ladew Topiary Gardens.

1 Tie the string to a projecting twig on the side of the hedge. Drape it so it hangs in the curve you desire, and tie the end to another twig. If you want a series of garlands, repeat this along the face of the hedge.

2 Cut away the lighter new growth to within a few inches above and below the string until you reach a darker layer, which is the previous year's foliage. Leave the hedge unclipped along and close to the string to roughly establish the shape of the garland. Gradually build out and refine the decoration in later trimmings.

Initials

These look nice when carved into the top of hedges that are waist high, but are equally effective on the side of a tall hedge. Draw the letters that make up your initials, or the numbers of your street address, on a sheet of heavy cardboard. Cut out each letter or numeral separately.

1 Arrange the cardboard patterns to form your initials or address on the top of the hedge.

2 Cut away the new growth on the top of the hedge around the cardboard patterns. Carefully go around the edge of each letter with hand clippers for a neat edge.

3 Save the patterns for use each time you trim the hedge. With each clipping, give the initials better definition and height.

Columns

To give your hedges a more substantial, truly architectural look, add some columns. To outline each column, you will need two bamboo or wooden stakes about a foot longer than the height of your hedge.

1 Sink a stake into the ground directly in front of the hedge, so it just brushes the foliage. Determine the width you want your column to be, and set a second stake that distance from the first stake. If you are a perfectionist, and want to be sure that the stakes are absolutely vertical, check them with a plumb line. Repeat these steps, setting a pair of stakes wherever you want a column.

2 For a three-dimensional appearance, the hedge is carved more deeply than for the other ornaments. Trim the surface around the decoration back a few inches into the dark green layer of last year's growth. If you don't have a thick enough layer of foliage, gradually bring out the column by leaving an inch of new growth on it in subsequent clippings.

3 Repeat Steps 1 and 2 if you want to contour the other side of the hedge.

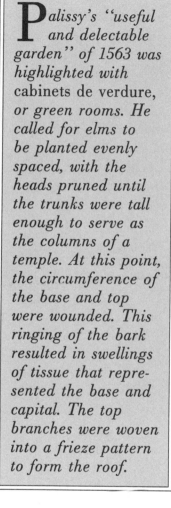

*P*alissy's "useful and delectable garden" of 1563 was highlighted with cabinets de verdure, or green rooms. He called for elms to be planted evenly spaced, with the heads pruned until the trunks were tall enough to serve as the columns of a temple. At this point, the circumference of the base and top were wounded. This ringing of the bark resulted in swellings of tissue that represented the base and capital. The top branches were woven into a frieze pattern to form the roof.

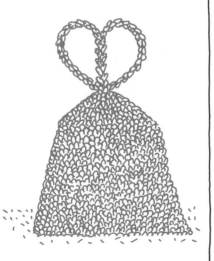

Crowning Touches

Once your hedge has reached its desired height, you may finish it off with topiary toppings. They can be simple globes, pyramids or finials—or even whimsical creatures.

Decide where the toppings will be placed, and allow shoots to grow out of the top of the hedge at these spots. Leave all shoots that appear around that spot until you determine which are best suited for training into the desired shape. For detailed designs, you must then set a wire frame on top of the hedge and tie the shoots to it. Simple birds and geometric toppings, however, are easily made without using a frame. Rounded shapes are formed by bending a branch downward and tying it to itself, for the natural resistance of the branch will hold the curve.

You will need:
—a well-grown hedge that has reached full height
—twine or other soft, sturdy tying material
—pruning shears

Crowns

Choose four sturdy shoots growing close together. Bend each shoot out and down, tying it securely to hold the curve. Trim the side branches of each shoot close to the main stem, so that each makes a dense ring of foliage.

Finials

A variety of rounded or pointed forms can be shaped. Allow a thick cluster of shoots to grow up, and trim them with pruning shears into the desired contour.

Birds

As with the finials, allow a cluster of stems to develop in one spot, and tie them together. Divide the shoots into two unequal bunches—the larger group will become the body and tail, while the smaller will become the head. Tie the large bunch together where you want to begin the tail.

Tie the smaller bunch where you want to define the neck. Take the two or three longest stems, bend them down and tie into a curve to create the head. The rough outline of a bird will be identifiable; clip into a well-defined shape as the stems grow.

GREEN ARCHWAYS

The following are several variations on the topiary arch, all of which make use of two hemlock trees. Norway spruce could also be used for a similar effect. Two of the designs come from Frank J. Scott's *The Art of Beautifying Suburban Home Grounds*, published in 1870. An opening of 4 feet is a good proportion for most paths, but this can be altered to suit your site. If you don't already have the right plants on your property, buy a pair of the tallest and fullest specimens you can find and afford. The 8- to 10-foot size is usually available.

Single Arch

You will need:
—two 8- to 10-foot hemlock trees
—pruning shears

—a 6-foot wooden stake or pole, notched at each end
—twine or other soft, sturdy tying material

1 Plant trees 2 feet away from, and on either side of, a 4-foot path (or 8 feet apart). Trim the inner sides back to 18 inches from the trunk to allow for new growth.

2 Take a stake or pole 6 feet long, notched at each end, and lash it horizontally between the trunks 7 feet up from the ground. This will bring the trees together and begin to define the opening.

3 When the trees have reached 12 feet or so in height, bend the tops above the stick until they join, twist them together, and tie them so they cannot come apart. Check ties frequently and adjust as necessary to prevent girdling. Begin trimming the outside to roughly resemble an arch.

4 When the tops are firmly intertwined, usually after two years, remove the ties. Once the trunks have grown rigid and hold the curve, remove the horizontal pole. Continue developing the figure by clipping regularly. The final height is a matter of personal preference.

Single Arch with Double Spire Variation

Twin spires are achieved by allowing the leaders of both trees to continue straight up, and twisting together side branches to form the arch and center pinnacle.

Single Arch with Bird or Beast Variation

For further amusement, create an arch with the side branches, and use the leaders to form the head and tail of a green animal or fowl.

Pavilion or Glorieta Variation

A pavilion or glorieta is formed using the same technique as for single arches. It would be lovely placed as a focal point in the center of your lawn, or at the intersection of two paths. Plant four trees in a square. Follow the steps described for an arch, twisting the tops of opposite diagonal trees together.

ARCHITECTURAL FORMS

Mazes

This maze is a simplified version of one designed by the Italian architect Serlio for his *Five Books of Architecture* in 1537. The design is made up of straight lines and right angles, so it is simple to lay out. It is really just a series of plain hedges. The goal in the center could be a topiary sculpture, a small fountain, or a chair as a reward for tired maze treaders. You do need a reasonable amount of space for a life-size game; this particular one occupies a 38- by 38-foot square.

Yew is unbeatable for making a maze—it will quickly make an attractive, narrow, and impenetrable barrier. Shredded bark

mulch, inexpensive and easy to handle, is a good material for the paths. It is handsome, gentle underfoot, keeps down weeds, retains soil moisture and protects the hedge's root systems from trampling.

You will need:
—thirty-eight short (12- to 18-inch) stakes
—several balls of sturdy twine
—hedging plants to make the design

1 Set one stake to mark the first corner. Tie twine to it and measure out 38 feet from the stake. Drive a stake into the ground at that point. Stretch the twine taut and tie it to the second stake. You have now established the first side, from which all subsequent measurements are taken.

2 Measure out the second and third sides of the maze in the same manner.

3 Measure out the last side as above. You will have to adjust the second and third sides until they form right angles.

4 Stretch string to mark out a diagonal line across the square from one corner to another.

5 Measure out the remaining diagonal. The intersection of both diagonals marks the center point.

6 Mark the halfway point of each side (19 feet) from each corner. Connect these points through the center of the square to form a cross.

7 Use these guidelines to lay out planting lines for the hedges, following the proportions in the drawing (at left). Measure 4½ feet between each row of bushes, which ultimately allows 2 feet in width for the mature hedges and 2½ feet for the paths.

8 Plant and shape as described on pages 280 to 281. In subsequent years, maintain the hedges by shearing.

Stilt Hedge Palissades

Here are directions for growing one of the simpler palissades, a square hedge raised on bare trunks. The famous Stilt Garden at Hidcote, England, is composed of double rows of pleached hornbeam that create rectangular rooms where walls of trees form the sides, framing a rectangular ceiling of blue sky.

Small-leafed linden is a pretty and dependable tree for training into a stilt hedge, but the instructions can also be followed for hornbeam or beech. Try to purchase trees that have straight trunks clear of branches up to an overhead height. A support system is used to act as an initial training guide, but if your trees' branches are already touching, they may be tied to each other without the aid of a framework.

You will need:
—a length of string and two short stakes for laying out each row
*   of trees*
—healthy, straight-trunked trees
—one 15-foot post for each tree
—wire, preferably vinyl-coated, to string between the stakes

1 To determine the number of trees in a row: First, measure the total length of the strip you want covered. You will want to space your trees at approximately 10-foot intervals, so divide that length by 10 to ascertain the total number of trees.

For example, if you want to cover a row 51 feet long, divide 51 by 10, which gives you 5.1. This rounds out to 5, which means you will need 5 trees.

Again the moss-grown terraces to raise,
And spread the labyrinth's perplexing maze;
Replace in even lines the ductile yew,
And plant again the ancient avenue.

—RICHARD PAYNE KNIGHT
from "The Landscape: A Didactic Poem," 1794

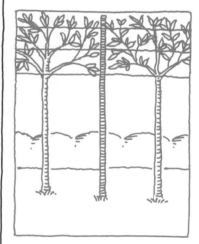

POLLARDING

The technique of pollarding is used to mold individual trees into a distinctive knobby head. Rarely seen in this country, it is common in Europe, where avenues of street trees are kept within bounds by cutting the main branches back almost to the main trunk. The practice was originally developed to produce firewood without losing trees—drastic pruning encouraged a supply of thin, new branches. Some pollarded trees have been yielding kindling continuously for hundreds of years.

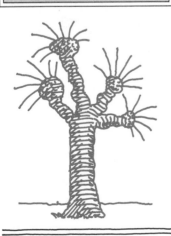

2 To determine the spacing between each tree: First, deduct 10 feet from the length of the row to allow for a 5-foot overhang of branches at each end. Then divide the remainder by the number of spaces between the trees, which is one less than the total number of trees.

If we use the same example as in Step 1, subtracting 10 from 51 feet leaves 41. The trunks of the two outer trees will be spaced 41 feet apart. Dividing 41 by 4 (spaces between the five trees), we find that each tree in the row will be spaced 10 feet 3 inches from the next one.

3 Sink the short stakes at each end of the row and stretch a string between them. Mark planting spots at the intervals determined in Steps 1 and 2, remembering that the two outer trunks should be placed 5 feet in from each end. Prepare the holes, plant trees and drive a 15-foot post 3 feet into the ground next to each tree. Secure the tree trunks to the posts.

4 String horizontal wires between stakes at 1-foot intervals. You can string five wires starting at 7 feet, or four wires beginning at 8 feet for a higher canopy.

5 When the trees are tall enough to begin training (at least 10 feet tall), all branches should be removed up to a height of seven feet from the ground. Any branches facing front or back should be cut off to within 2 feet of the main trunk to direct vigor into the side branches. Encourage side branches to spread toward adjacent trees by tying along the wires. Wherever branches from adjacent trees cross, they should be intertwined. Snip back the side branches to develop a thick growth of new stems. As new stems appear, tie them along wires or weave them into the older branches.

6 Once the top growth is full, clip the surfaces flat with hedge trimmers, using guidelines if necessary. The final depth of the hedgetop should measure about 5 feet.

7 For a truly breathtaking palissade, top it off with finials. In this case, use only the side branches for pleaching; let the central leaders grow up above the top wire and clip into tight spheres or any other shape you desire.

Leafy hallways provide cool shade from which to admire this 17th-century Dutch garden in the heat of the day.

66*Live hedges are already become objects of serious importance, particularly in those parts of the Union in which timber has got scarce . . . therefore, the sooner the citizens turn their attention to the cultivation and planting of them, the greater portion of their benefits will they themselves enjoy, and the sooner will they lay the foundation of a rich inheritance for their children, and of an ornamental and useful establishment for their country.***99**

—BERNARD MCMAHON
McMahon's American Gardener, 1857

❝As a boundary fence, especially upon the roadside, there is much to be said in favor of the hedge. Nothing gives a neighborhood such a finished rural aspect, as to have the roads bordered by hedges.❞

—GEORGE A. MARTIN
Fences, Gates and Bridges: A Practical Manual, 1887

PRESERVATION AND RENOVATION

Architectural topiary is an investment of time and effort. To preserve your creation, give it regular attention. Since plants are placed close together, competing for moisture and nutrients, they should be watered during dry spells and fertilized annually.

It is always better to renovate a hedge or arch than to start from scratch. Clean out dead or diseased branches. Holes and gaps can be eliminated quickly by filling in with new little plants. Weak or overgrown old forms can be restored by drastic pruning. Some details may be sacrificed initially, but the result is perfect beauty in the long run. Drastic reshaping must be accomplished in stages, however, so that a supply of leaves is left to feed the plants. Cut back one side and the top. When new growth emerges on the cut sides the following year, repeat the treatment on the remaining surfaces.

Evergreens are usually pruned in winter or early spring, and lightly trimmed at any point in the growing season. Deciduous plants can be heavily pruned whenever the sap isn't running, meaning anytime except the spring, although it is easier to see their structure after the leaves have fallen.

Sources and Resources

GLOSSARY

A

alley (or allee): a garden path or walkway bordered by rows of trees or hedges. A pleached alley is formed by training the pliable branches from two rows of trees to interlace overhead in a connected series of arches, in order to create a shaded tunnel.

apical: refers to the tip or apex of a stem. An apical bud is the bud at the end of a stem, and an apical shoot is the uppermost stem on a plant. An apical shoot that grows more rapidly than and inhibits the development of side stems is referred to as apically dominant.

arbor: a shaded tunnel of trees or shrubs that meet overhead, trained on an underlying framework. Often the wood or metal structure is decorative in its own right. Also called a berceau or gallery.

arch: in topiary, two shrubs or trees trained and shaped to meet overhead. They can be freestanding or incorporated into hedges where an opening is desired for a path. A radiating circle of arches is called a glorieta. A connected series of arches forming a shaded tunnel is known as an alley, berceau, charmille or arbor.

architectural topiary: outdoor trees and shrubs, usually elaborations of a basic hedge, trained and cut to form living outdoor walls, halls and rooms; often ornamented with architectural features such as windows, arches and columns.

auxin: a hormonal substance produced in the growing tip of a plant's shoots, or apical buds, that inhibits the growth of side shoots.

axil: the angle between a leaf and the stem on which it grows. Axillary buds or shoots are those that appear in this space between the leaf and stem.

B

berceau: a shaded tunnel of trees or shrubs that meet overhead, trained on an underlying framework. Often the wood or metal structure is decorative in its own right. Also called an arbor.

bud: a protuberance from which a shoot, leaf or flower will develop. A dormant bud is one that will not swell and develop until it has been stimulated by pruning to break apical dominance. An apical or terminal bud is the topmost bud on a stem. Adventitious buds are those that appear as a result of stimulation by pruning. Axillary buds are those that appear in the space between the leaf and stem. Lateral buds are found along the sides of the main stems, and will develop into shoots that grow out at an angle.

C

cambium: a layer of new, growing tissue between the bark and wood of all stems and branches, usually visible as a brighter green than the surrounding tissues. In order for a graft to succeed, the cambium layers of both plants must be aligned so that they grow together.

carpet bedding: a Victorian ground decoration consisting of designs or patterns formed on the ground of annual flowers and colorful foliage plants, instead of herbs or low-growing shrubs as in knot gardens or parterres.

charmille: a tree tunnel constructed by interlacing the overhead branches in a double row of trees. The name derives form the French *charmes*, or "hornbeam," a favorite tree for this purpose. Also known as a pleached alley.

cordon: the most basic espalier form; a single stemmed shape with severely shortened side shoots, which may be vertical, diagonal, horizontal or serpentine. The word derives from the French *cordon*, meaning "ribbon" or "cord."

crown: the multiple-branched top portion of a single-stemmed topiary, or standard.

cultivar: an abbreviation for "cultivated variety"; in contrast to a naturally occuring or wild variety, it is a form of a plant species that was discovered or developed in cultivation.

cutting: a portion of a stem or a leaf removed from the parent plant and partially immersed in water or a moist medium, such as sand or perlite, in order to stimulate the development of roots and create a new plant.

D

deciduous: a tree or shrub that annually sheds and replaces its leaves.

dowel: a round wooden pole, available in a range of diameters and lengths, used in the creation of mock topiary.

E

espalier: a term used to describe any plant trained into an open, flat pattern, as well as the technique used to achieve a two-dimensional effect.

estrade: an iron replica of a tiered, single-stem topiary popular in medieval times, in which a central pole supported trays filled with potted flowers, often festooned with metal balls to resemble fruit.

F

fedge: a word coined from fence and hedge, describing a solidly vine-covered fence that simulates a hedge.

fertilizer: a natural or artificial material added to soil, or dissolved in water, that nourishes a plant and stimulates growth or the production of flowers or fruit. Prepared fertilizers usually have three numbers separated by dashes on the label. The first number refers to the percentage of nitrogen, the second to the percentage of phosphorus and the third to the percentage of potash that the fertilizer contains. In general, choose a balanced formula such as 20-20-20. To promote the development of flowers or fruit, select a fertilizer with a higher phosphorus content, such as 5-10-5. To ensure the hardiness of outdoor plants, don't apply fertilizer containing nitrogen in late summer or fall.

flat topiary: also called a ground decoration, a plant design that carpets the ground in level beds made of low hedges, clipped herbs and flowering plants. Various styles are known as carpet bedding, knot gardens, or parterres.

frame: an open metal or wooden skeleton used to train plants into shapes.

framework: the skeleton of a tree or shrub; the main branches that define a plant's shape. Also used to describe a metal or wooden structure used to train plants into formal shapes.

G

gallery: a shaded tunnel of trees or shrubs that meet overhead, trained on an underlying framework. Often the wood or metal structure is decorative in its own right. Also called a berceau or arbor.

genus: in botany, a group of plants with common characteristics, usually comprising several species.

girdling: injury to a stem or branch caused when a tie or wire is too tight and constricts the plant, blocking the flow of water and nutrients. This leaves a permanent ring and usually results in the death of all tissue above the point of constriction.

glorieta: a group of trees trained and clipped into a radiating circle of arches to form an open pavilion. The glorieta originated as a Spanish garden feature, usually planted at the intersection of paths or water channels. A simplified version consists of two arches that cross each other.

grafting: uniting part of one plant, a bud or shoot (known as the scion), with the stem and root system of another (known as the understock) to form a single plant. This is done so that the desirable characteristics of two or more plants may be combined in a single specimen. As a rule, only closely related plants can be successfully grafted.

H

hardiness: the ability of a plant to survive in a specific area, primarily determined by its tolerance of low temperature, but also influenced by its adaptability to high temperature, differing soil and rainfall, and even air pollution.

hedge: a row of trees or shrubs planted and trimmed into a solid line; the basic element of architectural topiary. A stilt hedge or pole hedge is a square-cut shape raised on smooth trunks.

horticulture: the art and science of cultivating plants.

K

knot garden: a level bed ornamented with a pattern of intertwining lines formed with dwarf hedges or clipped herbs.

L

laterals: buds and branches growing out at an angle along the sides of the main stems.

leader: the main, usually central, stem of a plant, which is longer and more vigorous than other portions.

M

maiden: a young, unbranched single stem tree whose leader has not been cut. Also called a whip.

maze: sometimes called a puzzle-hedge; a network of paths framed by hedges to make a life-size game.

mock topiary: an instant creation that resembles a growing plant sculpture, actually assembled from cut dried or fresh foliage, flowers and other plant materials.

moss: botanically speaking, a minute, flowerless plant that grows closely together to form a dense material. The term is used loosely to describe several types of plant material used in the creation of portable topiary and mock topiary. Sheet moss comes in large flat pieces, is light green when alive, and dries to a golden brown. Mound moss is a fresh green color, and grows in rounded mounds of various sizes. Long fiber or coarse sphagnum moss is the main ingredient in filling stuffed topiary, with a fluffy texture composed of whole fibers that become spongy when wet. Milled sphagnum has the texture of fine powder and is impossible to use for filling frames. Reindeer moss has a popcorn-like texture, is naturally a grayish green but is often dyed other colors. Spanish moss is a distinctive, loose, curly gray type of plant material.

N

node: a point on the stem where a leaf or bud will grow. Also referred to as a lateral bud, which is found at the junction of the leaf and stem, or a terminal bud, which appears at the tip of the stem.

P

palissade: a large, ornate variation of the hedge; a row of trees or shrubs clipped into a wall, arcade or other architectural form. The stilt hedge, or pole hedge, is one version of the classic palissade, consisting of a square-cut head raised on high, smooth trunks.

palmette verrier: a tree or shrub trained into the open, flat shape of a six-armed candelabrum. A classic espalier design, named for Louis Verrier, a 19th-century French agriculturist.

parterre: a low, level bed ornamented with a pattern made of dwarf hedges, flowers, grass and colored stone. The name is French, from *par terre*, meaning "on the ground." A variation of the knot garden, usually larger in size, parterre designs generally consist of arabesques, open scrolls or fleurs-de-lis rather than intertwining lines.

pinching: also called pinching back or stopping out; the practice of removing the soft tips of stems, branches and leaders in order to encourage the sprouting of lateral buds for bushier growth. It may be done with the thumbnail and forefinger or with a small knife or scissors.

pleaching: a technique wherein branches from neighboring trees are woven together to form a solid wall or canopy. Deriving from the Old French *plessier*, "to twist" or "to plait," it is a method used to create many forms of architectural topiary, ranging from a rustic tunnel to the formal palissade. Initially support may be necessary, but eventually some of the intertwined branches will grow together, forming natural grafts that strengthen the structure.

pollarding: the technique used to mold individual trees into a distinctive knobby head and keep them from increasing in size from year to year. This is accomplished by annually cutting the main branches back almost to the main trunk to encourage a supply of thin, new branches. This is a common practice in Europe, where avenues of street trees are kept in bounds by this method; the original purpose was to produce firewood without losing trees.

poodle: a kind of single-stemmed topiary, or standard, with multiple disks or balls along the stem instead of a single crown of growth.

portable topiary: a technique wherein fast-growing plants are trained over a wire frame. Because the metal frame, rather than a plant's branches, provides structure and definition, this type of topiary can be any size and shape. There are two types: hollow portable topiary, where the frame serves as a hollow trellis over which vines planted in the pot beneath are trained; and stuffed portable topiary, in which the frame is stuffed with moss and potting mix so it can serve both as form and growing container.

pots: containers used to hold the growing medium and root system of topiary; in same cases, such as stuffed portable topiary and mock topiary, they may serve only a decorative function. In most cases, clay pots are preferable to plastic ones, because their heavier weight helps to stabilize topiary.

primary leaf: a leaf growing directly from the leader or along the central stem, also called a basal leaf.

pruning: shortening or removing a plant's branches, buds or shoots in order to change its shape, remove weak or diseased portions, or make it more vigorous. Pruning stimulates the sprouting of buds into healthy shoots, leaves and flowers. New growth may be removed while still in the bud stage by rubbing out or pinching off with a fingernail, while more mature stems and branches are cut off with tools such as scissors, pruning shears or a saw. New shoots will grow in the same direction the bud below the cut is facing. The cut should be slanted away from the bud to avoid injuring it and so that no unsightly stub remains.

R

rootstock: in grafting, the lower plant, used to form the roots and main trunk.

runner: on vining plants, a long stem that grows out from the main stem of a plant and develops roots.

S

sapling: a young tree whose main branches are still flexible.

scaffold: a major side branch on a shrub or tree, part of its framework, from which secondary growth develops.

scion: in grafting, the bud or shoot chosen for the top part of the new plant, which is joined to the rootstock.

shoot: the new stem that develops from a bud or node.

species: in botany, a closely related group of plants, which share many characteristics and can reproduce among themselves.

spiral: a form of single-stemmed topiary whose foliage is clipped so it appears to coil up and around the central stem, or whose central stem has been twisted in a corkscrew fashion.

sport: a new variety of plant, arising when a shoot or portion of a particular plant appears with a different leaf shape, color or growth habit. This is caused by spontaneous changes in the genetic material.

spur: a specialized branch structure on which some varieties of apples, pears and stone fruits bear flowers and fruit; the short,

gnarled twigs live for several years, elongating slowly.

stake: a wooden or bamboo stick, used to support and guide a topiary during training. Also used as a marker when laying out knot gardens or architectural topiary.

standard: a plant trained to have a crown of growth atop a single, erect, unbranched stem; a stylized form inspired by the trunk-and-crown silhouette of a tree. A grafted standard is produced by using one or more plants rather than training a single individual. Several buds or shoots, known as scions, are used to form the crown, while the trunk is furnished from another plant, or rootstock. A portable topiary standard consists of plants trained on a frame that resembles a standard shape. Mock standards may resemble a growing plant, but are actually assembled from cut branches, leaves, flowers and fruit.

stone fruits: members of the genus *Prunus*, such as peaches, cherries and plums, with a single hard pit in the center of a fleshy fruit.

T

template: an object, usually flat, used as a guide in carving shapes in plants or in bending wire to make a frame.

thinning: reducing the number of shoots and branches, and removing any dead material on a plant, so that light penetrates to shoots and dormant buds in the center of the plant in order to develop a denser layer of growth.

topiary: the art of shaping plants, by clipping and training, to create living sculpture.

trellis: a lightweight framework of wooden strips, usually in a diamond or grid pattern, used to support and train espaliers or vining plants.

trimming: the removal of the tips of branches and stems for a neat, well-defined appearance and even surface.

tying: attaching a branch or stem to a frame, stake or other structure, in order to provide support or guide the plant into a particular shape. A soft material that is strong yet "gives" should be used to tie the branches or stems. Good ties include raffia, soft string, old stockings, twine, osier or basket willow, and notched garbage bag closures. Ties should be checked periodically, as no material has infinite stretch and strength, to prevent girdling, chafing or broken ties. Branches never recover from severe girdling injuries, although it may take years for them to die.

U

understock: —see **rootstock**.

V

variety: a plant that has some variation from the species to which it belongs, which may mean different-colored flowers or foliage, a compact growing habit or a special leaf shape. It is identified by the third word of the botanical name. For example, *Taxus cuspidata* 'Aurescens' is a form of Japanese yew (*Taxus cuspidata*) with golden-tinted foliage.

W

wall aids: various devices used to attach espaliered trees or ivy to a solid surface. These include nails, screws, vine guides, eyebolts and antenna guides.

water picks: plastic tubes of various sizes, with pointed ends, that may be stuck into sphagnum moss, foam or vegetable forms for mock topiary. They are filled with water and have a rubber cap that seals around the flower stem. Used to add fresh flowers to a dry base, provide additional support and water for delicate flowers in a wet form, or for adding flowers as decorations on stuffed portable topiary.

whip: a young, unbranched single stem tree whose leader has not been cut. Also called a maiden.

wire: the main component of frames; many kinds are employed for topiary. It must be flexible enough to bend easily, but stiff enough to hold the shape you want. It is sized in reverse order to its thickness; the higher the number the thinner the wire. The size of wire is referred to as the gauge. Aluminum wire is soft and rustproof. It is more expensive than galvanized, but easier to bend. Galvanized wire is harder to bend than aluminum, but this means a thinner gauge will still hold its shape. The galvanizing process makes the metal rust resistant, but it will eventually corrode. Number 8- or number 9-gauge wire is sometimes sold as "fence wire." Chicken wire, a hexagonal mesh, can be used on its own to construct simple frames, or it can be added to wire skeletons. Hardware cloth, a sturdy wire mesh, is used to line the base of frames, or to create forms for training outdoor ivy sculptures. Florist's wire is thin, green-enameled, and available in straight lengths or coiled on spools.

Z

zone: a growing region of the United States and Canada, determined by the average annual minimum temperatures of the area. When a zone is specified for a particular plant, it indicates the northern or coldest region in which it usually grows, meaning that it will thrive in several zones to the south. Weather patterns are changing, and gardeners are experimenting with growing plants untested in their zones, proving that it is possible for many plants to succeed farther north or south than had previously been believed. The Hardiness Zone Map (at right) indicates the numbered regions referred to in THE COMPLETE BOOK OF TOPIARY.

HARDINESS ZONE MAP

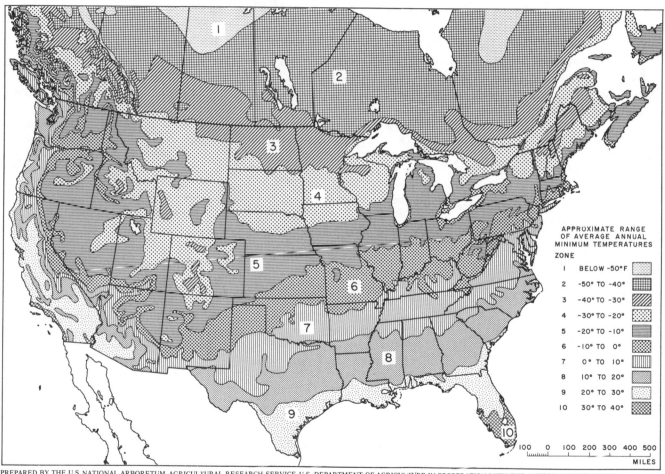

APPROXIMATE RANGE
OF AVERAGE ANNUAL
MINIMUM TEMPERATURES

ZONE	
1	BELOW -50°F
2	-50° TO -40°
3	-40° TO -30°
4	-30° TO -20°
5	-20° TO -10°
6	-10° TO 0°
7	0° TO 10°
8	10° TO 20°
9	20° TO 30°
10	30° TO 40°

100   0   100 200 300 400 500
MILES

PREPARED BY THE U.S. NATIONAL ARBORETUM, AGRICULTURAL RESEARCH SERVICE, U.S. DEPARTMENT OF AGRICULTURE IN COOPERATION WITH THE AMERICAN HORTICULTURAL SOCIETY.

TWELVE TOP PLANTS FOR TOPIARY

These plants have proven to be the most successful for a variety of topiary methods. We encourage you, however, to experiment with other plants, making use of different leaf sizes, colors and shapes. Apple and pear trees (which are the best material for espaliers) and ivy (great for all forms of topiary) are not included here, since whole chapters are devoted to their merits and needs.

Baby's Tears
(*Soleirolia soleirolii*)
hardy in frost-free areas/houseplant

Baby's tears is a popular choice for portable indoor topiary. It has a bright green moss-like appearance and a close-growing habit. The thread-thin stems root easily wherever they touch moss or soil. No pinning is necessary; simply snip off unruly growth. The 'Aurea' variety has golden-yellow leaves, perfect for a tiger's stripes. Uniform watering and a warm growing temperature are essential.

Boxwood
(*Buxus microphylla, Buxus sempervirens*)
hardy to Zones 5–6

Boxwood shears beautifully, is very long lived and has a bright green appearance that is different from any other outdoor evergreen. Grown primarily in the Middle Atlantic states and southern New England (up to and including Zone 6), it is quite possible that boxwood will succeed in other regions. Check with a local nursery to see if it is suited to your area. Choose a variety with an appropriate growth rate. For sculptures and low hedges, common boxwood (*Buxus sempervirens*) is unsurpassed. In the South, tree box (*Buxus sempervirens* 'Arborescens') grows to great heights and is trained into pleached alleys. As a young plant, it has a naturally pyramidal habit. For knot gardens use dwarf varieties, which grow at a rate of one to four inches a year. Try Dutch edging box (*Buxus sempervirens* 'suffruticosa'), or varieties such as Kingsville Dwarf (*Buxus microphylla* 'Compacta'), Korean boxwood (*Buxus microphylla* 'koreana'), or Vardar Valley (*Buxus sempervirens* 'Vardar Valley'). The latter is hardy to Zone 5.

Clipping is best done in spring before hot, dry weather sets in, so the new growth has a chance to harden before frost. The cut leaf edges may turn brown—this is unsightly but it won't hurt the plant. Some authorities recommend clipping just after a rain to prevent discoloration. The roots of boxwood rob the surrounding soil of moisture and nutrients, so if you use it to border flower beds, cut away the boxwood's roots on the inner edge of the beds with a sharp spade.

Creeping Fig
(*Ficus pumila*)
hardy to Zone 9/houseplant

Creeping fig is a dependable vine for portable indoor topiary that thrives in a range of temperatures and light levels and rarely succumbs to insects or diseases. The stems root easily where they touch moss or soil. Small green leaves are close together and lie flat against a stuffed form. 'Variegata' has the same habit, and white-splashed leaves. The oak leaf (*Ficus pumila* 'Quercifolia') and miniature (*Ficus pumila* 'Minima') varieties create an even finer, flatter cover than ordinary creeping fig but are extremely slow growing. Creeping fig can be used outdoors in mild climates—its one requirement is that it never be allowed to dry out.

Cypress
(*Cupressus arizonica, Cupressus macrocarpa, Cupressus sempervirens,* × *Cupressocyparis leylandii*)
hardy to Zones 6–8

Cypress, while not as hardy as many other species of evergreens, has a fine texture and takes well to close shearing into specimen sculptures or hedges. Arizona cypress (*Cupressus arizonica*) has pale to gray-green foliage and is hardy to Zone 6. It prefers dry, light soil. It is not a good plant for windy locations—because of its poor root system, it tends to fall over. Monterey cypress (*Cupressus macrocarpa*) is bright green and is hardy only as far north as Zone 8. It is a rapid grower, strong enough to withstand wind, and tolerates salt spray. There are golden varieties, such as 'Golden Pillar,' that provide color contrast in the garden. Italian cypress (*Cupressus sempervirens*) is dark green, and survives as far north as Zone 8. The varieties 'Stricta,' which naturally maintains a tall, narrow habit, and 'Horizontalis,' which stays low and broad, are useful for sculptures of these proportions. Leyland cypress (× *Cupressocyparis leylandii*) is a hardier, fast-growing hybrid with gray-green leaves.

Hemlock
(*Tsuga canadensis*)
hardy to Zone 3

Hemlock is a graceful, long-lived tree, particularly suited for large-scale architectural topiary such as tall sculpted hedges, arches, tunnels and summerhouses. The flexible main branches are easily bent and tied. Fine needles produce a delicate yet dense foliage texture that is excellent for carving into bas relief and detailed decorations. The branches droop naturally at the ends—for an interesting contrast, leave one side of a hemlock hedge unsheared. Unlike most plants, which naturally reach for the light, hemlock shoots have a peculiar habit of bending in toward the center. Before trimming, it is neccessary to rake out the inwardly curled growth.

Lavender
(*Lavandula angustifolia, Lavandula dentata*)
hardy to Zone 5/houseplant

Lavender is well loved, both for its aromatic foliage and spikes of flowers used for perfumes and potpourri. English lavender (*Lavandula angustifolia*) is useful for knot gardens or standards, with gray leaves and lavender-blue flowers, and is hardy to Zone 5. In order to enjoy lavender's blooms, hold off on clipping knots or standards until they finish flowering in June or July. English lavender generally grows about 24 inches as a miniature hedge; 'Munstead' is a more compact grower that stays about 15 inches tall. 'Hidcote' is a variety with deep purple flowers, and 'Jean Davis' has green foliage and white flowers.

French lavender (*Lavandula dentata*) is not as hardy as English lavender, but it is a good indoor plant for standards and poodles, grown for the appearance and fragrance of its toothed, light green leaves and purple flowers. 'Candicans' is a larger variety with silver leaves.

Myrtle
(*Myrtus communis*)
hardy to Zone 9/houseplant

Myrtle can be trained around a hoop for a two-dimensional portable topiary, or as a standard or other single-stem topiary shape. The leaves are shiny, bright green, narrow and tiny. Both foliage and twigs exude a spicy smell when cut or rubbed. Myrtle can be trained to virtually any height you desire, from 6 inches to 6 feet. White flowers and blue-black berries add seasonal interest. 'Microphylla,' the common variety, has closely set leaves less than an inch long. The variety 'Variegata,' with white-edged leaves, is more difficult to grow but has an unusual appearance. Mealybugs like myrtle, so check under leaves and inside ties for these cottony insects. Remove them with a swab dipped in alcohol.

Pine
(*Pinus strobus, Pinus densiflora*)
hardy to Zone 3

White pine (*Pinus strobus*) is a

native tree that can reach 100 feet or more in height, whose layered growth habit makes it a natural for training into large-scale cakestands and other tiered shapes. The needles are flexible and a lovely soft green, holding their color throughout the winter. White pine needs careful attention when shearing, since the needles are bunched toward the tip of the current year's growth. Be sure to cut in the middle of the needled portion, and not in the bare part of the branch, or the branch will die back to the previous year's needles. When pruning cuts are made in the correct place, buds will quickly sprout at the base of the needles. White pine tends to drop its lower limbs when it is older; you can take advantage of this habit to form palissades or bowers with a flat tabletop of foliage and bare trunked columns, or by raising your cakestand's tiers on a smooth trunk. Dragon's eye pine (*Pinus densiflora* 'Oculus-draconis'), hardy to Zone 5, is an unusual form of Japanese red pine whose yellow-banded needles give it a striking and distinctive appearance. It grows rapidly, ultimately attaining a height of about 35 feet, and would make a unique topiary conversation piece.

Privet
(*Ligustrum japonicum, Ligustrum lucidum, Ligustrum ovalifolium, Ligustrum vulgare*)
hardy to Zones 5–7

Privet is a good choice for outdoor plant sculptures and architectural shapes, with a dense coat of small oval leaves. It grows quickly and contentedly in a wide variety of growing conditions, is inexpensive and easy to obtain. It is known for its ability to grow near the ocean. Good species include Japanese privet (*Ligustrum japonicum*), hardy to Zone 7; glossy privet (*Ligustrum lucidum*), hardy to Zone 8; California privet (*Ligustrum ovalifolium*), hardy to Zone 6; and common privet (*Ligustrum vulgare*), hardy to Zone 5. There is little difference among these species in terms of appearance—ask your local nurseryman which grows best in your area. Privet is not evergreen, but the bare skeleton is handsome when set off against a background of snow or evergreens. The winter appearance is soon followed by a flush of new leaves and fragrant, tiny white flowers. It is good for practicing topiary, as it recovers quickly from any accidental disfigurement. A new supply of plants can be readily started by rooting cuttings from older bushes. Any major pruning should be done in the early spring before new growth begins. Since privet grows rapidly, it may require trimming as frequently as every two weeks during the summer.

Rosemary
(*Rosmarinus officinalis*)
hardy to Zone 7/houseplant

Rosemary has always been a popular herb for indoor potted topiary. It is suitable for simple or complex designs large and small, such as hoops, espaliers, standards, poodles and hollow-frame animals. In mild climates, it is a fine addition to the knot garden. The fragrant, needle-like leaves resemble those of yew, a favorite for outdoor topiary. The foliage color is a distinctive gray-green, joined intermittently by small flowers. There are lots of varieties, most of which are nearly impossible to tell apart, but it is easy to distinguish between the upright types, appropriate for standards and single-stem shapes, and the prostrate ones, which lend themselves to training on a frame. Rosemary generally has lavender blooms, but the varieties 'Alba' and 'Roseum' have white or pink flowers respectively. Depending on temperature and humidity conditions indoors, it may be prone to spider mites and whiteflies (hot and dry) or powdery mildew (damp and cool).

Yaupon
(*Ilex vomitoria*)
hardy to Zone 8

Yaupon is a native, drought-tolerant plant with small, glossy leaves that takes well to close shearing. It resembles boxwood and may be used as a substitute for it in sculptures and architectural topiary wherever summers are hot and dry. Yaupon is a type of holly, and it sets a heavy crop of red fruits on the previous year's growth. Dwarf yaupon (*Ilex vomitoria* 'Nana') is smaller growing and good for knot gardens, but it doesn't bear fruit.

Yew
(*Taxus baccata, Taxus cuspidata, Taxus × media*)
hardy to Zones 4–7

In most areas this dark green evergreen is the best plant for outdoor sculpture and architectural topiary. It grows well in a range of conditions, including deep shade, and its fine, dense texture makes it easy to give sculptures detail and character. The light green of the new needles contrasts with older foliage. Yew has the perfect rate of growth—not so rapid that frequent shearing is necessary, nor so slow that many years go by before the figure is finished. Topiary sculptures formed on a frame generally assume the desired shape in two to three years and have a mature appearance in five years. Yew has pretty red and black berries, but only on female specimens (nurserymen refer to this as a "pistillate" plant). Try to obtain a female for sculptures, planting a male nearby for pollination so that red and black berries will decorate your topiary. Yew leaves and seeds are poisonous so don't allow children or pets to ingest plants or berries.

By choosing the right

variety, yew can be trained into virtually any form, since there are upright, pyramidal and spreading types. For example, a sitting dog might have an upright yew planted at each paw to start the front portion, while a spreading variety could form the hindquarters and tail. Upright and pyramidal types are best for hedges, spreading types for low, rounded sculptures. English yew (*Taxus baccata*) has been trained into topiary for centuries in the British Isles, and there are many varieties. Most are not dependably hardy in the United States north of Zone 7, except 'Repandens', a flat-topped, low form that is hardy to Zone 6. Irish yew (*Taxus baccata* 'Stricta') has a distinctive columnar habit that resembles Italian cypress. Japanese yew (*Taxus cuspidata*) is a broadly pyramidal shrub hardy to Zone 5. 'Nana' and 'Pyramidalis' are slow-growing varieties with tufted, thick foliage, while 'Densiformis' is a fast-growing low mound. 'Aurescens' is a golden yew that looks striking next to other evergreens. The hybrids between Japanese and English yew (*Taxus × media*) are also hardy to Zone 5. 'Hatfieldii' is a dense, pyramidal variety, excellent for hedges or sculptures. 'Hicksii' resembles the Irish yew, and is usually female.

Yew is a greedy feeder. It will deplete nutrients from the surrounding soil, so leave some space between yew hedges or arbors and flower beds. Young plants should be sheared two or

three times during the growing season to promote compact growth, but established shapes can usually be maintained with one annual trimming. Trimming is ideally done early in the growing season, giving new buds a chance to develop. Overgrown plants can be restored to their former dimensions by pruning back severely in fall or winter, since yew readily sprouts new growth from old wood the following spring.

SOURCE GUIDE

Here is a selection of firms that offer frames, plants and finished topiary for indoor and outdoor display. The symbol "MO" indicates that a company will ship its products and plants by mail or parcel service. Some have shops, greenhouses and display gardens that you can browse through for inspiration. Don't overlook local nurseries, garden centers and plant shops, where plants are usually sold in larger sizes than can be shipped by mail. Many garden centers carry rose and other flowering standards in spring and summer.

Angelwood Nursery (MO)
12839 McKee School Road
Woodburn, OR 97071
(503) 634-2233

This greenhouse offers more than 100 varieties of ivy plants.

Dorothy Biddle Service
U.S. Route 6
Greeley, PA 18425-9799
(717) 226-3239

Flower arranging supplies for mock topiary, and florist's pins for training vines on portable topiary.

Carroll Gardens, Inc. (MO)
444 East Main Street, P.O. Box 310
Westminster, MD 21157
(800) 638-6334

Many varieties of yew, boxwood, holly and hemlock for outdoor topiary; herbs and perennials for knot gardens and indoor topiary.

Caprilands Herb Farm (MO)
Silver Street
Coventry, CT 06238
(203) 742-7244

Herb plants, as well as dried herbs and flowers for mock topiary. Also a lovely display garden.

Chicago Botanic Garden
Box 400
Lake Cook Road
Glencoe, IL 60022
(312) 835-5440

Wire topiary frames, along with florist's pins and cloth-covered wire for making portable topiary. They always have a topiary display in the greenhouses.

Exotic Blossoms (MO)
P.O. Box 2436
1149 South 12th Street
Philadelphia, PA 19147
(215) 271-2440

This company offers wire frames and stuffed or planted portable topiary by mail. They also have topiary on display for sale.

The Garden Contained
21 Everit Street
New Haven, CT 06511
(203) 773-1584

This firm trains herbs and flowering plants into standards ranging from tabletop size to four feet tall. They also offer antique English and imported terra-cotta pots. Open by appointment only.

Gilson Gardens (MO)
3059 U.S. Route 20
P.O. Box 277
Perry, OH 44081
(216) 259-4845

Many varieties of ivy are sold, in sizes ranging from small cuttings in cell packs to plants with long runners in 2½-inch pots, with discounts offered on large quantities.

Allen Haskell
787 Shawmut Avenue
New Bedford, MA 02746
(617) 993-9047

Beautiful standards and poodles trained from myrtle, lavender and other herbs, and unusual flowering plants. These must be picked up at the greenhouses.

Irene's Topiary (MO)
3045 North Academy
Dept. CIL
Sanger, CA 93657
(209) 875-8447

This firm offers a selection of frames, stuffed forms and planted portable topiary.

Ivies of the World (MO)
P.O. Box 408
Weirsdale, FL 32695
(904) 821-2201

Ivy plants in 2-inch pots. The catalog indicates which varieties are recommended for portable topiary or various outdoor uses.

The Kinsman Company (MO)
River Road, Dept. 451
Point Pleasant, PA 18950
(215) 297-5613

Steel and plastic frames for arches, arbors and summerhouses that can be assembled in any desired length. They also carry line markers for laying out hedges and knot gardens, lead nails for training espaliers, and wire hanging baskets for improvising standard or globe-shaped topiary frames.

Henry Leuthardt Nurseries, Inc. (MO)
Montauk Highway, Box 666
East Moriches, NY 11940
(516) 878-1387

A source for espaliered apples and pears in several designs. They also sell antique fruit varieties as young

whips for starting your own espaliers.

Logee's Greenhouses (MO)
55 North Street
Danielson, CT 06239
(203) 774-8038

An extensive catalog of plants for portable topiary and standards. They list creeping fig, ivy, geraniums, and herbs, as well as unusual plants for the home and greenhouse.

Kenneth Lynch & Sons, Inc. (MO)
78 Danbury Road
P.O. Box 488
Wilton, CT 06897
(203) 762-8363

This famous garden ornament firm makes stainless steel topiary frames, which range in size from a 3-foot rabbit to a life-size pony. They are quite costly, but made to last for years either indoors or in the garden.

Meadowbrook Farm (MO)
1633 Washington Lane
Meadowbrook, PA 19046
(215) 887-5900

Frames and moss-filled forms are available by mail; planted indoor topiary is sold only at the greenhouse.

Merry Gardens (MO)
Camden, Maine 04843
(207) 236-9064

This 40-year-old firm ships portable topiary in planted or kit form, and grows many varieties of plants for portable topiary and standards, including ivy, creeping fig, herbs and geraniums.

J. E. Miller Nurseries, Inc. (MO)
5060 West Lake Road
Canandaigua, NY 14424
(716) 396-2647 or (800) 828-9630

Fruit tree whips and young nut trees for espalier and pleaching.

Naomi's Herbs (MO)
11 Housatonic Street
Lenox, MA 01240
(413) 637-0616

Dried herbs, spices and flowers for mock topiary are available in the shop or by mail. Herb plants are sold at the store.

Noah's Ark (MO)
1299 Starkey Road #74
Largo, FL 34641
(813) 539-8590

Many portable topiary designs offered as frames or moss-stuffed forms, or planted in creeping fig.

Rosedale Nurseries
51 Saw Mill River Road (Route 9A)
Hawthorne, NY 10532
(914) 769-1300

A selection of outdoor juniper topiaries is available at the nursery, as well as a limited number of large yew figures.

**Stark Bros. Nurseries and
  Orchards Co. (MO)**
Highway 54 West
Louisiana, MO 63353-0010
(314) 754-5511 or (800) 843-5091

Their catalog is best known for
their dwarf fruit trees, which you
can train as espaliers, but they also
offer shrubs and trees for hedges
and architectural topiary at
quantity discounts.

**Sunnybrook Farms Nursery
  (MO)**
P.O. Box 6
9448 Mayfield Road
Chesterland, OH 44021
(216) 729-7232

A broad selection of ivy plants,
scented geraniums and herbs are
available by mail; a wider selection
of other plants is available at the
nursery.

Taylor's Herb Garden (MO)
1535 Lone Oak Road
Vista, CA 92084
(619) 727-3485

More than 100 varieties of herb
plants are shipped in 3-inch pots;
ask for unpinched plants if you
want to start standards. The
nursery has potted and field
displays of all the herbs offered for
sale.

Tohickon Glass Eyes (MO)
Box 15
Erwinna, PA 18920
(215) 294-9483

A leading manufacturer of glass
eyes to make your topiary figures
come alive.

Topiary, Inc. (MO)
41 Bering Street
Tampa, FL 33606
(813) 254-3229

This company has an illustrated
list of reasonably priced galvanized
wire frames, and planted portable
topiary. They also do special
designs on a custom basis.

Topiary by Lucky (MO)
Route 2, Box 434
Danville, KY 40422
(606) 236-1968

Wire frames, stuffed forms and
planted portable topiary. They
specialize in horses.

Totally Topiary (MO)
P.O. Box 191
Stockton, NJ 08559
(609) 397-2314

Owned by co-author Barbara
Gallup, specializing in custom
designs for frames and topiary.
Frames and stuffed forms can be
ordered by mail; or call for an
appointment.

Vine Arts (MO)
Janet Schuster
P.O. Box 03014
Portland, OR 97203
(503) 289-7505

Galvanized wire topiary frames in
an assortment of shapes.

Well-Sweep Herb Farm (MO)
317 Mt. Bethel Road
Port Murray, NJ 07865
(201) 852-5390

A broad selection of herb plants
are sold by mail; they also have a
limited supply of herbal standards,
available only at the nursery by
prior appointment. On the grounds
is an attractive example of an
herbal knot garden.

Weston Nurseries
East Main Street (Route 135)
P.O. Box 186
Hopkinton, MA 01748
(617) 435-3414

They offer hardy outdoor topiary,
including grafted evergreen
standards, poodles, and a number
of large boulevard cypresses
shaped into faces. They also grow
several varieties of boxwood and
yew for starting your own outdoor
figures. There is no mail service,
but they do deliver by truck within
the Boston area, or you can choose
plants at the garden center.

GARDENS TO VISIT

Following is a selection of gardens across the United States that feature some sort of topiary, including portables, standards, espaliers, knot gardens, outdoor sculpture and architectural features. They should provide plenty of inspiration and ideas for your own garden. We have not listed admission fees or schedules, since they change frequently. Most have regular hours of admission, but some are open only by prior appointment. It is advisable to write or phone any garden before planning a visit.

Brooklyn Botanic Garden
1000 Washington Avenue
Brooklyn, NY 11225
(718) 622-4433

One of the finest knot gardens in the country is found here, made of herbs, boxwood and dwarf barberry.

Callaway Gardens
Pine Mountain, GA 31822
(404) 663-2281

Portable topiary animals are always on display in the Sibley Horticulture Center greenhouses.

Casa Amesti
Old Capital Club
516 Polk Street
Monterey, CA 93942

For information, contact:
Monterey History and Art Association, Ltd.
P.O. Box 805
Monterey, CA 93942
(408) 372-2608

Behind the early 19th-century house is a formal Spanish garden, modeled after the Generalife at the Alhambra, and planted around 1918. It contains parterres and geometric shapes. Pollarded and cloud-pruned trees line the front walk. A property of the National Trust for Historic Preservation, it is open to the public only on Saturday and Sunday afternoons or by appointment.

Chicago Botanic Garden
Lake Cook Road
P.O. Box 400
Glencoe, IL 60022
(312) 835-5440

Portable topiary animals, some featuring unusual plants such as rosary vine and mondo grass, are displayed in the greenhouses, along with a collection of myrtle standards. A knot garden of santolina and germander forms the centerpiece of the outdoor herb garden, which includes heliotrope standards and fragrant herb varieties.

Henry Clay Foundation
Market Street at Sycamore
Lexington, KY 40502
(606) 266-8581

Geometric hollies and espaliered dogwoods surround a boxwood parterre garden.

Colonial Williamsburg
P.O. Box C
Williamsburg, VA 23187
(804) 229-1000

Many gardens have been recreated here, following maps and pictures, resulting in a living record of Dutch and English styles of the 17th and 18th centuries. The Governor's Palace is especially interesting for its holly maze, geometric topiary and pleached hornbeam alley, while several other gardens feature pleached arbors or espaliered fruit and nut trees.

Denver Botanic Gardens
909 York Street
Denver, CO 80206
(303) 575-3751

The Herb Garden, completed in 1965, contains a large design of five interlocking circles in a traditional bowknot design.

Disneyland
1313 Harbor Boulevard
Anaheim, CA 92803
(714) 999-4565

Since 1958, Disneyland has introduced millions of Americans to topiary. Most of the original figures, including Dumbo, waltzing hippos and a sea serpent, can be seen near the Dumbo and It's a Small World attractions.

Walt Disney World
P.O. Box 40
Lake Buena Vista, FL 32830
(305) 824-4500

The grounds contain many examples of geometric shapes and Disney animal characters rendered in traditional pruned topiary as well as large outdoor versions of stuffed portable topiary. Examples include unusual plants and combinations, such as a stuffed Mickey Mouse covered in wax begonias, a yaupon Mary Poppins shaded by a pyracantha, and a podocarpus swan. Most of the figures are in the Magic Kingdom, but there are additional topiaries at Epcot Center. Others in various stages of completion are in the Chlorophyll Zoo, which may be visited by reserving a place in a horticulture seminar.

Duke Gardens Foundation, Inc.
P.O. Box 2030
Highway 206 South
Somerville, NJ 08876
(201) 722-3700

A unique creation of eleven greenhouses, each containing a particular style of garden. Good examples of ivy trained in a formal manner, portable topiary animals, geometric shapes and a formal herb garden. Reservations are necessary.

The Elizabethan Gardens
P.O. Box 161
Manteo
Roanoke Island, NC 27954
(919) 473-3234

The garden was created in 1951 by the Garden Club of North Carolina, Inc., adjacent to Fort Raleigh, site of the first English colony in America. Inspired by English garden design of the 16th century, the Sunken Garden is enclosed by a pleached alley of clipped yaupon and features parterres accented with crape myrtle standards and a fine collection of garden ornaments.

Filoli Center
Canada Road
Woodside, CA 94062
(415) 364-2880

This property of the National Trust for Historic Preservation, located 25 miles south of San Francisco, consists of 16 acres of formal gardens in natural surroundings. There are two knot gardens, 250 Irish yews clipped into cylinders 22 feet tall, and a mile of hedges. A special feature is the Chartres

Cathedral Window Garden, where boxwood patterns are filled with colorful annuals in imitation of stained glass. Advance reservations are required for a tour of the gardens.

Garden Center of Greater Cleveland
11030 East Boulevard
Cleveland, OH 44106
(216) 721-1600

The Western Reserve Herb Society, part of the Herb Society of America, maintains a large herb garden at the four-acre Garden Center. The centerpiece is a knot garden, made of interlacing ribbons of different-colored herbs placed around five antique millstones.

The J. Paul Getty Museum
17985 Pacific Coast Highway
Malibu, CA 90265
(213) 458-2003

The gardens of this world-renowned art museum contain boxwood knot gardens and clipped geometric forms, recreating the first-century Italian gardens excavated at the Villa dei Papyri at Herculaneum. Reservations must be made in advance.

Green Animals
380 Cory's Lane
Portsmouth, RI 02871
(401) 683-1267

A dromedary, giraffe and elephant, along with more than 80 other shrub animals and geometric topiary of privet and yew, live among boxwood-edged parterres in this seaside garden near Newport. Developed around the turn of the century by industrialist Thomas Brayton and his gardener, Jose Carreiro, Green Animals shares with Ladew Topiary Gardens in Maryland the distinction of being the finest topiary gardens in America.

Gunston Hall Plantation

Lorton, VA 22079
(703) 550-9220

This was the home of George Mason, who helped to write the United States Constitution and the Bill of Rights. The formal boxwood parterres and dome-shaped hollies along the Potomac River were restored to his original design by the Garden Club of Virginia in 1950. A central alley of English boxwood, now 12 feet high, dates from Mason's original 18th-century plantings.

The Hagley Museum and Library

P.O. Box 3630
Wilmington, DE 19807
(302) 658-2400

The first home of the Du Pont family in the United States, known as Eleutherian Mills since it was also the site of the family's original gunpowder mill. The French Garden was completed by E. I. Du Pont between 1803 and 1834. It was planned for utility as well as beauty, so it contains mixed parterres of vegetables, flowers and herbs, bordered by extensive plantings of espaliered fruit trees. These include cordon and U-shaped apples, a Belgian fence of peaches and pears, a pleached alley of lady apples and unusual conical freestanding pear trees.

Hampton National Historic Site and Gardens

535 Hampton Lane
Towson, MD 21204
(301) 823-7054

Boxwood parterres in 18th-century French geometric designs are managed by the National Park Service.

Hodges Garden

P.O. Box 900
Many, LA 71449
(318) 586-3523

The display greenhouses in this 60-acre quarry garden contain at least a dozen examples of portable topiary in various sizes, the largest being a 5-foot giraffe.

Walter Hunnewell Pinetum

845 Washington Street
Wellesley, MA 02181
(617) 235-0422

In 1851 Horatio Hollis Hunnewell began what is now the oldest topiary garden in America, featuring gigantic geometric topiary hewn from native trees. The garden is not open except by prior appointment, but the terraces of the topiary-filled Italian Garden can be seen from the public lakeside walk below.

The Labyrinth

New Harmony State Historic Site
Part of the Indiana State Museum System
P.O. Box 607
New Harmony, IN 47631
(812) 682-3271

This was the site of the 19th-century communal religious group known as the Harmonists or Rappites. The restored formal gardens contain a maze of concentric circles of privet hedges and flower borders about 140 feet in diameter. It was replanted by the state of Indiana in 1939, near the site of the original, which was planted of privet, thorns, beech and dogwoods between 1814 and 1824.

Ladew Topiary Gardens

3535 Jarrettsville Pike
Monkton, MD 21111
(301) 557-9466

The 22-acre gardens outside of Baltimore were started by Harvey S. Ladew in 1929, who continued creating plant statues until his death in 1976. Along with Green Animals, Ladew is one of the finest American topiary gardens. The special appeal of Ladew is that the overall scheme, a series of enclosed theme gardens, is as inspiring as the individual figures. Shapes include a foxhunt scene, a giraffe, assorted fowl, various chess pieces, a yew Buddha, elaborate hedges and espaliered fruit trees.

Longwood Gardens

U.S. Route 1
P.O. Box 501
Kennett Square, PA 19348
(215) 388-6741

The Topiary Garden features geometric yew shapes, some over 75 years old, as well as several birds, a rabbit and a table and chair. Other permanent topiary attractions include a huge stilt hedge made of Norway maples, along with various examples of espaliered fruit trees and ornamental shrubs. Seasonal displays in the conservatory, which covers 3½ acres, often feature large stuffed portable topiary and flowering standards.

Magnolia Plantation and Gardens

Route 4, Highway 61
Charleston, SC 29407
(803) 571-1266

This estate dates from the 17th

century and is now managed by J. Drayton Hastie, a ninth-generation descendant of its founding owner. Amid acres of magnolias, azaleas and cypress ponds, topiary attractions include a zoo of topiary animals; a recreation of the Hampton Court maze made from camellia shrubs; and a formal Biblical Garden with Old Testament plants growing in a parterre shaped like the Star of David, across from New Testament plants arrange in a cross-shaped bed.

Mount Vernon

c/o Mount Vernon Ladies' Association
Mount Vernon Memorial Highway
Mount Vernon, VA 22121
(703) 780-2000

At the former home of George Washington, a boxwood-edged parterre garden ornamented with clipped American boxwood balls recreates the first president's original design. There are also more than 50 examples of espaliered fruit trees, including a fence of double cordons that lines the paths.

National Herb Garden

United States National Arboretum
3501 New York Avenue NE
Washington, D.C. 20002
(202) 475-4815

The National Herb Garden

occupies about two acres opposite the National Arboretum's Administration Building. A large area is devoted to a 25- by 50-foot contemporary interpretation of a knot garden, planted in dwarf evergreen plants for year-round interest, including varieties of Japanese holly, arborvitae and false cypress.

Nemours Mansion and Gardens

P.O. Box 109
Rockland Road
Wilmington, DE 19899
(302) 651-6912

Built between 1910 and 1935, the former estate of Alfred I. Du Pont has gardens inspired by France's Versailles, featuring extensive boxwood parterres in a fleur-de-lis pattern, a Maze Garden consisting of cube-cut pin oaks, and formal hedges of hemlock and Japanese holly. Reservations are recommended for individuals and required for groups.

Oatlands

Route 2, Box 352
Leesburg, VA 22075
(703) 777-3174

Located south of Leesburg on Route 15, this early 19th-century formal garden was restored in the early part of this century and is now a property of the National Trust for Historic Preservation. It features terraced parterres of dwarf boxwood, an allee of tree box, and several examples of espalier.

William Paca House and Garden

1 Martin Street
Annapolis, MD 21401
(301) 269-0601 or (301) 267-6656

The garden, built between 1765 and 1772, was neglected and covered by a hotel and bus depot until archaeological and restoration work was begun in 1965. The colonial garden features four separate parterre gardens enclosed by hedges. One is composed of boxwood, another of holly, a third is filled with flowers in the shape of the British flag, and a fourth with antique roses in a Persian rug pattern. Accents are provided by geometric boxwood forms, and espaliered fruit trees line the garden wall.

Sonnenberg Gardens

P.O. Box 663
Canandaigua, NY 14424
(716) 394-4922

Nine separate formal gardens can be viewed on this Victorian estate. The Italian Garden has archways and pyramids of yew, with carpet bedding in a fleur-de-lis pattern. The Colonial Garden features boxwood parterres.

Tryon Palace Restoration and Garden Complex

P.O. Box 1007
610 Pollock Street
New Bern, NC 28560
(919) 638-5109

The Palace was built in 1767, destroyed by fire in 1791 and abandoned until its restoration in 1952. Three separate areas feature topiary: curvaceous parterres in the Latham Memorial Garden, yew spirals in the Dutch-style Kellenberger Garden, and various clipped shapes in the Green Garden.

Vizcaya Museum and Gardens

3125 South Miami Avenue
Miami, FL 33129
(305) 579-2708 or (305) 579-4626

Built from 1914 to 1916, Vizcaya is an American rendition of a Renaissance Italian villa and garden, using native and exotic tropical plants. Extensive parterres in a carpet pattern made of clipped jasmine are complemented by columnar podocarpus, casuarina hedges, a stilt hedge of live oaks and a maze made of coco plum.

Woodland Park Rose Garden

50th Street and Fremont Avenue
Seattle, WA 98103
(206) 625-2246

Originally a late 19th-century private estate, this is now a city park. Bizarre large conical and cloud-pruned false cypress rise up to 14 feet high from formal gardens containing All-America Selection roses.

PICTURE CREDITS

Page 29: The Metropolitan Museum of Art, Rogers Fund, 1920.

Page 33: The Metropolitan Museum of Art, Dick Fund, 1941.

Page 52: *Mediaeval Gardens*, by Sir Frank Crisp, 1924.

Page 62: The Metropolitan Museum of Art, Harris Brisbane Dick Fund, 1926. (26.72.57)

Page 69, 77, 85: *Mediaeval Gardens*, by Sir Frank Crisp, 1924.

Page 90: The Metropolitan Museum of Art, Harris Brisbane Dick Fund, 1930. [30.22.(34), Pl 34]

Page 122, 154: *Mediaeval Gardens*, by Sir Frank Crisp, 1924.

Page 162: The Metropolitan Museum of Art, The Elisha Whittelsey Collection, The Elisha Whittelsey Fund, 1949. (49.95.2276)

Page 170: The Metropolitan Museum of Art, The Elisha Whittelsey Collection, The Elisha Whittelsey Fund, 1954. (54.501.4)

Page 193: Library of the New York Botanical Garden, Bronx, New York.

Page 200: Picture Collection, New York Public Library.

Page 223: *Mediaeval Gardens*, by Sir Frank Crisp, 1924.

Page 248: Culver Pictures.

Page 255: *The Formal Garden in England*, by Reginald Blomfield, 1901.

Page 274: Picture Collection, New York Public Library.

Page 279: Culver Pictures.

Page 295: Picture Collection, New York Public Library.